Maverick Autobiographies

Wisconsin Studies In Autobiography

William L. Andrews

General Editor

Maverick Autobiographies

Women Writers and the American West, 1900–1936

Cathryn Halverson

The University of Wisconsin Press

The University of Wisconsin Press
1930 Monroe Street
Madison, Wisconsin 53711

www.wisc.edu/wisconsinpress/

3 Henrietta Street
London WC2E 8LU, England

5   4   3   2   1

Printed in the United States of America

Library of Congress Cataloging-in-Publication Data
Halverson, Cathryn.
    Maverick autobiographies: women writers and the American West,
    1900–1936 / Cathryn Halverson.
        p. cm.— (Wisconsin studies in autobiography)
    Includes bibliographical references (p.) and index.
    ISBN 0-299-19720-4 (cloth: alk. paper)
    1. American prose literature—West (U.S.)—History and criticism. 2. Women and
literature—West (U.S.)—History—20th century. 3. American prose literature—Women
authors—History and criticism. 4. American prose literature—20th century—History
and criticism. 5. Women authors, American—Biography—History and criticism.
6. Women authors, American—Homes and haunts—West (U.S.) 7. Authors, American—Biography—History and criticism. 8. Authors, American—Homes and haunts—
West (U.S.) 9. West (U.S.)—Biography—History and criticism. 10. Women—West
(U.S.)—Intellectual life. 11. West (U.S.)—Intellectual life. 12. Autobiography—Women
authors. I. Title. II. Series.
PS271.H29 2004
818'.5208099287'0978—dc22   2003020567

To David

Contents

Preface

How do you catch a maverick? This question first struck me after I chanced upon *The Story of Mary MacLane* (1902), described by its author as "as full and frank a Portrayal as I am able of myself, Mary MacLane, for whom the world contains not a parallel." As I stood in the stacks, skimming through the small red book, I moved through MacLane's depictions of what she refers to as "her wooden heart, her good young woman's-body, her mind, her soul" before reaching the text's final words: "It is shining little gold coins from out of my mind's red leather purse. It is my little old life-tragedy. It means everything to me. Do you see?—it means *everything* to me. It will amuse you. It will arouse your interest. It will stir your curiosity. . . . But am I to suppose that it will also awaken compassion in cool, indifferent hearts?" With my interest aroused, curiosity stirred, and perhaps even compassion awakened, I flipped back to the opening pages to search for information about MacLane. I found only her photograph to study—enhanced, I was later to learn, by artful padding of bust and hips, making MacLane's gaze outwards to the reader appear all the more insouciant. My initial research revealed no recent MacLane scholarship, and so I began visiting archives and tracking down contemporary newspaper and magazine accounts, as well as later local ones. The problem of maverick-catching became increasingly insistent when in the midst of my research on MacLane, I encountered the autobiographies of her contemporaries, Opal Whiteley and Juanita Harrison. Just as compelling and iconoclastic, the two are even less known. I began similar investigations of these writers, investigations that often crossed each other's paths. All three were like no one I had read before, but how could they be brought to light? The question led to this book.

MacLane, Whiteley, and Harrison each wrote and published autobiography in the early decades of the twentieth century: *The Story of Mary MacLane* (1902) and *I Mary MacLane* (1917), *The Story of Opal* (1920), and *My Great, Wide, Beautiful World* (1936).[1] Each author was a so-called ordinary woman rather than renowned public figure, who wrote not in retrospect but in present-tense diary form; their autobiographies are their only significant publications. For each, the American West, both textually and biographically, figured prominently in their "fictions of selfhood,"[2] to borrow Sidonie Smith's term; they used the West as an imaginative and literal point of departure even while inventing for themselves other families and homes located elsewhere. Subsequently, each had brief but intense notoriety as producers of innovative texts that readers found revelatory of some essential truths about the West, women, childhood, or the human race. Illuminating the relations connecting autobiography, gender, region, and early twentieth-century print culture and celebrity, MacLane, Whiteley, and Harrison participate in and revise the romance of individualism that figures so prominently in American literary history.

MacLane became a national celebrity at nineteen with the publication of *The Story of Mary MacLane*, prompting a flood of imitations. Her two books discuss her conviction of her own genius and its relationship to her barren surroundings, her sexual desire and desire for worldly fame, and the claustrophobia she feels in her family home in Butte, that "uncouth, warped, Montana town." Her first book is threaded throughout with avowals of her love for her English teacher, Fanny Corbin, and her desire for the devil, who she dreams will rescue her from tedium and loneliness:

> "What would you have me do, little MacLane?" the Devil would say.
>   "I would have you conquer me, crush me, know me," I would answer.
>   "What shall I say to you?" the Devil would ask.
>   "Say to me, 'I love you, I love you, I love you.'"

MacLane was greeted as a prototypical writer of the provinces, revealing the possibilities and the limitations of America's imagined empty spaces. Causing a stir in high-brow and mass-market forums alike (from the accolades of Harriet Monroe and Hamlin Garland to the invention of the Mary MacLane Highball, "with or without ice-cream, cooling, refreshing, invigorating, devilish, the up-to-date drink"), the text's success led her from Butte to high-spending bohemian life in New York, Boston, and St. Augustine. Although she attracted renewed interest with *I, Mary MacLane* and her performance in an autobiographical silent movie, MacLane died in poverty in Chicago in her forties.

Opal Whiteley also published a diary when she was just out of her teens, *The Story of Opal: Journal of an Understanding Heart.* Whiteley, however, claimed to have written hers during her early childhood in a western Oregon lumber camp near Cottage Grove. As its subtitle suggests, the text focuses on Whiteley's empathy with other creatures, the animals and plants with whom she claimed she communed. Whiteley maintained that she was truly "Françoise," the daughter of French aristocrats, rather than the Oregon logging foreman and wife who raised her, and she portrayed the latter as forcing on her a childhood of household drudgery. *The Story of Opal,* in which Whiteley describes experiences in the woods and at home, is at times a coy record of a child's challenges to adult authority, at times an eerie account of a child's longing for love and freedom:

> Now I sit here and I print. The baby sleeps on. The wind comes creeping in under the door. It calls, *"Come, come, petite Françoise, come."* It calls to me to come go exploring. It sings of the things that are to be found under leaves. It whispers the dreams of the tall fir trees. It does pipe the gentle song the forest sings on gray days. I hear all the voices calling me. I listen. But I cannot go.

The initial acclaim that greeted the book, portions of which were first published in the *Atlantic Monthly,* fanned an enthusiasm for texts written by little girls. Yet hostility soon replaced the fanfare when skeptics cast doubt on the diary's child authorship. With the help of aristocratic patronage, Whiteley relocated to England, France, and India, where she devoted herself to genealogical research. She spent the last decades of her life in an English mental institution, until her death in 1992.

In contrast to these highly local texts played out in the small spheres of Butte and Lane County, Juanita Harrison's book chronicles eight years of travel in Europe, the Middle East, and Asia. *My Great, Wide, Beautiful World* opens

> A beautiful June Morning. I arrived at 9 A.M. with my two suit cases the larger one with 2 blue dresses 2 white dresses and one black aprons caps and references. The smaller one with my dress up cloths. and 2 jars of sour cucumber pikles which is so good to keep from being sea sick. Our cabins looked good. I always want a upper berth I don't want anybody making it down on me. I went to the 1st and 2nd Class. Their towels looked more linnen so I took two, the soap smelt sweeter so I took 2 cakes. I went up to the writing room and the paper was the kind you love to touch so I took much and tuked it away in my bunk.

This first entry inaugurates a persistent theme in *My Great, Wide, Beautiful World*, that of getting away with something — conning free food, cheap rooms, illicit entry. So too, on a much larger scale, through travel and travel writing Harrison got away with commandeering a life of freedom and adventure unavailable to her as a working-class black women in the United States. Claiming Los Angeles as her home, Harrison used her racially ambiguous appearance to "pass," not as a white American but as anything but: "I am willing to be what ever I can get the best treatments at being." At the end of her travels, as a consequence of entering the American literary marketplace, Harrison was "willing to be" recodified in narrow racial terms, even as her text itself contests this codification. She published her travel writings first in the *Atlantic Monthly* and soon thereafter as a book. Unlike MacLane and Whiteley, Harrison did not meet a tragic end; in the 1950s she was still traveling widely, and she listed her occupation as "author."

A contemporary's description of Whiteley's book holds true for MacLane's and Harrison's as well: "if ever the word unique is appropriate to a literary production, certainly it is here. . . . Nothing else is like it, or apt to be."[3] These texts are among what I call maverick autobiographies, self-writings not only far from the imaginary norm of autobiographies, but also striking for the oddity of the stories they tell, the oddity of the telling, and even the oddity of the circumstances under which they came to be told. The initial appearance of these authors as lacking origins, contemporaries, and influence, not to mention a corpus of their own work, makes them difficult to approach critically. So too does the fact that their texts can be categorized in multiple ways — in the case of the three I discuss, as autobiography, confession, diary, travel literature, nature writing, women's writing, western women's literature, African American literature, and children's literature — but seem to inhabit none of these genres or canons comfortably. This discomfort is demonstrated by the fact that although their names do crop up in academic circles (they are popular inclusions in anthologies), these writers have yet to find substantial representation in studies of western women's literature, African American literature, or autobiography. Instead, they serve only to provide introductory anecdotes, buttressing evidence, or footnotes for arguments concerning other, more easily categorized texts.

Although these writers are not widely known, their neglect does not derive from their total obscurity or even from lack of readers' enthusiasm. On the contrary, they continue to tantalize academic and general audiences alike: the unorthodoxy of their lives, the richness of their texts, the unlikelihood of their fame leave readers hungry for more. The 1990s saw a proliferation of reprints that made the work of MacLane, Whiteley, and Harrison far more visible than previously. Yet the same singularity that has generated this renewed interest has discouraged critical ventures, and relevant scholarship remains slim and scattered. The sustained discussions that do exist, with some notable exceptions, are written for a general audience and are biographically oriented, a tendency fostered by the extraordinary nature of these writers' lives.[4] Judith Fetterley's reflections in "Commentary: Nineteenth-Century American Women Writers and the Politics of Recovery" offer insight into the situation of my twentieth-century mavericks. Noting that little work has been done on many "recovered" women's texts, Fetterley writes, "I wonder if we have this investment in recovery because persons interested in these writers are having difficulty finding ways to write *about* them."[5]

My challenge, then, has been to transform MacLane, Whiteley, and Harrison from fodder for anecdotes into subjects of analyses. In doing so, I hope to help pave the way for studies of the multitude of other mavericks whose work has been similarly passed over, not out of lack of interest, but out of fear. Who has not encountered an unknown and wished to make it known? The delight of discovering a text points to our visceral sense of its significance. The problem lies in articulating this sense.

As I intend to demonstrate in the following chapters, a maverick autobiography might better be conceived not as an anomaly, but rather as a text that appears to be anomalous, as a text standing outside of any literary traditions. My experience with these three leads me to conjecture that the more incongruous a once best-selling writer may appear, and the more she resists classification in the standard renditions of literary history, then the more cultural insights her text may offer and the more urgent her claim to our attention. Her apparent singularity signals one of our own blind spots. In the case of these three early-twentieth-century writers, it also signals the market power of singularity in their own time. MacLane, Whiteley, and Harrison are not simply writers whom we cannot categorize: their uncategorizable nature was their selling point when they wrote.

Questions of historical and cultural significance aside, I think these books are important because they are good. Perhaps some generic considerations will justify such a bald-faced assertion. It has become a truism to note that the study of literature of the American West suffers from a tendency to read texts as documents rather than art. Likewise, autobiography in general and diaries in particular also attract attention primarily as documents. The works of MacLane, Whiteley, and Harrison defy such a tendency: aesthetically and imaginatively rich, they reward analytic inquiry and thereby offer footholds for inquiry into other western texts and memoir. With their double status as diaries and as western literature, these maverick autobiographies lead us to consider when and how to take a text beyond the level of artifact.[6]

Offering many rewarding rereadings, these books continue to absorb me. Like their contemporary readers, from the start I found them deeply pleasurable to read, sentence by sentence as well as page by page and chapter by chapter. Like their contemporary reviewers, I am tempted to depend upon lengthy quotations in an effort to represent them adequately. And, of course, representation does not suffice. They need to be read.

Although *Maverick Autobiographies* is a study of western women's autobiography, it is also a recovery project. As I conceive of it, the audience for these chapters is made up of both those who want to investigate the relationship between the early-twentieth-century West and women's self-writing and those who simply want to know more about the texts and lives of my three mavericks—those who had the same reaction I did when I chanced upon MacLane's book: tell me more! Ideally, these two groups are one and the same. If not, perhaps reading *Maverick Autobiographies* will make them so. Fetterley wonders why "positive passion" remains a taboo subject in formal literary study, despite the fact that such passion or its lack dominates responses to texts.[7] (What is the first comment so many undergraduates make about an assigned text?) I hope that throughout this study, whatever threads I pursue, my own positive passion remains clear.

Acknowledgments

This book took its earliest form as an eight-page paper written during my third month of graduate school for a seminar with Julie Ellison (surely a few of the original sentences are still there). Julie went on to become my dissertation advisor and mentor. Over the past decade her enthusiasm and counsel have been invaluable, through to the very final stages of this project. Thanks also to my other committee members at the University of Michigan: Kerry Larson, whose courses triggered my interest in American Studies and who agreed to guide me despite claiming that his knowledge stopped at 1865; Patsy Yaeger, who was especially encouraging as I made the transition from dissertation to book; and Susan L. Johnson, who asked that I remember that ideally paragraphs include topic sentences. I especially value my committee's willingness to leave me to my own devices, with the confidence that it would all work itself out in the end.

During graduate school, I was well served by a Rackham Pre-Doctoral Fellowship and Mellon Candidacy Fellowship, which enabled me to write while sojourning in youth hostels in New Mexico, Colorado, and New Zealand. The friendship and intellectual generosity of Stephanie Palmer, who so often shows me how to take my arguments further, has for years availed me. My friend and colleague at Kobe Gaikokugo Daigaku, Jim Kirwan, generously both edited my manuscript (twice) and offered some important ideas. I appreciate, too, the warmth of my senior colleagues, Kojiro Tagawa and Shiro Wada.

Most important, David Ginsburg's love and support, not to mention his research assistance with primary sources (gifted in tracking down the most elusive of references), sustained me throughout. So too did that of my family, who despite remaining unsure as to what exactly I *do*, have always believed that it must be of worth.

I would like also to thank those publishers with whose permission I reprint earlier work. A very early version of chapter 2 appears as "Mary MacLane's Story" in *Arizona Quarterly* 50.4 (1994), reprinted by permission of the Regents of the University of Arizona. My argument in chapter 4 on the reception of children's writing first appeared in "Reading Little Girls' Texts in the 1920s: Searching for the 'Spirit of Childhood,'" *Children's Literature and Education* 30.4 (1999). Chapter 6 was first published as "'Betwixt and Between': Dismantling Race in *My Great, Wide, Beautiful World*" in *Journal X: a journal in culture & criticism* 4.2 (2000). Last, a portion of Chapter 5 is reprinted from "Opal Whiteley's 'Explores': The Disappearing Region," *Western American Literature* (Summer 2002), Special Issue: Western Autobiography & Memoir. Editors and readers of these journals were of great assistance in helping me to develop my arguments, not to mention in editing my work. I would especially like to thank Kathleen Boardman, special issue editor for *Western American Literature,* and Jay Watson, former editor of *Journal X.*

I am grateful to the Newberry Library for permission to quote from material located in the Stone & Kimball Publishing Company archives; to the University of Chicago Library, Special Collections Research Center, for permission to quote from material located in the records of *Poetry: A Magazine of Verse;* to the Division of Special Collections and Archives of the University of Oregon Libraries, for permission to quote from material located in the Opal Whiteley Papers; and to the Massachusetts Historical Society, for permission to quote from material located in the Opal Whiteley special subject file of the Ellery Sedgwick Papers. I also appreciate the graciousness of Ellen Crain, director of the Butte–Silver Bow Public Archives, in guiding me to Butte–Silver Bow's Mary MacLane materials.

Finally, I would like to remember here my father Richard C. Halverson, journalist and editor, who gave me a sense of what the life of a writer could be like as well as scoffing, in true reporter fashion, at affectations of style. His ideal sentence did not exceed eight words.

Maverick Autobiographies
and the American West, 1900–1936

Introduction
Western Genius, Eastward Bound

Although I have been using the term "maverick autobiography" to denote unusual texts in general, "maverick" has regional connotations that make it particularly fitting for MacLane, Whiteley, and Harrison, with their claims on and rejections of Butte, Cottage Grove, and Hollywood, respectively. "Maverick," speculatively explained as the coinage of the seventeenth century English-born American colonist, Samuel Maverick, literally means an unbranded calf separated from its mother. The term is used more broadly now to refer to a dissenter. On the one hand, *maverick* is an apt term for these western texts written by independent women unregistered under any one brand. While not literally motherless, these writers cut themselves off from their mothers' ways of life in order to look to the East and other nations and carve out a cosmopolitan, urban existence for themselves. On the other hand, the fit of *maverick* is so neat as to threaten cliché: the American West teems with bars, restaurants, and dude ranches that include the word in their names, as do the titles of various books celebrating the "Wild West." Maverick has ranged far from cattle country to now attach itself to anything craving frontier chutzpah. Drive down the main strip of an Alaskan fishing town miles from the nearest "herd"—a 4-H project or two—and you will pass not only the Maverick Saloon, but also perhaps "The Maverick" in the form of a hefty RV. Head east towards Montana, and you can stop at Maverick Realty to shop for a ranchette, and then pick up "The Maverick" at the gourmet pizza shop next door. By labeling a writer like MacLane this way, it might seem that I have stereotypically packaged her, projecting the market's preoccupation with MacLane as a gutsy pioneer gal. Such a projection, though, is exactly the point. The word *maverick* simultaneously suggests the rugged individualism that these writers actually did possess and points to the ways in which western tropes yield commercial gain when yoked to the most unlikely of subjects.

In the case of real nineteenth-century cattle, the idea of rebellion associated with mavericks belies the fact that they were, after all, domesticated animals raised for profit (even if a few did get away). Controlled by corporations, they were driven to greener pastures north, and then shuttled through Chicago and other Midwestern cities to eastern and international markets. Such circulation resembled that of a legion of other western resources including not only livestock, grain, timber, and ore, but also writers and artists who capitalized upon the West and who, much like these other commodities, were liable to boom and bust cycles. (Just think of the spectacular rise and fall of Bret Harte and Albert Bierstadt, two of the earliest western chroniclers to saturate national markets.)[1] Like Willa Cather's Thea Kronborg — and arguably, like Cather herself — MacLane, Whiteley, and Harrison were transformed by a network of patrons and employers from regional raw materials into national commodities and transformed as well from westerners to easterners.

Unlike cattle and wheat, however, writers have agency. If MacLane, Whiteley, and Harrison can be read as exploited western resources, they also can be read as individuals who themselves exploited the West and the opportunities it afforded them. As Harrison stated, "I am glad I choosed Calif. for my home before I left as every one know it" (192). I like the name *maverick* for these writers because it suggests troublemaking: synonyms for *maverick* include *renegade, rebel, heretic,* and even *traitor.* For these women who manipulated the West in their "fictions of selfhood," this last points to the ways in which they betrayed popular representations of the West. In this respect they can be read as early-twentieth-century predecessors of Krista Comer's new western regionalists of the 1970s, who exhibit, Comer states, "female attempts to . . . recast the spatial field of the West."[2] MacLane,

Whiteley, and Harrison's texts ask us to consider several questions: What does it mean to be a western autobiographer? What role might region play in articulating identity and in reception? When is region present—and when absent?

This study examines the role the West played in these autobiographers' constructions of maverick identity as they revised western American myths and back-trailed to the East and Europe. It examines as well the West's role in their history of publication and reception as women at once provincial and outlandish, and argues for the close relationship between western and cosmopolitan identity. Comer contends, "Given that so many spatial maneuvers happen quietly, the first task in a study of regionally conceived spaces is to render spatial power plays more audible, even clamorous."[3] *Maverick Autobiographies* takes on this task: to show the ways in which places mattered in these mavericks' texts, careers, and lives. In so doing, it narrows the wide historical gap in the field of western women's literature left between Comer's study of contemporary texts, *Landscapes of the New West: Gender and Geography in Contemporary Women's Writing* (1999), and Annette Kolodny's now classic analysis of the fantasies of eighteenth- and nineteenth-century white female settlers and writers, *The Land Before Her: Fantasy and Experience of the American Frontiers* (1984).

In the latter, Kolodny examines the strategies by which, in contrast to male fantasies of western landscapes as a seductive or maternal woman's body, white women made a literal and imaginative space for themselves in the American West as they "claimed the frontiers as a potential sanctuary for an idealized domesticity" and dreamed of small-scale "gardens."[4] Yet the relationships Kolodny describes among women, the West, and their writing (her study concludes in the 1860s) have little application to the early twentieth-century writers I discuss. By the turn of the twentieth century, both the American West and American women writers were very different from their mid-nineteenth-century counterparts. The ideology of separate spheres had lost some of its sway, and the era is marked by a proliferation of writers who moved away from the professional identity of the domestic fictionists to present themselves as artists.[5] By this time, as well, the West had been largely "settled." The region was home to many

Euro-American cities and towns possessing histories that already comprised several generations, communities that in many respects resembled eastern ones more than they differed. Their populations included, of course, numerous women who had been born in them.

These women, unlike some of their foremothers, did not feel the need to assert the credentials that justified their writing about the West. They did not question their own status as westerners. On the contrary, their sense of profound familiarity with the region was a source of discontent: the white writers I discuss represent their social landscape as having become banal. Jean Stafford maintained of her western girlhood that the exotic West "existed only in memory, and I could not wait to quit my tamed-down native grounds. As soon as I could I hotfooted it across the Rocky Mountains and across the Atlantic Ocean."[6] Since one of the most pressing needs of these mavericks was to escape the "tame" life expected of them, the fantasy of the garden in the West was the very one that they would reject. It is the eastern United States and other nations, not the West, that they perceived as the alluring territory inviting trespass. Personal identity, these writers show, can depend upon a dream of an East that encompasses Europe and even Asia, a dream that extends across social classes.

Kolodny's continuing dominance in the field is an indicator of the dearth of work in western women's literature. With the prominent exceptions of Comer, Brigitte Georgi-Findlay, and Susan J. Rosowski, no scholar of Kolodny's stature has followed her, either to examine the ways in which women of succeeding generations write about the West, or to examine those nineteenth-century women who allowed their imaginative engagement with the West to range beyond domestic fantasies.[7] It is this absence I address in exploring the ways in which women used the West to write about themselves, to succeed as published authors, and to find adventure. The lives and texts of MacLane, Whiteley, and Harrison, along with those of their fiction-writing contemporaries, both supplement and challenge Kolodny's arguments about western women. They not only show the ways in which post-frontier western women related differently to the West than did their settling forebears, but also suggest that even prior to the 1860s, some women may have used the West in very different ways than those Kolodny describes.

Kolodny focuses on women who moved to the West; I focus on those who moved out of it. And the West itself, of course, "moves"—often unevenly, and the line between "Midwest" and "West" is rarely clear. Throughout the nineteenth-century and into the twentieth, the West included urban areas as well as frontier. As wild as parts of the nineteenth-century West may have seemed, many were easily reached by railroad (a traveler on a Pullman in Nebraska in 1871, remembered his coach as "like a slice out of one of the Eastern cities set down bodily in the midst of a perfect wilderness").[8] Development pressed in from the Pacific seaboard as well as from the Atlantic, and also moved on a north-south axis. Georgi-Findlay notes, "Urban and agricultural frontiers, mining and Indian frontiers develop and continue to exist simultaneously in the American West, overlapping, determining, and complementing one another."[9] Such discrepancy accounts for why Portland residents found Whiteley just as fantastic as Bostonians did.[10]

Even more so than with other regional identities, the variability of the West has vexed the question of what makes a writer "western." First of all, where *is* the West, and must the western writer be born, bred, or die there? Must she take the West as her central subject? Espouse a distinctly western sensibility? Arguably, none of the mavericks I discuss fulfill these criteria. Born in Winnipeg and having had a Minnesota childhood, MacLane set both her texts in Butte and spotlighted the city and its environs. Her main focus, however, was herself and her desire to be elsewhere; she examined her environment only insofar as it affected her. Whiteley did grow up in western Oregon and set her text there. Yet although various details serve to place the text, her fairytale scenes of forest harmony often seem generic, her Oregon woods indistinguishable from any other woods; her narrative, moreover, reflects her deep yearning for other lands and other times. Both writers fled the West when barely out of their teens: MacLane to eastern urban centers, returning to Butte only under duress; Whiteley to these same centers and then abroad.

Harrison was already overseas by the time she began writing about herself as a Californian. Of the three, my claim to Harrison as a western writer is surely the most vulnerable. I cannot include Harrison in some of my arguments about western women since she focuses on how travel, rather than environment, implicates

identity. With the exception of a Hawaiian epilogue, Harrison sets
none of her text in the West, and she spent only a handful of years
in Los Angeles before devoting her life to travel. Los Angeles and
Hawaii, moreover, are places associated with movies, surf, and
Chicano/a and Asian ethnicity rather than the open range of the
cattle industry and cowboys and Indians; they are, therefore, especially susceptible to charges of inauthenticity as western locales. So too, as Comer suggests, does Harrison's identity as an
African American woman make her invisible in most conceptions
of the West.[11] These very difficulties, however, make it all the
more critical to read Harrison through a western lens, to resist the
total association of the West with rural spaces and whiteness.[12]
Harrison had a choice of origin stories and chose the West for a
reason—for the romance and the breakdown of rigid hierarchies
it connoted. Yet for all of her bragging of Hollywood, Harrison
also chose not to stay in the West or, for that matter, the continental United States. Despite having established in L.A. close ties
with white employers and friends, Harrison nevertheless left
as soon as she was able—out of a desire for adventure and in-
dependence and, perhaps, out of an aversion to the racism that
permeated all American regions, as Hollywood productions so
clearly revealed. Like MacLane and Whiteley, Harrison too re-
acted against the limitations of the West.

These writers' regional articulations were engendered by their
cosmopolitan aspirations, a consequence of western love of, and
nervous need for, mobility. Like maverick cattle, they did not stay
where they were expected to. Their record of their intense desire
to relocate themselves—physically, psychologically, genealogi-
cally—is perhaps what most vividly distinguishes them from
other autobiographers. By moving, they hoped to alter their class
status, less so in material than aesthetic terms. As young women,
they had images, often seeded by books and magazines, of what
they wanted their lives to be like. They fantasized achieving a
lifestyle appropriate to an inner aristocracy that derived not from
family or wealth, but from taste and sensibility. Therefore, they
had to move: the way of life befitting such sensibility, their texts
maintain, is simply unattainable in the places they find themselves.

None of the mavericks I discuss suggests (as men's narratives often do) that she wishes to leave her native community because she is precluded from privileges there that she hopes to attain elsewhere. Nor do the three authors express any envy for the lives of those around them. Whereas men's texts often portray relocation as an attempt "to escape . . . the chains of social class,"[13] as Frederick Turner put it in his frontier thesis, to find the freedom, space, and economic opportunities that afford autonomy, women's texts are more likely to depict moving as a way to *find* class — in other words, to find a certain kind of lifestyle.[14] One might expect, for example, that Harrison chafed to leave Mississippi "only" because of racism and her lowly status there. Yet the preface suggests otherwise, maintaining that, inspired by a travel magazine, Harrison resolved to "sail faraway to strange places" because "Around me no one has the life I want. . . . not even the rich ladies I work for" (ix). Harrison fled not just her own position in Mississippi, but the society as a whole. Analogously, MacLane's text contends that no one in Butte, no matter what their wealth or power, operates outside of a system of bad taste she is desperate to escape ("From insipid sweet wine; from men who wear moustaches; from the sort of people that call legs 'limbs'; from bedraggled white petticoats; kind Devil deliver me. From unripe bananas; from bathless people; from a waist-line that slopes up in the front; kind Devil deliver me" [78]). The only way she can be "delivered" from such affronts, MacLane asserts, is by deliverance from Butte itself. Faulkner has made infamous the love/hate relationship one might have with a region. But rarely do critics stress the hate side of the equation.

That these writers do not engage the themes traditionally considered western surely contributes to their exclusion from overviews of western women's writing. Early-twentieth-century autobiographers, MacLane, Whiteley, and Harrison neither describe the non-native nineteenth-century experience of newly adapting to the West nor, as in contemporary literature, the experience of returning to one's western roots. Even more important, although the West plays a central role in their texts and self-presentations, these writers identify themselves only intermittently as westerners. Their contemporaries read them in the same way. Sometimes Whiteley and MacLane were perceived as Oregon or Montana writers; at other times, categories of gender or class eclipsed geography. Harrison's racial identity made it impossible for readers ever to conceive of her as western, despite her own assertions.

We rarely highlight the sporadic nature of regional identity and its consequences. Despite the demonstration of the interrelated nature of race, gender, class, and place in fields such as women's and African American studies, studies of western texts often do not emphasize that region exists in complex relationships to factors that inflect or even overshadow it. Take the example of the critical reception of Stafford's "The Mountain Day." The story's narrator first details her family's summer home in the Colorado mountains, including its horses, antiques, carefully rustic decor, and servants. She goes on to describe a wonderful day during which she, her sister, and their fiancés ride and picnic in the hills. On their return, they discover that the family's two Irish maids have drowned, triggering for the girls an epiphany about the nature of love. Drawing on insights into differences between men and women's experiences in the West, critics concur in reading the story as one depicting the perils of the West for women. As well-intentioned as this reading may be, however, it obscures the class dynamics at work. "The Mountain Day" shows that although the West is dangerous for working-class women, for wealthy women it serves as a private playground and an arena for personal growth. Suffused with class longing, "The Mountain Day" is not simply a story about women and the West, but a story about the differing relationships between women of different classes and the West. Region may initially seem a relatively safe, uncharged category. As a category of analysis, however, the West can still camouflage large portions of the population, whether women, peoples of color, or the working classes.

Western literary scholarship has often been accused of lacking sophistication, and various theories circulate in explanation.[15] Yet a fundamental and particularly thorny problem in Western studies is simply an excessive insistence on region. One of the most fascinating aspects of the maverick autobiographies I discuss, as well as the hardest to pinpoint, is the slippage between their appearance as Western texts and their appearance as simply American ones. Region is both present and not present, important and not important.

In part, region unevenly colors texts and writers because region itself suffuses into larger domains. The West has always been a part of national and global economic and social networks. John Keeble asserts, "It's important that Western writers not become entrenched in their Westernness, because the world doesn't operate that way anymore. . . . The Alaskan fishery is controlled by the Japanese; you can't write poems about salmon without knowing that."[16] We might question Keeble on his use of the word "anymore": did the West ever operate independently?

Consider Whiteley, living in a turn of the century logging camp. Tracking Whiteley through archival materials can feel surreal for the researcher — these materials seem so different from her text. Especially on first reading, *The Story of Opal* can seem to be a portrait of some universal, ahistorical nature child begat by the luxuriant abundance of her forest home. Yet Whiteley's childhood collection of books reveals her as very much a participant in a modern American marketplace. The collection includes a how-to guide on writing for magazines, Gene Stratton-Porter's hugely best-selling *A Girl of the Limberlost,* and issues of the catalog *Birdskins,* distributed by W. F. H. Rosenberg: "Naturalist and Importer of Exotic Zoological Collections, Dealer in Mammal and Bird Skins, Birds' Eggs, Reptiles, Batrachians, Fishes, Lepidoptera." Even overlooking the fact that Whiteley lived in a settlement predicated on the transformation of trees into lumber, her "raw" materials reveal themselves as deeply implicated in "cooked" enterprises.

The relative mobility of its writers reflects the West's network of connections with other regions, especially in its role as provider. T. M. Pearce remarks that Cather, when compared to other regionalists such as William Faulkner and Sarah Orne Jewett, "seemed almost a wanderer," her movements spanning the Great Plains, the Southwest, New England, Europe, and the Atlantic Maritimes.[17] The trajectory of any of the writers I discuss is as complex and far flung as Cather's. It isn't news that regional writers cover ground.[18] Yet I would build upon Pearce's observation and contend that compared to New England and Southern regionalists, western writers logged more miles. This greater wandering was due in part simply to the distances between western locales and the eastern urban centers often necessary to liter-

ary production. It was also due to perception. Western intellectuals usually wanted to be, and believed that they needed to be,
versed in the East.

This predilection for mobility — or sense of the urgency of mobility — appears as a salient theme in the work of early-twentieth-
century western women. Their texts emphasize their protagonists'
resistance to their home communities and the necessity of leave-
taking. The conviction of being out of place is often expressed
through a portrayal of the heroine's affinity both with others who
are racially more closely associated with the West and, paradoxi-
cally enough, with unpeopled western landscapes.

In this regard, *The Song of the Lark* (1915) is surely a prototypical text. Cather's novel both contributes and responds to early-
twentieth-century conceptions of western women artists, in trac-
ing the emergence of Thea Kronborg from obscure beginnings
in small-town Moonstone, Colorado, to opera glory in New York
City. Thea's artistry is rooted in a complex interplay of genealogy
and geography, the grafting of her pure-blooded Scandinavian
inheritance onto the vitality of a new yet ancient world. Thea's
blond hair both marks her as a Swede and reflects her affinity
with the American desert, with its "yellow prickly-pear blossoms
. . . not so sweet, but wonderful."[19]

In contrast to the white Philistines who dominate the town,
Cather depicts Moonstone's ethnic minorities as having an innate
endowment of artistic sensibility. A German educates Thea, and
Mexicans sing with her. However, her teacher is timeworn, and
though talent carries a charge of estrangement and hard work for
Thea, the Mexicans sing and play communally and only for pleasure. Cather symbolizes Thea's difference through contrasting
her voice with theirs. "How it leaped from among those dusky
male voices! How it played in and about and around and over
them, like a goldfish darting among creek minnows, like a yellow
butterfly soaring above a swarm of dark ones."[20] The "yellow"
quality of Thea's soaring voice suggests a racial superiority as
well as a gendered one. Cather more fully expresses her concep-
tion of Thea as the flower of an advanced civilization in her description of the girl's sojourn among the cliff-dwellings of Panther
Canyon, where empathy with the vanished, childlike cliff-
dwellers fans her ambition. Primitive stepping stones leading to
the pinnacle of high culture, the "folk" cultures that Thea en-

counters in America do not transform her but rather enable her to realize her essential self.

In contrast to Thea's comfortable cultural borrowing and linear progress, consider the tortured self-conflict of the mixed-race heroine of *Cogewea, The Half-Blood*.[21] The Okanogan author, Mourning Dove, aspired to the status of artist just as ardently as did the white writers I discuss, despite what may have been different motivations, and chronicled such aspiration in her novel. *Cogewea* depicts the longings of its Montana heroine, half-white and half-Okanogan, to find a place in the world that satisfies both her Native attachments and Euro-American ambitions. Unable even to imagine such a place, Cogewea attempts a near disastrous elopement. The novel ends in stasis with her engagement to another half-blood and their agreement to remain in the "corral" to which they and their kind have been consigned.

My mavericks, resisting identification with the white middle-class circles that dominated their home communities, liked to imagine themselves as "multiculturally" sophisticated, privy to less hegemonic cultures and standing outside of an Americanness that they saw as generic and provincial. Harrison achieved this insider/outsider status, not wholly out of choice. For MacLane and Whiteley and other white western writers, however, this was more often envisioned than achieved. Although these women imagined a kind of cultural or even ethnic hybrid nature for themselves and their heroines, their cross-cultural interactions mostly took place under controlled and exceptional circumstances. MacLane made a point of how much she enjoyed talking with an Italian peddler woman, but the conversation she describes occurred not inside her house, but at the threshold. Whiteley liked to dress up as an Indian maiden, but is not known to have had any actual contact with Native American cultures. It is no coincidence that Mourning Dove's text rather than Cather's dramatizes uneasy cultural dualism rather than easily digested lessons. My intention here is not to chastise middle-class white writers for their inability to make themselves or their characters authentically "hybrid." Rather, it is to show that the needs of white women were often met more by the imagination than by the literal facts of their lives, more by the subjective than by the social.

In the end, the early twentieth-century texts of white women often demonstrate more sustained relationships with western landscapes than western peoples. And such relationships with the land, of course, are made possible by these writers' "legacy of conquest" and the fantasies of ownership it engenders.[22] They emphasize the degree to which they experience the land around them as theirs, and describe a sense of ownership running far deeper than that bought with legal title. This sense derives from their artistic, epistemological, or emotional commitment to the land. Georgia O'Keeffe expressed it in declaring of a mountain she often painted, "It's my private mountain. It belongs to me. God told me if I painted it enough I could have it."[23]

Even as these women make such profound claims to the region, however, they also express a sense of dislocation and their conviction that they must leave. This conviction, again, is often expressed through racial theories. Whereas Mourning Dove invokes a fusion of culture and race to show where Cogewea belongs, Cather uses race to show where her heroine should not be: Thea's Swedishness precludes lazy desert life. Likewise, MacLane depicts her "barbaric" and "passionate" Scottish blood as proving that she is unsuited to the tameness of Butte; Whiteley, even more isolated from direct contact with Old World cultures, maintains that her aristocratic French blood makes her out of place in an Oregon lumber camp.

Such texts portraying the West as a place that fledgling artists must leave remind us that an essential chapter of western history remains unwritten: the "back migration" to the East that was as pervasive as pioneering out.[24] It is easy to forget that as a young married woman, Laura Ingalls Wilder headed southeast from South Dakota to spend the rest of her life in Missouri. Yet in their autobiographical texts, many early twentieth-century women writers depict the West not as destination, but as origins from which they must escape. In contrast to Horace Greeley's urging of young men to "go West" in order to "grow up with the country," these young women present the region as a hindrance to their growth. Although they portray their kinship with its outdoor spaces as forging their characters, this kinship is not that of classic frontier lore: they enter less populated territory not to escape from "civilization," but rather to escape from settlements they regard as undercivilized. Their longings are not so much for solitude as for more congenial social landscapes; they describe solitude as a second-best alternative. Countering notions of the

West as a site of freedom, they suggest, moreover, that the unpeopled spaces that could be intermittently liberating for unconventional women were also responsible for their claustrophobia, by virtue of having separated them in the first place from more compatible communities. Cogently expressing this view, Stafford has one of the narrators in her ironically titled collection "Cowboys and Indians, and Magic Mountains" recall "We stared west at the mountains and quailed at the look of the stern white glacier; we wildly scanned the prairies for escape. . . . 'If only we were something besides kids! Besides girls!'"[25]

In representing the inadequacy of their home communities in their texts, these women recall the turn of the century American school dubbed by Carl Van Doren as "Revolt from the Village": "a superior youth, of rebellious energy and somewhat inarticulate ambition, detaches himself in disgust from his native village and makes his way to the city."[26] Yet Van Doren's "youth" is explicitly male, while western women writers reveal that their frustration arose from the limited scope that their communities allowed them as women. Consequently, whereas "Revolt from the Village" texts often contrast the banality of a place with the glory of its frontier past, this narrative of decline is conspicuously absent from the texts I discuss. As Melody Graulich points out, the roles available to women in frontier myths are not likely to appeal to aspiring women artists, and thus they are not likely to turn to these myths.[27] This might account for why MacLane in her own self-mythologizing did not exploit the legend of her father, "Flatboat MacLane," westerner extraordinaire, but instead touted her Scottish heritage. Likewise, Whiteley disowned a pioneer ancestry in favor of a royal French past. Mary Austin countered hagiographic representations of pioneering by describing her California homesteading experience as a "perpetual picnic" that struck her as "quaintly ancestral";[28] Mourning Dove claimed her mixed-blood heroine as the embodiment of the frontier;[29] Harrison identified the West through the movies it produced.

These women's texts, significantly different in their cultural positions, all decline to long for the West that was. Their indifference to or overt rejection of frontier myths thwarts the nostalgia characteristic of western writing that has contributed to its dismissal. Thus, even as frontier myths made the West resistant to women writers, its exclusion of them helped them write a West of the present.[30] Rudyard Kipling, traveling by train from San Francisco to Portland, pleasurably settled back as he "waited for the flying miles to turn over the pages of the book I knew. They brought me all I desired."[31] In contrast, these women writers from the West wanted new books.

In writing these books, they moved far from tired western scripts. Their texts depict a region that can seem "Midwestern" in its provincialism and rigidity, and yet deeply western in its thinly populated spaces and signs of the human extraction of resources from the land. They cover an expanse of varied terrain: Cather's prairies, MacLane, Mourning Dove, and Stafford's high plains and mountains, Austin's southwestern deserts, Whiteley's northwestern forests, and Harrison's L.A. Yet with perhaps the exception of the last, several factors unite these areas, including a remoteness from cultural centers that contributes to a provincial small-town atmosphere; ready access to large stretches of relatively uninhabited land; a frontier past at only one or two removes either geographically or historically; and a relatively recent or ongoing Native American presence. Despite their many differences, this shared regional experience fosters a certain similarity among early- to mid-twentieth-century western women writers. As a group, they are linked by the ways in which they use the West to portray themselves as women of superior sensibility; such a portrayal often reflects racial and class fantasies. In negotiating an identity as westerner and artist, these writers work to distance themselves from their families and social milieu and avow an innate aristocracy. Asserting their genius without kinship, they produced a distinct kind of regional American individualism. Their self-portrayals as western iconoclasts were not only personally but also professionally significant, winning them wide readerships.

At the very same time that Owen Wister was fixing the West as frontier in popular imagination, another far more interesting image of the West was being created: as an empty place so devoid of culture or fulfillment as to fill its inhabitants with dreams of mobility and of fusion with other, more passionate races. Publishers were interested, for mildly exploitative reasons, in these women's attempts to use their writing both to abet and to chronicle their escape from the West. In editing and marketing their texts, they tried to turn the real West into a generic, safe, possessable West;

journalists, subsequently, used these writers as figures around which one could rally to express admiration, envy, longing, and contempt for East, West, and South. As a result, the real women were often left, to use Harrison's phrase, "betwixt and between." Nevertheless, countless readers were able to keep in sight these mavericks as mavericks, responding to their fierce individuality even as they turned to them for gratification.

1

The Devil and Desire in Butte, Montana

> I wish to give to the world a naked Portrayal of Mary MacLane: her
> wooden heart, her good young woman's-body, her mind, her soul.
> Mary MacLane, *The Story of Mary MacLane, By Herself*

With no published work to her name, shortly after her high school graduation MacLane sent a manuscript entitled *I Await the Devil's Coming* to Chicago, that typical first destination for a westerner intent on flight. She chose as her prospective publisher Fleming H. Revell Company, self-described "Publishers of Evangelical Literature." George Doran recalled

> a most extraordinary manuscript coming to our office. . . . *I Await the Devil's Coming*. It was unusual but still might easily come within the range of a premillenarian's thought and expression. I thought no more about it until I sat down to read. The dedication was far from pious or prophetic. As I recall it ran, "To that devil with the steel-grey eyes who some day, who knows, will come to this weary wooden broken heart of mine, I dedicate this my book.". . . I read on into the book—done in most perfect and painstaking handwriting. I discovered the most astounding and revealing piece of realism I had ever read. Clearly we could not publish it, but Mary must have a publisher. The next day I sent it to dear old Ned Stone, of Stone & Kimball, publishers, and son of Melville. He arranged for its immediate publication but under the

simple title Mary MacLane. Its success was so great that Ned invited Mary to come from the dunes of Butte, Montana, to visit
Chicago. She came.[1]

The previous chapter discusses how some women wrote about
the West in order to escape it: both the West's literal geographic
domain and the staid way of life they regarded endemic to it.
MacLane's early practice clearly illustrates such use. In her
middle years, she found that both economic and aesthetic factors led her to return to the West to continue her life project of
writing about herself. As a young woman, however, she conceived of her writing in terms only of the escape its success could
bring her, not of the rootedness it might require. And, as Doran's
account suggests, her exodus and her transformation from westerner into easterner fascinated her readership. Her words in *The
Story of Mary MacLane* proved prophetic: "Let me but win my
spurs, and then you will see me—of womankind and young—
valiantly astride a charger riding down the world, with Fame following at the charger's heels, and the multitudes agape" (21).

Naked-Soul Ladies

Although *The Story* is thematically complex, it is simple in shape
and subject. Written in diary form, the text describes three months
in MacLane's life, "very like the three months that preceded them,
to be sure, and the three that followed them—and like all of the
months that have come and gone" (123). At the time MacLane
lived in her parents' home in a middle-class Butte neighborhood,
occupied only by writing, walks, some desultory housework, and
her frantic desire to leave. Each entry is dated, but so little appears
to happen in her life that one day is indistinguishable from the
next. Staged against the wasteland around Butte, the text consists of analyses of MacLane's mental and emotional states inter-
spersed with pleas for rescue. It dramatizes the stagnancy of her
life through its own repetition, returning again and again to her
solitude and loneliness, femininity and sensuality, youth, genius,
and longing.

    MacLane presents her self as a work of art and invests with sig-
nificance the seemingly insignificant—her penchant for fudge,

the way she mends a tear in her skirt. As she asserts in her sequel text, *I, Mary MacLane* (1917), "I could go on writing all night these seemingly trivial but really significant details relating to the outer genius. But these will answer. These to any one who knows things will be a revelation" (264).[2] She focuses on herself instead of her history, thereby addressing Virginia Woolf's critique of autobiography: "They leave out the person to whom things happened."[3] At the same time, she provides relief from her self-portrayal by her vignettes of Butte life and Butte middle-class hypocrisy, visions of distant landscapes, speculation about the ramifications of publication on her life, professions of love for her "anemone lady," and torrid imagined scenes with the devil. *The Story*, held together by tropes such as "the Sand and Barrenness," "My Soul," "the Gray Dawn," "the Red Red Line," and, most important, "the Devil," reveals MacLane as heir to the New Woman writers of the 1890s. These women experimented, as Elaine Showalter shows, "with new fictional forms that they called 'keynotes,' 'allegories,' 'fantasies,' 'monochromes,' or 'dreams'" in an effort to "explore a hitherto unrecorded female consciousness."[4] MacLane's language is usually vivid, spare, and exact.

Referring to her text as if it were already published, MacLane directs the reader's attention to its frontispiece photograph: "You can see by my picture that my [shirt-]waist curves gracefully out. Only it is not all flesh—some of it is handkerchief. It amuses me to do this" (99). In playing such games with her readers, she confirms that she has not written this so-called diary as a diary at all, sitting down each night to record the day. Hers is a calculated, literary production. MacLane uses the premise of diary to establish her literary legitimacy via links to Continental autobiographers. She, like these others, emphasizes the authentic sincerity of her "naked Portrayal" (17) even while alluding to plans for publication. Although the aggressiveness of MacLane's "I" tempts one not to look past it, *The Story of Mary MacLane* was far from sui generis.

MacLane was deeply influenced by one of the most notorious texts of the 1890s, *Journal de Marie Bashkirtseff,* and the traditions from which this text sprang. Bashkirtseff, a Russian expatriate, lived in Paris and wrote in French. Her book consists of close to one thousand pages edited from the diary she kept between the ages of fourteen and twenty-six. A protest against the restricted lives of bourgeois women, it records her busy days along with her endlessly unsatisfied desire for love, fame, and artistic success — "all that I have been crying for since the world began" (278). As Doran's account demonstrates, the arrival of MacLane's book out of "nowhere"—literally and literarily—makes a compelling story. A close look, however, at Bashkirtseff's use of the genre of diary to voice outrage; the intense interest in reading women's autobiography that the publication of her diary fostered; and Bashkirtseff's own predecessors goes far towards understanding the literary climate in which MacLane acted. A *Mademoiselle* journalist later wrote, "By 1902, Marie had been dead for a generation but the pollen of her life story was still lazily adrift. Some of it had floated as far as Butte, Montana, of all places."[5] Her incredulity is typical. But as MacLane's work shows, Butte was neither as distant from nor as unlike Paris as most imagined.

Bashkirtseff states in her text, "a man who is indignant . . . mounts the platform and makes himself a reputation. But a woman has no platform at her disposal . . . she grows indignant, but can only be eloquent before her dressing-table; result, zero" (420). Although the diary had by then become an established place for a young lady to wax "eloquent," by planning from the onset to make hers public, Bashkirtseff transformed the genteel practice into a "platform." She discusses in the diary itself her plans to publish it:

> If I [die young], I will have my journal published, which cannot fail to be interesting. But as I talk of publicity, this idea of being read has perhaps spoilt, nay, destroyed, the sole merit of such a book? Well, no! To begin with, I wrote for a long time without a thought of being read, and in the next place it is precisely because I hope to be read that I am absolutely sincere. If this book be not the exact, the absolute, the strict truth, it has no right to exist. (Author's Preface, xxxi)

Asserting "I am my own heroine" (31), rejecting ideals of girlish self-repression and domesticity, Bashkirtseff describes herself as split between her masculine interior and "diabolically feminine envelope." This split is mirrored by her use of the genre of diary. On the one hand, in France diaries had come to be marked as feminine when dedicated to moral or religious musings. Yet with her sustained focus on her self, Bashkirtseff adopted a mode that, if not masculine, was certainly read as unfeminine, more typical of men active in the public sphere than of well-bred young women.

The diary was published by her family in 1887, and its renown was immediate.[6] Bashkirtseff served as a rallying figure for the New Woman debate in America and Europe, either lauded or condemned. Bernard Shaw, for example, noted a critic's claim that she was "anything you like but a natural woman with a heart to love, and a soul to find its supreme satisfaction in sacrifice" and went on to counter "of all the idealist abominations that make society pestiferous, I doubt if there be any so mean as that of forcing self-sacrifice on a woman under pretense that she likes it. . . . The manly man is he who takes the Bashkirtseff view of himself."[7] Bashkirtseff's text inspired the same kind of hyperbole that would later greet MacLane's: "It is this Journal with which the world is now ringing, and which it is hardly too much to say is likely to carry the fame of Marie Bashkirtseff over the face of the civilised globe." After William Gladstone declared it "a book without a parallel," the diary, it was said, was translated "into nearly every civilized language."[8] Publishers issued new editions and companion volumes up until the 1920s, and well into the twentieth century it was read as a kind of cult text.[9] Bashkirtseff's notoriety in the United States laid the groundwork for MacLane's celebrity and, less directly, for Opal Whiteley's.

Like MacLane herself, Bashkirtseff is often presented as an anomaly, ahead of her time and operating outside of prevailing literary forces. Yet despite the fanfare that greeted her revelations, she was not alone among writers of her era in making such a public record of a private self. Philip LeJeune documents that throughout the nineteenth century, French girls had both assiduously kept their own diaries and read the published diaries, real and fictional, of other girls and young women. Diary texts were "codified" by the influence of Mlle Monniot's fictional *Journal de Marguerite* (1858) and Eugenie de Guerin's diary (1862), and the market in publishing and selling such texts boomed.[10] Bashkirtseff's journal can also be grouped more directly with the era's *journaux intimes,* such as that written by Henri-Frédéric Amiel. *Journaux intimes* are characterized by the same insistence on sincerity and complete revelation that marks Bashkirtseff's text, with the diarist himself being "the absolute focus of attention."[11] Although George Sand's *Histoire de ma Vie* played an influential role in the development of the genre,[12] published journals were associated more with men than women, especially men of advanced years and some prominence. Differing from these diarists by virtue of both her sex and youth, then, Bashkirtseff contributed to diverting the *journal intime* from its established course—from a medium of distinguished European men—to one that eventually included young and unknown American girls.

Even as late as the 1940s, Bashkirtseff was still remembered as the source of the practice among American girls and young women of writing "psychological" diaries—with MacLane abetting her. Of "the girl who started the fashion in confession," *Mademoiselle* maintained in an article entitled, "Dear Diary—Will Secret Scribblings Bring Fame to a New Marie Bashkirtseff or Mary MacLane?"

> Within a generation . . . her mirrored image had multiplied into the millions. The world seemed to be full of girls who kept diaries. They had this in common with Marie: each girl was writing a book, and each was her own heroine. . . . The Journal's effect upon the imaginations of young women was profound. All over the world, girls sat down before mirrors and looked soulfully into their own eyes. "What am I?" they asked themselves. "Not the Me the world knows, but the Real, Suffering, Wonderful Me?" Diaries, which till then had been fairly factual, became psychological jam sessions.[13]

Other accounts suggest that Bashkirtseff inspired young women not only to write revealing self-portrayals but also to circulate them: "since [the publication of Bashkirtseff's journal] we have learned that thousands of girls have been thinking the same thoughts that Marie thought, but have usually lacked her literary ability to give them expression."[14] These hordes were not content simply to stare into their own mirrored eyes, and, although described as not displaying "literary ability," many of their texts attracted considerable interest. So too did those penned by professional writers posing as young women.

Such texts are characterized by a focus on the narrator's desires and hitherto hidden nature, especially in regard to her sexuality. They thus could be read as "low-brow" versions of more literary New Woman texts such as George Egerton's and Olive Schreiner's, which likewise sought to explore, in Egerton's words, the *"terra incognita* of herself."[15] In addition to that of di-

aries, they take the form of love letters, "confessions," "reflections," "comments," or some other first-person mode. Written by
men as well as women (often published under a pseudonym or
anonymously), they are always, however, about a woman and
presented in her voice. Even Mark Twain participated, parodying
the genre in *Eve's Diary*. Of her newly-discovered reflection, his
Eve remarks, "When I found it could talk, I felt a new interest in
it, for I love to talk. . . . I am very interesting, but if I had another
to talk to I could be twice as interesting, and would never stop."[16]
Typically, *Eve's Diary* first appeared in *Harper's Monthly* (1905):
such texts abound in similar magazines. Already divided into
convenient short units, the diary entries and letters, the "confessions" and "comments" suited the increasingly popular "middle-
brow" magazines well.

The vogue for publishing young women's revelations was decried as a sanction of excess and morbidity, and as salient enough
as to constitute a "school."[17] Hugh M. Stutfield stated in an 1895
essay for *Blackwoods*, "Tommyrotics," that "it cannot be denied
that women are chiefly responsible for the 'booming' of books
that are 'close to life'—that is to say, as viewed through sex-
maniacal glasses."[18] A disgruntled reviewer of *The Story of Mary
MacLane* wondered if the book was

> a fake that some one has perpetrated, possibly, to show us the real
> tommyrottenness of all this latterday business of the woman who
> wants to go about exposing her "naked soul" to the atmosphere,
> just so we can see that it has as many spots as a coach-dog. These
> "naked-soul" ladies are a great affliction. They are all so inveter-
> ately young; so incorrigibly green; so mentally chlorotic; so utterly
> rapt in the contemplation of their own imaginary desirability and
> their own diseased desirousness.[19]

The *Detroit Free Press* similarly conjectured that *The Story* might
be a "'roast' on the 'Love Letters' and 'Confessions' and soulful
yearnings generally, which have been more or less periodic in appearance since Marie Bashkirtseff unburdened an egotist's mind
for public edification."[20] Certainly, some of these texts are hardly
compelling. (The heroine of the not unrepresentative *The American Diary of a Japanese Girl* muses that "without beauty woman is
nothing. I prefer death, if I am not given a pair of dark velvety
eyes. One stupid wrinkle on my face would be enough to stun

me."[21]) Yet impatience towards these texts was often expressed with a misogynist tone, suggesting that it arose as much from a predisposition to dismiss the diary texts as a "feminine" mode as from dissatisfaction with their actual quality.

Responses to "naked-soul lady" texts are notable for their suggestion that each book is a version — often a parody — of another, with Bashkirtseff the originating source. They and the women they portray appear as distinguished primarily by vagaries of geography. Havelock Ellis is typical in describing Miles Franklin's *My Brilliant Career* (1901), a diary recording the tribulations of its young, rural, Australian heroine, as "the confessions of a Marie Bashkirtseff of the bush."[22] Contemporaries thus emphasized Bashkirtseff's influence on MacLane and variously dubbed her "the Bashkirtseff of the West," "a Montana Bashkirtseff," "the Butte Bashkirtseff," "the Backwoods Bashkirtseff," "the Rocky Mountain Bashkirtseff," "A Montana Girl. . . . a la Bashkirtseff," a Marie Bashkirtseff "burlesque," "another of the sham Bashkirtseff[s]," "a skit on Marie Bashkirtseff," and "a Marie Bashkirtseff without a conscience, strong where the Russian girl was weak."[23] MacLane encouraged the connection by comparing herself favorably to her in *The Story of Mary MacLane:*

> As for that strange notable, Marie Bashkirtseff, yes, I am rather like her in many points, as I've been told. But in most things I go beyond her. Where she is deep, I am deeper. Where she is wonderful in her intensity, I am still more wonderful in my intensity. Where she had philosophy, I am a philosopher. Where she had astonishing vanity and conceit, I have yet more astonishing vanity and conceit. (14)

The *New York Times* saw MacLane as having introduced in the United States what had been a Continental tradition, noting on her death that "[MacLane was] called the American Bashkirtseff, because she wrote the first — or one of the first — of the personal diary-and-confession books ever written in this country."[24] Yet MacLane did more than just replicate Bashkirtseff's work on American soil. Without question, Bashkirtseff's influence was profound. *The Story of Mary MacLane* centers around the same themes as the *Journal:* an avowed objective to lay the self bare, but a growing belief in the impossibility of doing so; desire for fame and love, anguish at being alone and misunderstood, and a conviction that the journal is the sole place where its writer finally can be known. MacLane's allusions to dying young—in a narrative that otherwise extols her perfect health—appear to be borrowed directly from Bashkirtseff's book. Yet her assessment that she "go[es] beyond" her predecessor is accurate, in that she strips the model Bashkirtseff gave her of all the daily events, characters, and conversations recorded over the course of years, transforming the "real life" diary genre into a much sparer, more literary form. By doing so, she creats an even more concentrated record of longing and self-absorption. One critic put it, she is "Marie Bashkirtseff raised to the 9th power." (Admittedly, in full this critic offers, "If one could imagine Marie Bashkirtseff raised to the 9th power of ignorance, indecency, and an illimitable absorption, with a dash of delirium tremens added, we shall pretty nearly arrive at Butte, Montana, and Mary MacLane."[25])

Whereas Bashkirtseff declared of her journal, "It will only be published after my death, for I cannot lay myself quite bare to the world in my life time" (133), MacLane hoped by publishing hers immediately to transform her life. At the time, she had no money or career prospects and only a summarily terminated education. Like so many westerners, MacLane suffered from attempts to work the West to extravagant gain: through mining speculation her stepfather had lost the money reserved for the children's college expenses, as she learned only as she was about to leave Butte for Stanford.[26] Afterwards she made a desultory effort to get a library position, but searched for no other employment.[27] Denied college, trapped in a city that offered her no palatable work, and determined not to marry, there was little for MacLane to do but step into "the outward role of a family daughter with no responsibilities" (*IMM*, 10)—and, of course, to write. Presenting her autobiography as a powerful agent *in* her life rather than a mere record *of* it, she concludes, "Now I will send my Portrayal into the wise wide world. It may stop short at the publisher; or it may fall still-born from the press; or it may go farther, indeed, and be its own undoing. That's as may be. I will send it. What else is there for me, if not this book?" (123–24). She pleads with her readers for help: "You have the power to take this wooden heart in a tight, suffocating grasp. You have the power to do this with pain for me, and you have the power to do it with ravishing gentleness. But whether or not you will is a different matter" (70); "My life is a dry

and barren life. You can change it. . . . Stranger things have happened. Again, whether you will—that is a quite different thing"
(70); "Do you understand this? That I am telling you my young,
passionate life-agony? Do you listen to it indifferently? Has it no
meaning for any one? For me it means everything" (68).

MacLane's fear of the world's indifference, at least, proved un-
founded: she became, according to Gertrude Atherton, "the most
talked-of young author in the country."[28] Shortly after publication
her book was the number two best-seller in Chicago;[29] nationwide over 80,000 copies were sold within a month, with demand
exceeding supply. *The Story of Mary MacLane* ultimately earned
MacLane $17,000 in royalties and was translated into over thirty
languages.[30]

Invading New England

In passing *The Story* on to Herbert S. Stone & Co. (originally Stone
& Kimball), George Doran did MacLane a good turn. The renown
of Stone, "dedicated to the new and to a sense of the printed book
as an art object in itself," generated interest in *The Story* from the
start.[31] The company was owned by the brothers Herbert S. and
Melville E., sons of the head of the Associated Press, Melville E.
Stone, and was best known for its influential magazine, *The Chap-
Book* (1894–1898), which had garnered it a reputation for avant-
garde production.[32] Stone had published Kate Chopin's *The
Awakening* the previous year, in 1901. The succès de scandale of
Chopin's novel may well have influenced the house in accepting
another book revealing a woman's shocking inner self, especially
considering that Lucy Monroe, its "chief reader and literary editor," had urged the publication of Chopin's book and also cham-
pioned MacLane's.[33] Although Doran does not explain why he
chose Stone for MacLane's manuscript, the house made a fitting
match for MacLane's elegant prose and her generic innovation.
So too did its arty image accord with the aesthetics of absence she
mapped for Butte, a place made weirdly beautiful by all it lacked.

Before publishing *The Story*, Stone & Co. sought to mitigate the
excesses it perceived. Punctuation was made more standard and
the book's dedication to the devil cut along with passages judged
inopportune, including the whole of the entry for February 19,

"Am I not intolerably conceited?"[34] Most significantly, it changed the title from "I Await the Devil's Coming" to "The Story of Mary MacLane," probably out of a desire both to tempt the appetite of a public hungry to sound the soul of some young woman and to avoid too scandalous a title.[35] The change gave Stone a handle on this strange book, reflecting its choice to stress MacLane's connections to other women's "stories"—the autobiographical texts that were coming into vogue—rather than exploit more fully a claim to the bizarre. Like its *Chap-Book,* the publisher was less "decadent" than its renown, which stemmed largely from canny packaging and marketing.

Stone skillfully promoted *The Story,* too. It sent out cryptic notice of its plans to release the "book of the year for 1902."[36] Advertisements quoted Harriet Monroe's praise and claimed *The Story* as "the work of insanity or genius."[37] Most important, Stone exploited its family tie with the Associated Press so that on April 27, 1902, newspapers across the country ran a review.

MacLane was an instant celebrity. Readers were intrigued, as they pondered whether her book was "the work of insanity or genius" and whether western hinterlands could foster true genius. Her impact is suggested by the extent to which she permeated American popular culture. A rash of MacLane songs and cartoons circulated.[38] The vaudeville team of Weber and Fields ran for months "The Story of Mary McPaine," featuring a terrified devil. The Floradora Hextet, a popular singing group, offered MacLane $300 a week to join them.[39] Parodies of *The Story* quickly appeared, including *The Story of Willie Complain, The Devil's Letters to Mary MacLane, By Himself,* and *The Story of Mary MacJane.*[40] MacLane had a brand of hot sauce named after her and endorsed silk stockings; Butte named its local baseball team "The Mary MacLanes";[41] a cigar company bought the rights to "Mary MacLane" and her picture for $500; and Butte's Newboro Drug Store advertised the "Mary MacLane Highball," "with or without ice-cream, cooling, refreshing, invigorating, devilish, the up-to-date drink."[42]

The nature of the response to MacLane's book reminds one of eighteenth-century "Werther-fever" in Europe. A similar portrait of youthful angst (and of course laying the groundwork for MacLane's), Goethe's *The Sorrows of Young Werther* was reworked into parodies, dramas, dances, songs, paintings, and merchandise.[43]

The text, tremendously versatile, both influenced the actions of earnest individuals and lent itself to popular culture and commodification. Yet although it did have such precedent, the enthusiasm for *The Story of Mary MacLane* was also typical of a particular moment in American publishing history, when such enthusiasms were no longer singular but multiple. Fascination with Bashkirtseff's text was thus succeeded by fascination with MacLane's. According to Frank Luther Mott, the entire decade of the 1890s was one of "Literary Fevers," during which "enthusiasms for certain books and authors gathered force suddenly and spread widely through the country with all the exaggerations and the delirium of eulogy that follow upon such epidemics."[44] Suddenly, popular books were enjoying, according to one contemporary, "enormous and absolutely unprecedented sale."[45]

Mott's description of the reception of Walter du Maurier's *Trilby* is evocative of MacLane's ("A new town in Florida was named Trilby. . . . There were Trilby hams, Trilby sausages, and a Trilby hearth-brush"[46]). Literary texts were packaged as products to the extent that one reviewer was moved to complain, "there have been, annually, so many 'novels' of the year that one grows quite dizzy trying to remember their names. And now they are on the verge of giving away a beautiful celluloid paper knife or a cake of soap with every copy."[47] At the same time, as the literal selling of MacLane's name indicates, authors themselves increasingly appeared on sale. MacLane's portrayal of her unrecognized, lonely genius, ironically enough, was an extravagant mass-market success.

From the start, MacLane recognized that she was peddling her own self, asserting in *The Story* "the fact that I am exchanging my tears and my drops of red blood for your gaily-colored trifles is not a thing that thrills me with delight" (81). After publication, she represented herself as helpless before the market, forced, for example, to endorse cigars for a company in order that it not name a whiskey after her. She likewise regretted that anyone who chose could "name all the puppies, babies and highballs after me and I cannot help myself."[48] Her reservations about commercialism may have contributed to her intermittent resistance to publicity efforts. She dodged reporters, to her publisher's frustration, and teased him in writing, "A person has written to you—or will do so—about a French edition of that little book you brought out this spring—the Mary MacLane book. . . . I believe that I consented to some arrangement. I am not prepared to say just what arrangement it is—I've forgotten."[49] Well aware of the power she commanded, MacLane made a display of taking lightly the success she yearned for in *The Story*. Yet despite her shows of carelessness, MacLane closely monitored her own publicity. She did, after all, agree to endorse the cigars.[50]

MacLane's text not only hit the market hard, but also drew deeply personal responses from readers. In a newspaper forum set up for the purpose, earnest fans pledged their devotion:

> Mary MacLane is a genius. She is a great genius, in that she recognizes herself and has the courage to announce it. She distinctly portrays the wall of the human heart for that indefinable something that we never possess in this world. She appeals to the tragic side of life. . . . Mary MacLane's attitude is at all times introspective, and therefore original. I cannot understand how any one can condemn her. She tells the unvarnished truth. I can see the sand and barrenness is [sic] every life with which I come in contact. (Lily May Ivy, New York, New York)

> Is Mary MacLane a genius? Yes. She is more. She is grandly, deliciously beautiful and I believe she is good. She dares to tell to all the world what most people try to keep profoundly guarded. . . . I think she is more intense than she really knows. . . . I love you, Mary MacLane! Not because you say you are a thief and a liar and are not afraid of the devil, but because you are yourself. (Spokane, Washington)[51]

Readers such as these explicitly responded to MacLane's ideas and personality. Equally ardent, critics lauded MacLane for the quality of her writing. Monroe proclaimed "yes, Mary MacLane is a poet. . . . There are splendid sounds and harmonies in her thrilling, vibratory prose."[52] Another reviewer maintained, "only two writers in the western hemisphere have produced faultless English—Nathaniel Hawthorne and Mary MacLane."[53] Monroe and Maria Louise Poole likened her to Emily Brontë,[54] and she was described as "a feminine Walt Whitman . . . who began younger."[55] In accord with Hamlin Garland's admiration of MacLane's "crisp, clear, unhesitating use of English," H. L. Mencken stated, "She is one of the few damsels in this republic . . . who actually knows how to write English. . . . She senses the infinite resilience, the drunken exuberance, the magnificent power and delicacy of the language. She knows words; she has style."[56] Supporting MacLane's claim that she was just as good a speaker as writer, Atherton reported of an interview that she spoke "in a mixture of slang and prose of an almost classical purity."[57]

Although MacLane's book was a best-seller, her audience was perceived as a "high-class" rather than "pop" one.[58] Her most passionate fans appear to have been an intriguing mix of intellectuals and adolescent girls (she "fluttered Vassar," according to Mencken [59]). For different reasons, perhaps, neither group objected to the alleged immorality, the "vulgarity and filth and unwholesome ideas [veiled] in suggestive and carefully worded English," that her detractors perceived.[60]

A remark about one of Bashkirtseff's paintings could well be made of MacLane's self-portrayal: "It is a picture to make people scream, especially if it is known that it is by a woman—a young girl" (*Journal*, 434). Lionel Johnson perhaps locates the source of such hostility in urging Bashkirtseff's admirers to consider, "What would life become were most women like Mdlle. Bashkirtseff? Could any man wish to have a wife, a daughter, a sister, like her? Is it for her qualities that any man loves his mother?"[61] For some of her female readers, MacLane offered the pleasure of vicarious daring, but she appalled many others, particularly men. Decrying her "incoherent ramblings," MacLane's critics were united in their insinuations of insanity. *The Story* was declared "foul, foolish, and futile" and "unmitigated 'rot,'" and MacLane herself "silly, ineffectual" with "a savage jerky soul."[62] Mary Cass Canfield later charged that MacLane "approached Miss Gertrude Stein in a sort of frenzied lack of meaning, and a twisting and crippling of the English tongue."[63] In a sinister evocation of Charlotte Perkins Gilman's "The Yellow Wallpaper" (1892), the *New York Herald* asserted, "It is only charity to think that Mary MacLane is mad. If she is not she ought to be. She should be put under medical treatment and pens and paper kept out of her way until she is restored to reason."[64] The *New York Times*, in keeping with this theme of "restoration," fantasized about properly punishing MacLane for her temerity, incorporating in its rebuke a tribute to American industrialism and a jab at the West:

'Twould be a fearful thing . . . to spank a girl of nineteen. Not at all the proper caper. . . . But the genius of the West is inventive no less than that of the East. And might there not be contrived an automatic slipper, which would rise and fall with the force and unerring precision of the stamps in silver mills, not on the just and unjust, but where it would do the most good, and for the special benefit of Miss Mary MacLane, way out there in Butte, Montana, where she belongs?[65]

MacLane's youth, home, gender, and even appearance contributed to the atmosphere of incredulity that surrounded her book. Readers found it hard to connect the text they read with the young woman claimed as its author. A *Washington Post* review, hailing the work by the "mysterious, lonely, loving, elfish Mary MacLane" as "the most astounding book that has been brought out in years," remarked "the publishers state that the 'girl is a real girl of the name she uses'. . . . One can hardly believe it." Like the outright attacks on MacLane, this generally positive review goes on to insinuate incipient madness: "Who could think of a young woman of nineteen, putting down her innermost thoughts, some of the strangest thoughts, too, that ever coursed through the brain of an erratic mind."[66]

Another suggested that "'The Story of Mary MacLane by Herself' was written by a man, and the appearance on the scene from Butte-Montana of the extremely pretty young person who is supposed to be the authoress is all part of a tremendous advertising scheme."[67] This reader's suspicion is generated by familiarity with a literary market increasingly dependent on "personality" and "schemes" combined with a notion of what young women can plausibly express. The reference to MacLane's "appearance on the scene from Butte-Montana," moreover, points to a widespread impression of the West as a murky, unknowable site of origins. As with Whiteley in the almost inconceivably remote forests of Oregon, one source of the distrust accorded MacLane was the fact that she had "appear[ed]" from "way out there in Butte, Montana,"[68] too far away to be accounted for. Both Whiteley and MacLane attracted detectives to their home towns to investigate whether they actually existed, one of whom concluded, "there is no doubt that Mary McLane [*sic*] . . . is a real person. I have made inquiries in Butte, Mont., where Miss McLane lives, and find that she is all that she paints herself."[69] The West, John D. Dorst reminds us, has long been associated with the duping of naive easterners.[70] The uncertainty of whether these authors were playing a western trick contributed to their appeal—at least until it was concluded, as in Whiteley's case, that one had, indeed, been duped.

In connection with the notion that "naked-soul lady" texts were simply versions of one another, others suggested that if not an outright hoax, at the least *The Story* was "a caricature, invented by some evil minded journalist, intent on making the worst possible picture of a woman."[71] As cited, the *Detroit Free Press*, concurring with suspicion that the book was "a fake that some one has perpetrated, possibly, to show us the real tommyrottenness of all this latter-day business of the woman who wants to go about exposing her 'naked soul,'"[72] declared, "the only possible excuse for the printing of such stuff as 'The Story of Mary MacLane' resides in the supposition that it is in the nature of a 'roast' on the 'Love Letters' and 'Confessions' and soulful yearnings generally, which have been more or less periodic in appearance since Marie Bashkirtseff."[73] These comments point to a perception of such texts as proliferating in threatening, indiscriminate abundance.

To some, therefore, the nation's enthusiasm for MacLane appeared as evidence of its own degeneracy: "'Whither are we drifting?'"[74] Canfield remarked on the "danger that [MacLane] may be embraced by a certain section of the public, which is always full of that hyper-sentimental curiosity that in this country washes up like a great sloppy sea at the feet of 'Personality—capital P.'"[75] H. W. Boynton, referring to "the swaggering journal of the ignorant girl whose name filled the national mouth not long ago," argued in the *Atlantic Monthly*,

> It is impossible to have any sort of attention to the passing show of fiction without being struck and struck again with the extreme cleverness of the performance. . . . What [the public] really enjoys is a certain brilliancy, sometimes of a smooth workmanship . . . and sometimes of a dashing irregularity which it takes for a sign of genius. . . . Why should the hysterical confidences of a morbid precocity have recently gained our serious attention?

Such comments point to a perception of a national indulgence in emotion that approached dangerous proportions, a perception stemming in part from awareness of popular literature trends.[76] One maverick, it was feared, could unleash a host.

Not surprisingly, MacLane most directly influenced aspiring girl writers. The *Anaconda Standard* reported that in the wake of *The Story*, eight Montana girls were writing books like Mac-Lane's.[77] The author of *Confessions of a Chorus Girl*, describing her escape from a rural town to New York City, suggested Mac-Lane's influence in declaring "I had always been an insatiable book-worm, eating into everything from Chaucer down to Mary McLane [*sic*]—a long way down. . . . It was here in New York that I began to keep a diary, though at the time I had no intention of ever 'confessing' its contents."[78] MacLane also inspired one Ida Monroe, who sent the *New York World* a clipping about MacLane, specimens of her own poetry, and a letter declaring "Special to the World! Inspired at the kitchen fire: Literary Cinderella!" The *World*, typically focusing on regional difference, ran an interview with Monroe with the headline, "New York Produces a Composer that Beats Butte's Wonder a Block": "I've had so much woe that I think the Lord has sent me the gift of poetry as compensation. I am the Genius of Woe. My pathos is exquisite. . . . Think of it— writing poetry by the kitchen fire on old grocery bags that I cut up."[79] Groups of girls across the country, particularly in the East, formed "Mary MacLane girl clubs."[80] Members read and studied MacLane's writings and worked to produce their own versions thereof, along with behaving in what they imagined to be a Mary MacLane manner. In a 1917 Chicago review that emphasizes MacLane's sheer replicability, Fanny Butcher recalls,

> I have only the vaguest memories of "The Story of Mary Mac-Lane." I was too young to read it either with understanding or in-terest. I remember only that some of the older girls in the school went around constantly urging the kind devil to deliver them from something or somebody, that they had a pompous little se-cret club and called themselves the M. M. L.'s, and that if it hadn't been for Mary MacLane and her confessions I should never have learned how to sew a button on with a safety pin, which was the only secret of the M. M. L.'s that was divulged. I didn't realize that it was all in a book. It seemed like some part of the social system of the universe, like the G.A.R. . . . or like the Masons . . . [After *I, Mary MacLane* is read] there will probably be the same M. M. L.'s spring up [*sic*], hundreds of little groups, hundreds of individual

M. M. L.'s who will read "I, Mary MacLane". . . . and say to themselves "I, too . . ."[81]

Though expressed childishly, Butcher's account suggests agency.
Girls used the book in staging their own acts. The press, however,
represented such fans as MacLane's prey. *Butte Intermountain*
dubbed the "Head of Local Mary MacLane Society" a "Victim of
MacLaneism" in reporting on the sixteen-year old Chicago girl
who stole a horse, it was claimed, in order to gain the experience
needed to write her own book.[82] The *Tribune-Review*, elaborating
on this notion of victimhood, ran an article entitled "The Harvest
Begun: The Story of Mary McLane [*sic*] Drives Young Girl to Suicide in Kalamazoo, Michigan":

> Morbidly mad from the reading of Mary MacLane's book in the
> nude, Francis Goodrich Stout . . . satiated her physical appetite
> with a feast of confectionery and cakes and put an end to the vain
> imaginings and longings inspired by reading the diary of the neu-
> rotic Montana authoress by taking arsenic. . . . She got a copy of the
> book a few days after its appearance. The influence of the book on
> the quick imaginings of the girl became evident at once. She
> likened her lot to that of Mary MacLane. She complained of being
> misunderstood. She told her girl friends that she had the same
> imaginings and feelings expressed by the Rocky Mountain Marie
> Bashkirtseff. She found pleasure in pointing out to the other girls
> that she was plain as to face and misunderstood as to mind. . . .
> When she was discovered writhing in the awful agony of arsenic
> poisoning, the book was still clasped in her hand.[83]

Whereas MacLane is the Rocky Mountain Bashkirtseff, Stout is
the (much less successful) Michigan MacLane. Its distant Montana genesis notwithstanding, with its profound cultural pene-
tration *The Story of Mary MacLane* is seen to threaten heartland stability. The book falls on fertile ground—victims are eager to take
action themselves. Clergymen, perceiving the beginnings of a girl
rebellion, preached sermons that sought to mitigate MacLane's
influence.[84]

"Mary MacLane," then, became for a time a national catch-
phrase—one that East and West could rally around, as I will discuss further in chapter 2, to express their admiration, envy, contempt, and resentment of each other. At the same time, both
westerners and easterners were intrigued by MacLane's having

transformed a French model into a seemingly new and peculiarly American kind of women's autobiography. MacLane was perceived as both a child of the wild and a child of the provinces, and so, too, her autobiography as a product of both.

Stone's rendering of "I Await the Devil's Coming" into *The Story of Mary MacLane* bore profitable fruit: readers could extrapolate from the text their own and others' "stories." Avid interest in "naked-soul lady" texts and a prevailing American climate of "literary fevers" contributed to making MacLane a sensation. MacLane deeply stirred countless readers, who responded to her text in very personal ways. In contrast to such fans, as well as the professional writers who admired her prose style, her equally vehement detractors were united in implying that her work was the product of a diseased mind. They perceived the nation's interest in her as a sign of its own decadence, and of young (white) womanhood at risk. MacLane's text was seen as having a forceful effect not just on women's textual production, but also, more profoundly, on their behavior and very way of thinking. As *The Chicagoan* queried after MacLane's death,

> How did it happen that a revolution in manners, a transvaluation of values in the female code of behavior, started, or seemed to start, with an unruly young woman who couldn't bear the sight of the tooth-brushes hanging up in the family bathroom at Butte, Montana? What seed fell upon that austere provincial soil to produce this amorous diarist with a narcissus complex?[85]

A Woman, of a Kind

The Story of Mary MacLane seeks to answer the *Chicagoan*'s closing question: to account for the "why" of MacLane in relation to the "austere provincial soil" of her home. Its central premise is that the accident of having been born female and living in Butte has determined who MacLane is and how she experiences the world. Following the heading "Butte, Montana, January 13, 1901," the opening words of *The Story of Mary MacLane* are "I, of womanhood." MacLane depicts "womanhood" as at once empowering and debilitating. Thus, although she claims the label of woman over that of girl, she qualifies it: "I am not a girl. I am a woman, of a kind. I began to be a woman at twelve, or more properly, a genius" (61). MacLane will call herself only a woman "of a kind" because she refuses the term's full implications, replacing it with a category that fits herself "more properly," that of the masculine genius. Like Bashkirtseff ("As a man, I should have conquered Europe" [676]), MacLane portrays her stagnation as rooted in the accident of gender: "I have the personality, the nature, of a Napoleon, albeit a feminine translation. And therefore I do not conquer; I do not even fight. I manage only to exist" (17).

Carolyn Heilbrun discusses how claiming male attributes and denouncing, in Bashkirtseff's words, a "diabolically feminine envelope" were typical moves for restless nineteenth-century women.[86] She quotes George Eliot from *Daniel Deronda:* "You can never imagine, what it is to have a man's force of genius in you, and yet to suffer the slavery of being a girl. . . . A woman's heart must be of such a size and no larger, else it must be pressed small, like Chinese feet."[87] In invoking bound feet, Eliot implies that the disparity between masculine genius and female destiny leads to a sense of conscription within the female body so profound that it can only be coded as racial difference. Yet MacLane refuses this dimension in laying a fiercely pleasured claim to her body—often figured through the trope of walking—even as she denounces the warping of her character and life that gender conventions cause. Throughout the text she celebrates the sensuality, sexuality, and sheer exuberance of her body, one that operates outside of a heterosexual economy yet remains "very feminine." Depicting herself as split into parts, she claims her "woman's-body" even in regretting other failures: "we three go out on the sand and barrenness: my wooden heart, my good young woman's-body, my soul" (18). If MacLane professes to possess "the personality, the nature, of a Napoleon"—the quintessence of masculine power and aggression—then to espouse a woman's heart or soul would be to contradict herself. She can, though, specify her body as a woman's body, since in her physical life she finds such delight.

At the same time, MacLane makes clear that biology will not determine her course. She compares a woman's life of rearing offspring sired by "a male thing" to that of snakes, dogs, birds, and toads ("A female snake is born out of its mother's white egg, and lives a while in contentment among weeds and grass, and dies" [48]) and concludes "the name—the plague-tainted name branded upon her — means woman" (49). Yet the text conveys her own struggle to resist such a destiny through rejecting the modes of womanhood conventionally available to her. These modes include that of the "girl," "heroine," "lady," and "virtuous woman" (the last a "monstrosity" who prostitutes herself through marriage [38]). No oft-played female role, MacLane asserts, truthfully represents herself. The "lie" is revealed by "close inspection" of her body, which appears in the text as the true repository of her self: "I am no lady — as any one could see by close inspection, and the phrase has an odious sound. I would rather be called a sweet little thing, or a fallen woman, or a sensible girl — though they would each be equally a lie" (98).

The "girl," she suggests, is a figment of popular imagination. In a passage that bears one of the text's running themes, that of MacLane's identification with legendary peoples in rugged environments, she asserts:

> Though I am young and feminine — very feminine — yet I am not that quaint conceit, a girl: the sort of person that Laura E. Richards writes about, and Nora Perry, and Louisa M. Alcott — girls with bright eyes, and charming faces. . . . I felt as if I had more tastes in common with the Jews wandering throughout the wilderness, or with a band of fighting Amazons. I am not a girl. . . . And then, if one is not a girl one is a heroine — of the kind you read about. But I am not a heroine, either. A heroine is beautiful . . . walks with undulating movements . . . falls methodically in love with a man — always with a man. . . . I do none of these things. (61)

MacLane maintains that the models urged upon girls are the creation of novelists: you "read about" heroines rather than meet them. In emphasizing that their realm is that of fiction, MacLane points to how unnatural and indeed unreal girls, heroines, and ladies are, not just for herself with her masculine genius, but for all women, who are expected to live up to examples they encounter only in books. MacLane was not interested in the "heroine's text" so prominent among women's reading, which, as Nancy K. Miller discusses, assumes "a woman's life has a single (often sexual) 'determining event.'"[88] Instead, she declares her devotion to J. T. Trowbridge, a popular boys' writer whom she "takes in" daily while eating fudge ("no sweet girl makes fudge and eats it, as I make fudge and eat it" [104]). And it is telling that MacLane alludes to her leaning towards female–female erotic love—"I do none of these things"—in voicing her resistance to the ideals of femininity girls' books espouse. She thereby portrays heterosexuality itself, "fall[ing] methodically in love with a man—always with a man," as a matter of following melodramatic romantic scripts. MacLane seeks to escape these scripts of gender. A central way by which she does so, as the following pages discuss, is through making claims on the environs of Butte.

Sand and Barrenness

MacLane's self-styling as a genius hinges upon her western locale, including the city of Butte and the plains and mountains that surround it. She continually reminds the reader of where she writes from. Yet although the place is essential to her identity, its incongruity is a central theme in her work: "Can I be that thing which I am—can I be possessed of a peculiar rare genius, and yet drag my life out in obscurity in this uncouth, warped, Montana town!" (17).

MacLane's reviewers usually read her as "western," in a typical instance remarking on "HER red red sunset" which "glowed in the West, always in the West."[89] In contrast, in *The Story*, MacLane herself never calls upon "The West" in elaborating her personal myth. Her sense of place is localized; it is just "Butte-Montana" or occasionally "Montana" alone to which she refers. MacLane locates Butte in the provinces, as opposed to in the West. She does sometimes invoke Butte's status as a fantastically booming, rambunctious, polyglot community: "For mixture, for miscellany—variedness, Bohemianism—where is Butte's rival?" (51) Such references to an urban frontier, however, only occasionally disrupt her depiction of Butte as a representative site of small-town America. MacLane's dull Butte prefigures the fictional western towns soon to appear in American novels, including Sinclair Lewis's Gopher Prairie, Cather's Moonstone, and Austin's Taylorville. The site against which she defines her genius is one where nothing happens.

Despite MacLane's avowals of superiority and distinction, Butte's "Main Street" identity leads her to align herself with ordinary women across the nation. In a rare gesture of solidarity she asserts in *I, Mary MacLane:*

> While I sit here this midnight in a Neat Blue Chair in this Butte-Montana flat I know a legion-women of my psychic breed may be sitting lonely in neat red or neat blue or neat gray or neat any-colored chairs—in Wichita-Kansas and South Bend-Indiana and Red Wing-Minnesota and Portland-Maine and Rochester-New York and Waco-Texas and La Crosse-Wisconsin and Bowling Green-Kentucky: each feeling Herself set in a wrong niche, caught in a tangle of little vapidish cross-purpose: each waiting, waiting always—waiting all her life. (21–22)

MacLane depicts location as the source of these women's problems: they have been "set in a wrong niche" in which waiting is the only course of action available. Responding to news of the Kalamazoo suicide, she made an even stronger claim for the pernicious effects of such a setting in a 1902 interview: "I read of the Kalamazoo girl who killed herself after reading [*The Story*]. I am not at all surprised. She lived in Kalamazoo, for one thing, and then she read the book. Who should be blamed, me or Kalamazoo?"[90] Outlandish places, she suggests (and "Kalamazoo" makes an easy target), literally kill women. Throughout her texts, MacLane argues that place determines who you are and the quality of your life, and even whether it is worth living. Gender misplacement and literal geographic misplacement operate similarly: to be a genius living in Kalamazoo is akin to suffering Napoleonic genius imprisoned in female destiny. MacLane thus portrays provincial American arenas as a lethal version of femininity.

Such an association accords with MacLane's distance from views of the western United States as an insistently masculine region and an arena of self-actualization and growth. Her texts work to undercut myths of the American West, in part simply by refusing to acknowledge the myths. MacLane does not make regional generalizations; she focuses instead on local sites such as Butte, Red Wing, or Kalamazoo. She also troubles prevailing images of western landscapes. Montana, with its associations of Indians and cowboys, mountain men and miners, is the setting *par excellence* of formula westerns. Yet MacLane does not offer the reader the privileged landscape that westerns have conditioned us to expect: one of glorious plains, awesome mountains, and inspirational skies. Instead she describes a wasteland devastated by copper smelting. A place of stagnation rather than growth, MacLane's Montana is blighted, characterized above all by what it lacks.

In its disinclination to look to a heroic western past, celebrate the land, and assert male primacy, *The Story of Mary MacLane* is just the opposite of that other western best-seller of April 1902, Owen Wister's *The Virginian* — a book now recognized as "one of the most important forces in the early production of the modern textual West."[91] *The Story of Mary MacLane* and *I, Mary MacLane* propose none of the "theses" that Robert Murray Davis describes as staples of western texts, including the "Huck Finn thesis," the "Rambo thesis," and the "Frederick Jackson Turner thesis."[92]

In articulating her myth of herself MacLane completely ignores the romantic possibilities of her father, James MacLane, a local notable. MacLane's decision *not* to play up her father's past is arresting, considering the story-book character of his life. A former participant in the California gold rush, James MacLane was known in the Minnesota town that he helped develop as "Flatboat MacLane." The *Great Falls Tribune* recounted,

> Mary's father gained his name from his boating experience on the Red River of the North. In the early days before railroads he owned boats carrying freight and passengers between Fargo and Fort Garry, which was then an outpost of civilization near where Winnipeg now stands. In this way he gathered together considerable money, and he added to his pile occasionally by taking a hand of poker — and it was said that he beat them all there. . . . While society looked askance at the family from the rumors that the father had made considerable of his money by gambling, he was everywhere liked and a more generous man to the poor of any community never lived.[93]

Another article similarly noted that MacLane, once of "humble circumstances," had "carr[ied] supplies to the far outposts of the Canadian Arctic" and had moved with his family to the United States after the 1885 Riel Rebellion.[94] Mustering big-hearted gambling, an Indian war, a bootstraps rise, and "outposts of civilization" as remote as the Arctic, these accounts figure his life as replete with all the elements of Old West piquancy. MacLane later left Minnesota, adding another notch of classic western enterprise to his belt when he went into the cattle business in Montana. He died of meningitis during Mary MacLane's childhood, leaving his family in comfortable circumstances.

His replacement was a far more prosaic figure, MacLane's step-father, H. G. Klenze. MacLane both disliked Klenze and was affected by the economic stringency his business failures caused the family.[95] In her texts, however, she does not look back with longing to her lost father, and certainly not to the era in American history that he could be said to represent. On the contrary, she makes a point of dismissing his influence: "Apart from feeding and clothing me comfortably and sending me to school — which is no more than was due me — and transmitting to me the Mac-Lane blood and character, I can not see that he ever gave me a single thought. . . . It is a matter of supreme indifference to me whether my father, Jim MacLane of selfish memory, lived or died" (14-15). Through such strenuous protest, MacLane ignores or even renounces an arguably rich frontier heritage. She uses her father to avow not a western bootstraps genealogy, but instead a rebellious Scottish one:

> I am peculiarly of the MacLane blood which is Highland Scotch.
> My sister and brothers inherit the traits of their mother's family
> which is of Scotch Lowland descent. This alone makes no small de-
> gree of difference. . . . There are a great many MacLanes, but there
> is usually only one real MacLane in each generation. There is but
> one who feels again the passionate spirit of the Clans, those bar-
> baric dwellers in the bleak but well-beloved Highlands of Scot-
> land. I am the real MacLane of my generation. The real MacLane in
> these later centuries is always a woman. The men of my family
> never amount to anything worth naming.[96] (15, 25)

Akin to her identification with "wandering Jews" and "fighting Amazons," MacLane claims her distant Scottish ancestors as well as a matrilineal line of descent.[97] Although her father bestowed upon her the name MacLane along with "Highland Scotch" blood, both his sex and the throwback nature of the "real Mac-Lane" make of him a mere transmitter. As Cather does for Thea Kronborg and Whiteley for herself, MacLane exacts from Europe an inheritance that, although a matter of blood, none of the rest of her family share. Unlike Cather and Whiteley, though, for

MacLane Europe does not connote a highly evolved life of culture. Instead, it is the source of a "passionate" and "barbaric" sensibility that transcends the tameness of a middle-class upbringing in a provincial American city.

MacLane prefers the imagined Highland warriors of her distant ancestry, whose "bleak" homeland she associates with the empty spaces around Butte, to the real working immigrants that throng the city itself. In an entry remarkable in *The Story* for its devotion to a subject other than herself, MacLane describes a typical Butte street holiday, "some Fourth of July demonstration, or . . . Miners' Union day":

> The heterogeneous herd turns out—and I turn out, with the herd and of it, and meditate and look on. There are Irishmen—Kelleys, Caseys, Calahans, staggering under the weight of much whiskey . . . there is the festive Cornishman, ogling and leering. . . . There are suave sleek sporting men just out of the bath-tub; insignificant lawyers, dentists, messenger-boys, "plungers" without number; greasy Italians from Meaderville; greasier French people from the Boulevarde Addition; ancient miners—each of whom was the first to stake a claim in Butte; starved-looking Chinamen here and there; a contingent of Finns and Swedes and Germans; musty, stuffy old Jewish pawn-brokers who have crawled out of their holes for a brief recreation; dirt-encrusted Indians and squaws in dirty-gay blankets, from their flea-haunted camp below the town; "box-rustlers"—who are as common in Butte as bar-maids in Ireland, swell, flashy-looking Africans . . . heavy restaurant keepers with tooth-picks in their mouths; a vast army of dry-goods clerks—the "paper-collared" gentry; miners of every description; representatives from Dog Town, Chicken Flats, Busterville, Butchertown and Seldom Seen—suburbs of Butte. (51–52)

MacLane's account captures well the vitality of Butte's streets, to the extent that it has been of documentary interest.[98] Everyone in MacLane's colorful description, though, appears degraded, whether greasy, dirty, starved, or flashy. The creatures composing Butte's masses, uniform in their marginality, appear in high contrast to the narrator with her superior detachment and commanding gaze. MacLane may declare that she is "of the herd," but her description reveals the sense of distance she feels, making unsurprising her conclusion "the souls of these people are dumb" (54). Whereas MacLane finds her "female skin" uncomfortable, she is at ease in her white, middle-class one and uses the bodies of the Butte herd to affirm her sense of superiority.[99] Her sensitivity to the prescriptions of gender notwithstanding, throughout her life MacLane was never to reveal any interest in or even intimation of other kinds of oppression. She can be startlingly racist and class-conscious, as in her statement to Stone, "I like, not niggers but one aesthetic nigger. (And I'm almost weary and forlorn enough, with my fever-wracked head, to call him up and marry him now.)"[100] MacLane enjoys a sense of daring in associating with others she considers definitively beneath her.

Her descriptions of two elderly immigrant women are somewhat more sympathetic than that of the public parade dominated by male workers, and although she still makes clear that class and ethnic differences ultimately create an unbridgeable gap, here she makes a more concerted effort to demonstrate her feelings of kinship. Both figures — an ostracized Irish woman and a traveling Italian peddler — are single women who reject marriage, whom MacLane encounters in the private setting of the home as opposed to the street. The former lives in Butte's rough Dublin Gulch alone with her notorious reputation. "When she sees me picking my way towards her house," MacLane asserts, "her hard, sour face softens wonderfully and a light of distinct friendliness comes into her green eyes. Don't you know, there are few people enough in the world whose hard, sour faces will soften at sight of you. . . . We are equals" (64). Of the peddler, she explains that she was happy to visit with her because "I had always wanted to talk to a peddler-woman, and my mother never would allow one in the house" (117). (Although tellingly, Mac-Lane speaks to her not in the house, but while standing in the doorway.) Their conversation is mostly about the woman having left her "no-good" husband back in Italy; she recommends that MacLane too choose peddling over marriage.

In the same way that she declares herself "a genius, a thief and a liar" (18) in order to distinguish herself from girls, heroines, and virtuous women, MacLane declares her affinity with Butte's impoverished immigrant women, in particular those outside conventional marital arrangements. Like MacLane herself, they oppose the middle-class Butte respectability that her mother represents. Complementing such moments of identification, however tangential, MacLane's sense of distance from "Red Indians," specifically male Red Indians, further aids her perception of herself as approaching Old World sensibility and Highland genius.

In the description of the Butte holiday, we have already encountered the single instance in which Native Americans explicitly appear in *The Story of Mary MacLane,* as "dirt-encrusted Indians and squaws in dirty-gay blankets." They are to reappear in MacLane's work only once, in New York. In a review of an opera performance that, for good reason, was to remain unpublished, MacLane declares,

> A Red Indian, fresh from his native reservation, sitting in his unspeakable blanket, looking and listening to the opera "Aida," by Caruso and Eames, would, no doubt at all, stare about him in the most block-headed boredom and mystification — indifferent to the marvelous circling harmonies — till he dropped wearily in his tracks. There would be no little doors in the adamant hard dome of his ignorance to open and let in rhythmic light. One's advance over the Red Indian, proportionately, is with the number of one's little doors. Nightly, to the Opera, to hear Caruso, go countless greasy little Italian barbers and waiters. To whom it's very true, Shakespeare and even Dante are not even names — and their wan souls seemed filled by it with pure and informing delight. By that token they are a big advance on the Indian. I myself have known — sufficiently known — Indians on their native city-dumping grounds, and it is a question of much doubt in my mind whether anything in God's world could so with delight fill them — save perhaps the dumps. Which isn't the same sort of delight. I envied the barbers and waiters theirs.[101]

MacLane's transformation of real individuals into the stereotypical "blanket Indian" and native lands into city dumps belies her claim that her authority rests on first-hand experience. She sets up a racial hierarchy based upon the appreciation of art and, more broadly, upon refinement of sensibility: "the number of one's little doors." This hierarchy depends on inherent racial or ethnic sensibility alone. Therefore, in contrast to that of the hard-domed Indian, who appears to have nothing she desires, MacLane's portrayal of the "greasy Italians" reveals a complex mixture of contempt and envy. Their foreign bodies and working-class status provoke her snobbery, yet she also invests them with an enviable fineness of feeling beyond her reach. She thereby undermines her attempt to depict her own "advance."

Contacts with the working class, then, are central to MacLane's sense of self. Far more so than the city of Butte with its teeming crowds and refugees, however, the seemingly vacant mountains and plains around Butte dominate her self-portrayal. In the end, western spaces matter to her more than western peoples. Mac-Lane's ultimate negation of Butte's crowds is bound up with her fantasy of the blighted land as empty, a site she can claim as her "setting":

> We three go out on the sand and barrenness: my wooden heart, my good young woman's-body, my soul. We go there and contemplate the long sandy wastes, the red, red line on the sky at the setting of the sun, the cold gloomy mountains under it, the ground without a weed, without a grass-blade even in their season—for they have years ago been killed off by the sulphur smoke from the smelters. So this sand and barrenness forms the setting for the personality of me. (18)

MacLane's emphasis on Montana's barrenness reflects to a degree conventional nineteenth-century views of the Rocky Mountain region as part of the "Great American Desert."[102] It is no coincidence, either, that her best-seller is exactly contemporaneous with a surge of well-received texts that argue for the austere allure of American deserts.[103] Yet MacLane makes clear that the land in which she dwells is "barren" due not to nature, but to human influence. Ultimately, she suggests, the land is resilient and even fruitful. She maintains as well that she herself, likewise, is desolate not by nature but as a result of social forces. Thus, depicting her outdoor rambles as orgies of solitude at once miserable and ecstatic, she aligns herself with the land as a source of both her impoverishment and her strength: "Hour after hour, as I walk, through my brain some long, long pageants march: the pageant of my fancies, the pageant of my unparalleled egotism, the pageant of my unhappiness, the pageant of my minute analyzing, the pageant of my peculiar philosophy, the pageant of my dull, dull life,—and the pageant of the Possibilities" (18).

MacLane, in looking at a seemingly bleak landscape and perceiving "Possibilities," could be read as kin to the nineteenth-century women Kolodny describes, who overlaid their frontier homes with visions of gardens. Yet the softer elements she perceives in the land around her arise from nature asserting itself over man-made blight, not from patches of potential domestic cultivation. From MacLane's perspective, Butte suffered not from too little "civilization," but from too much. She cannot afford to envision a domesticated land because it is the domestic sphere from which she longs to escape. The "sand and barrenness" offers her relief from a claustrophobic bourgeois family life "signified" by its household effects: "The obviousness of those six tooth-brushes signifying me and the five other members of this family and the aimless emptiness of my existence here . . . makes my soul weary and my heart sick. . . . Oh, to leave this house and these people . . . ! But where can I go, what can I do?" (55–56).

Her answer to this last question is a surprising one. Seemingly at once in jest and in utter earnestness, throughout *The Story* MacLane posits turning to the devil as a solution to her problems. The figure of the devil is central to the text, as its original title, "I Await the Devil's Coming," asserts. At its simplest level, the devil is the rescuer astride a white horse: "All girls of nineteen are wait-ing for somebody that many of them call the 'prince,' many oth-ers the 'ideal,'" MacLane explained in an early interview. "I called him my 'devil.'"[104] MacLane's devil also offers her relief from her own self. She conceives of the devil as "a man with whom to fall completely, madly in love" (46) and, in one of her more memo-rable passages, imagines a torrid conversation with him:

> "What would you have me do, little MacLane?" the Devil would say.
>
> "I would have you conquer me, crush me, know me," I would answer.
>
> "What shall I say to you?" the Devil would ask.
>
> "Say to me, 'I love you, I love you, I love you,' in your strong, steel, fascinating voice. Say it to me often, always—a million times."
>
> "What would you have me do, little MacLane?" he would say again.
>
> I would answer: "Hurt me, burn me, consume me with hot love, shake me violently, embrace me hard, *hard* in your strong steel arms, kiss me with wonderful burning kisses—press your lips to mine with passion, and your soul and mine would meet then in an anguish of joy for me!"
>
> "How shall I treat you, little MacLane?"
>
> "Treat me cruelly, brutally."

"How long shall I stay with you?"

"Through the life everlasting—it will be as one day; or for one day—it will be as the life everlasting."

"And what kind of children will you bear me, little MacLane?" he would say.

"I will bear wonderful, beautiful children—with great pain." (46)

Allowing that her tone is light here—a parodic representation of sadomasochism—the dialogue suggests that MacLane's longing for the devil stems from her longing to escape her wearying self-consciousness ("Conquer me, crush me . . . consume me with hot love"). On leaving Butte with the devil, she states outright, "my life will be borne far out of self, and self will sink quietly out of sight. . . . 'It is the last—the *last*—of that Mary MacLane,' I will say, and I will feel a long, sighing, quivering farewell" (66). Mac-Lane suggests throughout the book that the devil will allow her to encounter some reality—the "red, red line"—that she perceives as cloaked by her insistent individuality.

Yet in *The Story*, the devil is an overloaded trope that works in multiple ways (as he always does). MacLane uses the figure of the devil not only to represent the possibility of self-transcendence, but also as means to eroticize and masculinize the Montana landscape, even as she identifies the landscape with her "very feminine" self. MacLane's close association of her "sand and barrenness" with her alluring devil renders it both a masculine arena and a potential stage for female desire.

In describing the land MacLane does not attempt to present it realistically; she is no naturalist. On the contrary, she works in quite the opposite direction: she grants her surroundings significance only in relation to herself, whom she names as "only one grand conglomeration of Wanting" (69), and continually associates the natural world with her own desire. She shows it as inciting desire: "the deep, deep blue of the summer sky stirs me to a half-painful joy. The cool green of a swiftly flowing river fills my heart with unquiet longings. The red, red sky convulses my entire being with passion" (74). She also uses it to figure desire's fulfillment: "Think, oh, *think*, of being happy for a year—for a day! How brilliantly blue the sky would be, how swiftly and joyously would the green rivers run, how madly, merrily triumphant the four winds of heaven would sweep round the corners of the fair earth!" (21) She most frequently makes her trope of the "red, red sky" represent the object of desire itself: "Oh Devil, Fate, World—some one, bring me my red sky! . . . . Bring it to me intensely red, intensely full, intensely alive! Short as you will, but red, red, red! . . . Bring me, Devil, my red line of sky for one hour and take all, all—everything I possess" (25).

While MacLane presents the devil as an imaginary object of desire, she also presents an actual flesh and blood counterpart, her former English teacher, Fanny Corbin. By the time MacLane wrote her book, Corbin had already left Butte for Boston, and she was desperately missed. MacLane writes of her as much as she does the devil, and addresses to her similarly passionate paeans: "To you—And don't you know, my dearest, my friendship with you . . . contains infatuation, and worship, and bewitchment, and idolatry, and a tiny altar in my soul-chamber whereon is burning sweet incense in a little dish of blue and gold?" (120) She polarizes the devil and Fanny as sexual opposites and as the two aspects of her Montana surrounds: while she depicts the devil as a carica-ture of masculinity and associates him with barren desert plains, she characterizes Corbin, "the anemone lady," with a tiny moun-tain wildflower and portrays her as gentle, loving, and redemp-tive.[105]

Fanny Corbin's imagined presence in the open spaces of Mon-tana adds another layer to the devil's function in the text, in that he appears as a displacement of the workings of same-sex desire. MacLane's yearning for the devil to rescue her from "sand and barrenness" is complemented by her wish that she herself could spirit Fanny away to "some little out-of-the world-place high up on the side of a mountain for the rest of my life" (27). In MacLane's imagination, a mountain idyll shared with another woman offers an alternative to the devil's plains. This idyll is located at the priv-ileged male site of western dominance, the high mountain with its overlook of the world below.[106] MacLane later explicitly portrays her love for Corbin as entailing a desire for masculinity:

Oh there is not—there can never be—another anemone lady! My life is a desert—a desert, but the thin, clinging perfume of the blue anemone reaches to its utter confines. And nothing in the desert is the same because of that perfume. Years will not fade the blue of the anemone, nor a thousand bitter winds blow away the rare fragrance. I feel in the anemone lady a strange attraction of sex. There is in me a masculine element that, when I am thinking of her, arises and overshadows all the others. "Why am I not a man," I say to the sand and barrenness with a certain strained, tense passion, "that I might give this wonderful, dear, delicious woman an absolutely perfect love!" And this is my predominating feeling for her. So, then, it is not the woman-love, but the man-love, set in the mysterious sensibilities of my woman-nature. It brings me pain and pleasure mingled in that odd, odd fashion. Do you think a man is the only creature with whom one may fall in love? (76–77)

Even as MacLane celebrates her "woman's-body" and "woman's-nature" elsewhere, she here suggests that she wants less to have the masculine other than to be it—both in order to give Corbin "an absolutely perfect love" and to control her own destiny. MacLane turns to a demonic character to figure incorporating within herself male sexuality and the power it connotes. By associating the devil with her own "setting," she projects onto the land the same masculinity she claims as "set in the mysterious sensibilities of my woman-nature."

MacLane's plains are inhabited by a party of four: herself, Fanny, the devil, and the missing Indian. Dorst notes that Native Americans are popularly portrayed as commanding the privileged gaze, the gaze that knows the West. Yet in *The Story*, Montana natives do no looking—or rather, their looking is indistinguishable from that of the Finns and the Cornishmen and the rest with whom they share the street. In MacLane's work, the Red Indian's only gaze of note is misplaced, as he "stares" at a New York opera in a futile attempt to understand it, in such contrast to the receptive Italians. Both by relocating the Indian's gaze and emptying it of comprehension, MacLane makes the Montana plains her own site of vision and desire.

In an article entitled, "Photographic Relations: Laura Gilpin, Willa Cather," Jonathan Goldberg shows the ways in which Gilpin and Cather depend on the native peoples dwelling in the southwestern landscapes they depict to express female-to-female sexuality: "Cather's dead Indians and male-male couples speak to her desires much as Gilpin's staged 'living' Indians are projective sites for hers. Access to same-sex female desire occurs along these highly conflicted routes."[107] Goldberg's discussion of Gilpin

and Cather's homoerotic western landscapes offers useful context for considering MacLane's (including his warning against
summarily dismissing texts for their "bad politics"). MacLane too
makes a western landscape an enabling setting for same-sex desire. In her case, however, it is not through focusing on native
inhabitants, but through rendering them almost, but not quite, invisible. The actual "Red Indian" is replaced by an explicitly imaginary and explicitly red devil.

Yet in the end, the same-sex idyll she imagines is troubled and
ultimately "overrun" by the parodic masculinity of the red devil,
who appears to suggest at once the absurdity and inequities
of normative heterosexuality—and also its seductive power.
Though she can project her fantasy of union with the devil into
the realm of marriage and sexual union, MacLane cuts short her
dream of life with Fanny, a real woman. The devil precludes her:
if MacLane herself is "fertile soil," then once "planted thickly" by
the devil "with rank wild mustard," she contends, "There would
be no room—no room at all—for an anemone to grow. If one
should start up, instantly it would be choked and overrun with
wild mustard" (106). In her text a biblical voice, wielding the language of marital vows, sternly reminds her, "'Thy friend is always
thy friend; not to have, nor to hold, nor to love, nor to rejoice in:
but to remember'" (27). And, MacLane pragmatically concludes,
"Miss Corbin would doubtless look somewhat askance at the idea
of spending the rest of her life with me on a mountain. She is very
fond of me, but her feeling for me is not like mine for her, which
indeed is natural" (27). Clearing the landscape of all traces of Native culture, she can perceive mountain tops as sites available for
same-sex love and mountain flowers as reflecting the spirit of her
beloved. These moments of fantastic fulfillment, however, in
MacLane's imagination are eclipsed by her masculine devil, figured by the red sun presiding over the entire scene.

2

After *The Story of Mary MacLane*

Lying on the Ground under a Warm Setting Sun

In her use of Montana landscape, MacLane is heir to a western women's tradition that Georgi-Findlay traces to the early nineteenth century and shows as dependent on the United States' Indian removal policy: women travelers and settlers incorporating themselves in a range of personal narratives as innocents turning to the emptiness of the West for self discovery and emotional growth.[1] Despite such continuity, MacLane's work also suggests a very modern twentieth-century female use of the land that does not appear in the texts of her forebears. Contrast her sexualized landscape—and those of her contemporaries—with the relationship between women and western spaces that Mary Hallock Foote suggests. Best known for her book *A Victorian Gentlewoman in the Far West,* Foote describes one of her works in a tone at once self-effacing and defiant as "not a woman's story. *How* I wish I had a son who would put his name to my stories. One could write so much better if one were not a woman—a wife and mother of small girls—the fields beyond which only men may tread. I know as much about the men who tread those fields as a man could—more—but I don't know the fields and don't wish to appear to."[2] Foote refers to a culture based upon male primacy and female childbearing—ideally of sons rather than "small girls"—within which she must work in defensively asserting her knowledge of the land; MacLane explicitly lays claim to the Butte plains as a way of denouncing Butte more. MacLane's and Foote's brands of self-assertion arise from quite different historical moments.

At first glance, early-twentieth-century women's depictions of the West may seem closer to those of their male predecessors than their female ones'. Kolodny argues that from its earliest exploration by whites, male writers have imagined the West as a woman's body in fantasies that omitted the presence of actual non-Native women.[3] The women writers I discuss replicate this identification of the land with a female body. However, through identifying the land with their own selves, they represent the land as not sexualized object but rather sexualized subject.[4] They thereby reject both sides of Kolodny's coin: the landscape is neither transformed by men into a woman to seduce, nor domesticated by women into a garden to manage.

These writers stand as predecessors to the "new westerners" of whom Comer writes: "This time, it is *women's desires* that are being explored or represented via western stories."[5] In the early twentieth century, too, women were exploring their desires in the West. The writers I discuss render the land a reflection, setting, or extension of their protagonists' subjectivities; its erotic energies are their own. Their rugged landscapes suggesting hidden riches mirror the nascent sexuality of their often adolescent heroines, who anticipate a riotous blossoming; they prompt feminine development, too. Although formula westerns also show how "characters reflecting *on* the landscape find themselves gradually reflected *in* it,"[6] these women's images of finding, emergence, extension, and shelter are different in degree from the images of radical transformation often associated with western male figures.[7] The experience, moreover, is explicitly portrayed as a female one. As MacLane asserts, "there is a worldful of easy . . . beautiful sensuality in the figure of a young woman lying on the ground under a warm setting sun. A man may lie on the ground — but that's as far as it goes. A man would go to sleep, probably, like a dog or a pig. He would even snore, perhaps — under the setting sun. But then, a man has not a good young feminine body to feel with" (23).[8]

In moving away from certain kinds of male-oriented western myths, white writers drew from and inscribed a different myth concerning the western female artist or genius. Their work is linked by a recurring set of associations between women and the West that is neither stable nor ubiquitous but nonetheless persistent: that of a woman with an affinity with western landscapes that arises from both her sense of dislocation in her human community, and from a real or imagined Native or aristocratic European sensibility.[9]

Today, this western female aesthetic is perhaps most evident in the figure of Georgia O'Keeffe. The works of MacLane, Austin, and Cather especially provide a precursor for the O'Keeffe icon, linking artistry, solitude, and the West to the figure of a strong woman. The O'Keeffe legend emphasizes the artist's communion with a sublime southwestern landscape and her responsiveness to Mexican and Native cultures, to the extent that she was sometimes figured as an Indian. Terry Tempest Williams's "In Cahoots with Coyote" proposes: "Through the years, [Coyote] brought her bones and stones and Georgia O'Keeffe kept her word. She never painted Coyote. Instead, she embodied him."[10] O'Keeffe also becomes the raven, "uplifted and free from the urban life she left behind."[11] The southwestern Native cultures to which the coyote and raven are central, however, remain invisible in the story: O'Keeffe can access their familiars directly through her art and her closeness to the land. Unnecessarily, Williams adds, "Perhaps the beginning of O'Keeffe's communion with Coyote began in Canyon, Texas." It is hard to imagine such an intensely landscaped scene of cultural appropriation set outside the West.[12]

Laura Gilpin's *The Prairie* (1917), a photograph of a woman standing with outstretched arms at the edge of a vast, seemingly empty plain, offers a useful literal picture of the solitary white woman and her relationship to the West. Gilpin's later work usually portrays human beings, especially Native Americans and ethnic Mexicans, in a comfortable relationship with the land. In this portrait of an apparently white, middle-class woman, however, the figure's dramatic stance suggests her sense of separation. The woman self-consciously responds to her surroundings, indicating that although they may stir her to heights of emotion, she does not experience them as home. Her outstretched arms appear to express both love of the prairie and yearning for what lies beyond it. The elaborate, long white dress she wears appears out of place as well, suggesting that just outside the frame of the picture lies some small-town community, the woman's usual domain from which, perhaps, she has escaped for a moment of solitude on the plains. With such an imagined scenario, *The Prairie* can be read as a meditation on the relationship between the West and a certain kind of white female subjectivity. The woman uses the landscape to explore and affirm her sense of difference.

As a landscape photographer of the West, Gilpin had no female contemporaries.[13] *The Prairie,* however, does link her to white, middle-class, western women writers between 1900 and 1920, in that it mirrors the way they use and represent their homes in articulating an identity as a female artist. (Mourning Dove's *Cogewea* points to the pervasiveness of this kind of scenario, in spite of the different inflection of race and class.) In the autobiographies and autobiographical fiction that describe their development as children or young women, these writers present themselves as both at home and not at home in the West. They identify with the magnificent or pastoral landscapes into which they make solitary forays. Typically, they see them as a reflection or extension or setting—often a sexualized one—of themselves. At the same time, they define themselves negatively against the white social circles they inhabit.

Their texts thus reflect the popular notion of the West that is associated with the questing white male: it is an arena in which one forges a defiant, independent, anti-social selfhood. Indeed, they sometimes echo male texts in showing their heroines' inroads into wild spaces as an evasion of women and domestic ideology. Thus, while in a larger sense these writers rebel against a patriarchal society that creates the limiting scripts available to them as women, it is personally against the mother and her values that they wage their fiercest war. Nevertheless, their texts fundamentally differ from those of their male counterparts in that they sidestep the overt connection between the West and action, and instead claim western landscapes for their own introspection.

White middle-class women could afford to identify with the natural world to assert a sensuality and sexuality that their culture denied them. Unlike women of color, they did not need to resist dehumanizing associations with nature, and they often had the leisure and security that enabled them to make solitary ventures into western spaces in the first place.[14] Yet racial privilege does not eliminate gender troubles, and MacLane's text reveals that be she white and well-heeled and well-buffered from the herd or no, her staid life was a hard one for her to bear. Heilbrun discusses in "Non-Autobiographies of 'Privileged' Women" the tribulations of relatively privileged women: rather than being trivial, they demonstrate how deep the tyranny of gender can run.

MacLane's difficulties were not only inherently middle-class but also a by-product of a middle-class sensibility that was geographically inflected. The popular notion that an unconventional western milieu nurtured unconventional women—Annie Oakleys and Calamity Janes, "Legendary Ladies of Texas" and "Wild Women of the West"—did hold true for some women.[15] For some, the West was a liberating place where gender roles could and did break down. Yet historians show that western settlements were often closely modeled after eastern ones.[16] Middle-class circles in western communities, laboring under a sense of social and cultural inferiority coupled with a defensive regional pride, could be even more strictly shaped by propriety than those of the East. Such a stance led to an especially constrictive code of conduct for women. Butte's outrage over *The Story of Mary MacLane* was predictable. Atherton's *Perch of the Devil* (1914), extensively researched in Butte, portrays the city's white, middle-class women, as well as those of other western towns, as circumscribed and under greater pressure to conform in comparison to their eastern counterparts. Atherton suggests that this condition arose from westerners' resistance to eastern conceptions of the West as a rough and lawless outpost; it is the East, therefore, that appears in her book as the site of relative freedom.[17]

Even within the span of a single girlhood the West could become progressively more restrictive for women, as Wilder's "Little House" series demonstrates. Showing that the "settling" of the West models the "settling" of girls, Ann Romines describes how the sisters in the series become increasingly bound by the little houses they inhabit. As they grow from girls into young women, the excitement of being in the Big Woods, on the Prairie, or at Plum Creek is tempered by increasing confinement and expectations of domesticity.[18] "The pivotal event of Laura's childhood," Romines argues, "a wild wagon journey across the plains, gives way finally to the housebound months of *Long Winter. . . .* The *House* was more and more pressingly the container and the context of the series."[19] In her autobiography, *Earth Horizon,* Austin goes so far as to define the West according to the role of its women: the moment women surrendered function to ornament marked the moment they and their environment became "middlewestern," thereby threatening the very existence of the West.[20] "Frontier freedom" is volatile, dependent upon class as well as era and locale.

To return again to Butte, Mary Murphy suggests that although the city's booming economy, anything-goes atmosphere, and strong unions may have provided opportunities for working-class women, they did not do so for those like MacLane who defined themselves as middle-class or above. Murphy notes that in 1910—almost a decade after MacLane left—the most common occupations for Butte women were still those of servant, boarding-house keeper, teacher, prostitute, and dressmaker.[21] In covering MacLane's high school graduation, a local reporter noted that while the boy graduates "presented every appearance of giving a good accounting of themselves in life," the girls simply "looked lovely."[22] It is tempting to draw conclusions such as that made by Virginia Terris, that MacLane and her work were "tied closely to influences found only in the West, including the expanded role that women were allowed in Montana and other western states."[23] In actuality, though, MacLane's western "influences" occasioned her less freedom than she may otherwise have had— and made her need even more the region's open spaces.

The Dunes of Butte

MacLane, as we have seen, was not alone in using the West to write about herself. Nor was she unique in her haste to leave the region so central to her identity. In the sections that follow, I consider the range of reactions to MacLane as a westerner before mapping the course her life took after the publication of *The Story of Mary MacLane*. My intent is to round out a discussion of the role of images of places in her reception with a discussion of the role of actual places in her life.

Reviewers, even in discussing seemingly unrelated issues, emphasized MacLane's western origins. Yet she was often perceived not so much as an indigenous phenomenon as a western version of another hailing from some more cultured place. In the same way that she is a feminine Whitman or Rousseau, so too is she a "Rocky Mountain Marie Bashkirtseff" or a "Young Messalina Out of the West."[24] Even when dismissive of MacLane herself, labels such as "the Backwoods Bashkirtseff" point to Americans' satisfaction over having a regional, homegrown version of a Continental celebrity—a version that sometimes outshone the original. Hamlin Garland declared, "The most remarkable of her powers (to me as to [Henry] Fuller) is her crisp, clear, unhesitating use of English. It is annoying to find that an unlettered young girl can write with such precision and such power. Critics are already comparing her confessions with those of Marie Bashkirtseff; but in truth this Montana maid has no need to fear the comparison."[25]

A remarkably similar avowal, fifteen years later, of a besting of Bashkirtseff—this time at the hand of O'Keeffe—indicates the role the West could play in the reception of iconoclastic women artists:

> The recent work . . . of Miss Georgia O'Keeffe of Canyon, Tex., speaks for itself. . . . [O'Keeffe] has found expression in delicately veiled symbolism for "what every woman knows," but what women heretofore have kept to themselves. . . . Marie Bashkirtseff, the little Tartar of a Russian . . . in Paris . . . wrote many audacious hints and intimate self-revelations in her famous diary; but she did it more or less unconsciously, and in any case she was a temperamental variant from the average femininity. Georgia O'Keeffe, offspring of an Irish father and a Levantine mother, was born in Virginia, and has grown up in the vast provincial solitudes of Texas. Whatever her natural temperament may be, the loneliness and privation which her emotional nature must have suffered put their impress on everything she does.[26]

Suggesting that the "loneliness and privation" of "vast provincial solitudes," in contrast to the social intricacies and plenitude of an urban milieu, leads to transparent work that "speaks for itself" in revealing women's nature, this reviewer appears unaware—or at least does not want to consider—that O'Keeffe grew up in Wisconsin. The image of the artist as nurtured by the great open West may have been too seductive to resist. Responses to MacLane and O'Keeffe suggest that the plains and desert West was especially conducive to interpretations of women's work as rendering their inner selves clearly visible. Just as MacLane was represented as baring her soul to the Montana expanse, discussions of O'Keeffe, so closely associated with the Southwest, frequently use the trope of nakedness—her being "nakedly, starkly Georgia O'Keeffe" in a "nakedly revealed world" making "unqualified nakedness of statement."[27]

"Montana," open to a range of interpretations, often rendered MacLane as exotic as foreign origins would have done. Her eastern and midwestern readers could invoke Montana's "backwoods," "fastnesses," "dunes," and "bleak and lonely moor." Their interpretations are linked by a conviction that the region is a "mental desert," a conviction that worked to confirm for them MacLane's claim to genius. Despite *The Story*'s allusions to her wide reading, therefore, Garland perceived the "Montana maid" as "unlettered," making her achievement all the more stunning. Similarly, the *Canadian Press*, linking MacLane to English genius, declared "the wonderful thing about this book is not that it was written, but that this child of ignorance wrote it. Coming from this young girl, it should rather inspire a feeling of awe. You can no more explain Mary MacLane than you can explain Charlotte Brontë. Shut up there in the bleak and lonely moor, she is the genius she proclaims herself."[28] Taking the opposite tack, the *Chicago Record-Herald* evokes the tradition of women's westering accounts in reading MacLane as the Everywoman of pioneer history: her "bitter cry of loneliness and of revolt against the barren sands of Butte might be the concentrated voices of all the pioneer women who have pined in the mental deserts of the West since its settlement began."[29] In a widely quoted statement, the Chicago socialist Oscar Lovell Triggs made the most explicit connection between MacLane's home and her literary production, avowing, "Such a book as the one written by Mary MacLane never could have been written by a woman living in the East. . . . Only a life spent in a barren region of the West could have given a woman the power to write such a work. A reader of this book will see the life of a woman laid bare."[30] Triggs here makes the familiar move of declaring that the West, as a region itself barren, is conducive to seeing "a woman laid bare." Even as the West as frontier was being fixed in popular imagination, an alternate image of the West was being deployed, as an empty place so devoid of culture or fulfillment that it forces gifted women to turn inward and cultivate

their own power, even while they dream of mobility and communion with other races.

Consequently, the allusions to the romance of her desolate
landscape notwithstanding, MacLane's contemporaries saw
Butte as a site of deprivation rather than plenitude. They echoed
MacLane in asserting the impoverishment of her social and cultural environment. Although they often regarded Montana as the
source of MacLane's originality, they also read Montana as a site
of American provinciality, as less "western" than "midwestern,"
less distinctive than representative. Mencken thus described
MacLane as "a Puritan wooed and tortured by the leers of beauty,
Mary MacLane in a moral republic, in a Presbyterian diocese, in
Butte . . . in brief, an absolutely typical American."[31] Mencken's
depiction of Butte contrasts with that of the exuberant MacLane
mini-revivals of the 1970s and 1980s, which identify Butte as a
raucous frontier community. As early as the 1920s, romantic references are made to Butte as a "camp," as in a description of Mac-
Lane's book as "peculiarly characteristic of the spirit of the mining camp: bald, defiant and unconventional."[32] The West so very
quickly reified into the frontier, due in part to the power of formula westerns. In 1902, however, frontier readings of MacLane's
text are largely absent, even though so many of the era's popular
texts rework frontier myths; and Butte appears as a small city, not
a camp. While Butte's working classes may well have been "defiant and unconventional," most of MacLane's contemporaries
show they were well aware that the circles she moved in were not.

Rather than a mythic West, a site of nostalgia, responses to
MacLane showed a modern West, a site of contention. As a scape-
goat for regional animosities, eastern presses used MacLane to
deride western crudity and materialism; western presses used
her to sneer at eastern pretension and immorality. Such sparring
was too topical to allow frontier reverie. Portraying Triggs' admiration of *The Story* as evidence of the limitations of both Chicago
and Triggs, the *New York World* sarcastically queried, "Where is
the woman living in the East who has ever written a burning
thought [like MacLane]?"[33] The *New York Times*, too, thought it
appropriate that it was a Chicago house that had published such
a one as MacLane.[34] From the other side, the *Butte Miner*, aware of
the East's view of Butte as bizarre, complained that "to the eastern mind, more or less warped concerning the trend of thought in

the West, this book advertises itself as a reflection of the ideas and sentiments quite likely to take root in Butte, as mushrooms might flourish on a moldy dungheap." Regarding the "insane craving for sensationalism manifested by some of the eastern press in the case of this unfortunate girl," the *Miner* concluded, "if the culture of the East is not equal to an appreciation of such evident truths, Butte ought to offset the popular impression by proving that freak productions of a doubtful character do not constitute our highest ideals."[35] Taking the moral high ground, the city of Butte banned *The Story* from its public library, thereby increasing local demand enough to drive its price to five dollars a copy.[36]

Invading New England

Considering the local tumult, MacLane was perhaps fortunate to have left Butte as soon as she published her book. Her fervent wish that *The Story* spring her escape had been granted: her publisher's first impulse towards the strange Montanan creature was to remove her from Montana. Initially, it contemplated a European tour and syndication.[37] The trip didn't come about; apparently as a next-best alternative Stone sent MacLane on a tour of eastern cities including Chicago, Boston, and New York. "The effete East welcomed [her]," as it was said, and the venture was hugely successful.[38] With special interest in her impressions of the East compared to the West, the press followed her every move.

MacLane explained before the trip, "My publishers have told me I must get away from Butte . . . that there is no literature here; nothing to write about; and they advise a complete change, no half-way change, such as a residence in Chicago, would be. . . . So I am going, and perhaps I may never come back. But I shall miss my sand and barrenness."[39] MacLane writes in spite of Butte, not because of it, and thus is urged east for her own literary good. Stone, itself a Chicago publisher of quality texts, "half-way" between east and west, is here portrayed as endorsing views of the West as having neither literature nor literary subject matter, able only to stunt aspiring artists. Stone's central role in Chicago's astounding literary naissance makes such an assertion hard to credit. However, playing as it did upon popular notions made for good publicity. The *New York World* seized on it to proclaim that

The Marie Bashkirtseff, of Butte, Genius by her Own Admission, Having Exhausted Life and its Artistic Possibilities in the Boundless West, will NOW INVADE NEW ENGLAND for inflammable literary Material. Accompanied by Miss Fannie, Her Instructress and Her Only Friend in her Dreary Montana Existence. . . . Let the timid, shrinking East veil her modest face that blushed even in the cool rays of the rising sun, for the Bold and crimson West comes to these Atlantic-washed shores . . . to invade the land of Priscilla and the Quaker maiden.[40]

The *World's* account is rife with contradictions about East and West identity — and shows perfectly how "West" and "Midwest" were all of a piece. The counterpart of the East's "Priscilla and the Quaker maiden," MacLane, as a representative of the West, is a fierce warrior woman. Yet despite being "Bold and crimson," the West affords her only a "Dreary Montana Existence"; although "Boundless," its "life" and "artistic possibilities" can readily be "exhausted." "Timid, shrinking" and "modest" as the East may be, therefore, for westerners it is a source of "inflammable literary material." MacLane, in a reversal of western conquest, must "invade" the older, milder place.

Undoubtedly, the primary motive behind sending MacLane east was not to introduce her to literature, but to promote *The Story.* On leaving Butte, MacLane first sojourned in Chicago at the home of Lucy and Harriet Monroe.[41] Chicago greeted MacLane with fanfare so great that the *New York World* suggested it revealed the city's lack of sophistication.[42] The *World* represented New York too as sycophantically eager to receive MacLane, "the most interesting woman of the new West," in demand to lecture "on the new literature of the new West and why the East needs it."[43] MacLane complained, however, of her reception in Boston, "utterly intolerant of anything that may come down out of Butte-Montana."[44] Perhaps this assessment stemmed in part from her rejection by Radcliffe College, where, following the success of her book, she had hoped to study chemistry.[45] Although MacLane was in earnest,[46] there were rumors that her interest in Radcliffe was only one of Stone's publicity ploys.[47] The idea of this girl from the "dust and mines of Butte" attempting to infiltrate the most high-brow eastern stronghold of them all made copy that seemed too good to be true. [48]

Consistently outrageous, MacLane's performance during her

tour appears as an extension of her literary one. In interviews and receptions, she was remarkable for her egotism and insults. ("Do you know what you all remind me of, you fat rich women? A lot of hogs with your feet in a trough."[49]) Such behavior only increased her popular appeal. Perhaps accounting for its previous spate of coverage, in August of 1902 the *New York World* hired MacLane to provide five Sunday articles discussing her "impressions of the mysterious East," including such renowned locales as Newport, Wall Street, and Coney Island. Reversing the mission of Lewis and Clark, Parkman, and so many other chroniclers of the West, she was to discover the Old World and interpret the East to itself, orientalized with the term "the mysterious East." The lucrative possibilities of such a reversal had already occurred to Garland, who recalled exclaiming to a "back-trailing" Oregonian, "What an opportunity! You must discover New England. Just as a Bostonian might visit and describe Oregon, you must write of Massachusetts. . . . I see an amusing and successful book in your hand."[50]

MacLane insists throughout her first article for the *World*, "Mary MacLane at Newport," on the differences between "Butte-Montana" and the East, naming the former all told eighteen times:

> I am come down out of Butte-Montana into the mysterious East. I go here and there in trains in the mysterious East and gaze at things. . . . Upon occasion I have read in the well-filled Bible about the pomps and vanities of this wicked world. And I have wondered what it meant. . . . But all upon a bright summer morning I anchored my bark at Newport and lo—I, of Butte-Montana, straightaway walked into the midst of the pomps and vanities of this wicked world![51]

Such naming of the East as such was new for MacLane. She does not allude in *The Story* to an east-west polarity, conceiving of herself as living just in Butte, not "the West." Nor was it to the East that she wished to escape—*The Story* does not once refer to "the East" or discuss specific eastern sites—but rather simply to "the world." Yet for the *World* she becomes a westerner, and the western "gaze" she turns on the East is the series' central motif, as she confounds the curious gaze her readers would turn on her. This East does not appear bound by the United States' borders, but to signify the East in its more capacious sense — with its resonance of the Orient, tyrants and their courts, authority, submission, riches, splendor. East/West is a false polarity, but it can be an enormously useful one when considering western writers who, as they are integrated into a literary culture, tend increasingly to deploy it.

Even prior to her incarnation as westerner, MacLane worked to stage and control how she was viewed. "You may rise in your seats and focus your opera glasses," she counsels her readers, "stare with open mouths, stand on your hind-legs and gape — I will myself turn on glaring green and orange lights from the wings" (96). *The Story of Mary MacLane* directs readers to the frontispiece portrait that lends the textual one authority: "you may gaze at and admire the picture in the front of the book" (22). In the characteristic gesture of the "confessions" of her time, MacLane decries the fact that even her most valiant efforts must fail to deliver nakedness. At the same time, though, she consistently undermines attempts to get at the truth of MacLane: "You can see by my picture that my [shirt-]waist curves gracefully out. Only it is not all flesh — some of it is handkerchief"(99). Her behavior in an interview with Zona Gale seemed so contrived that at its end Gale demanded, "Don't you want to speak quite frankly for a minute and let us talk about whichever is not the pose?" MacLane replied, "'But I pose all the time. . . . I never give my real self. I have a hundred sides. . . . I am playing a deep game."[52]

The several months following the publication of *The Story* constituted the high point of MacLane's career. Her text stirred the nation, and she enjoyed playing the role of spokesperson for the West. This period, however, was all too brief, and was succeeded by life-long financial problems as she struggled to make a living as a writer in the face of increasing obscurity. MacLane was not to produce a text comparable to *The Story* until 1917 with *I, Mary MacLane* and was never again to approach the renown of 1902. The rest of her public life is characterized by a series of dramatic disappearances and reappearances.

After concluding her work for the *World,* she moved to Boston to write her second book for Stone, *My Friend Annabel Lee.*[53] The book is set in Boston's Boylston Street and consists of a series of conversations with a porcelain Japanese doll. The work reflects the period's voguish interest in Japan and Japanese aesthetics.[54]

But it also reflects the same impulse to eastering that MacLane's *World* articles dramatize. In *My Friend Annabel Lee*, MacLane proffers a version of the East doubled back on itself—portraying a sensibility imagined as Asian and housed in a building in central Boston, the New England stronghold of high culture that MacLane was seen as "invading." She attempted to look as far east—as far away from Butte—as possible. (Whiteley had a similar impulse, and effected a long sojourn in India.) The book, though, was a failure—a "hodgepodge of miscellaneous reflections [that] utterly lacked the passionate tone of [*The Story*]."[55] MacLane was surprised by the difficulty she had writing it, and attributed her problems to her locale: "There are certain advantages to be derived from sand and barrenness when one would write."[56] The West compensates for what it lacks, she suggests, by promoting inspiration.

Her writing was perhaps also troubled by her opting for prudence, her agreement with Stone to make the book a "cater" in order that "even Boston cannot object to it on high moral grounds."[57] By writing a text above reproach, MacLane earned praise for what was perceived as a new maturity, but lost her readership.[58] In the months and years following the publication of *The Story*, MacLane was unable to please readers and publishers despite her willingness to "cheapen" herself with "inexpensive paragraphs . . . [to] suit the masses."[59] Up until 1918 she was occasionally contracted for freelance work, especially for Sunday newspapers, and at times found herself deemed incapable of the task of playing her own self. In one case she sought to make her writing "terse, flippant and marymaclanesque—a cater to the 1-cent public,"[60] but was fired by an employer who complained "I'm afraid that she has lost the knack of thinking and writing about it, and has taken to whining, which isn't at all the Mary MacLane idea."[61]

In 1902, the *World* described MacLane as follows: "Her face is oval, tanned, and slightly freckled. Her nose is what the French term 'retrousse.' Brown hair, gray eyes, red lips and fine teeth show that the desert winds have done well by the young woman. She weighs not more than one hundred and eighteen pounds."[62] This comment is telling of attitudes towards the western woman artist. The characterization of Montana as a desert suggests the solitude in which MacLane is presumed to dwell. The "oval, tanned, and slightly freckled face," "fine" features, and light body imply a physicality that is at once robust and delicate; the winds foster MacLane's sensual coloring while her French nose (no matter that it be pug) hints at refinement. This description appeared at the zenith of MacLane's success, just after she left Montana to begin her commanding eastern tour. In contrast, consider the comment that a year later accompanied her picture and a review of the unsuccessful *My Friend Annabel Lee*, in the *Chicago Record-Herald*: "Judging from the picture, Miss MacLane has toned down in personal as well as literary style since last she appeared in print. Her face has lost some of that keenness procured by hard mountain winds, no doubt, and has taken on a more ingratiating softness."[63] The statement points to a belief in an essential connection between MacLane's literary prowess, her personal appearance, and her regional locale. Just as the mountain winds no longer inscribe the keen West on MacLane's face, so MacLane herself no longer writes keenly; she has "toned down." Since she now inhabits the city instead of the lonely western wastes, she has acquired a mien more acceptable in women than keenness. Her gain in sociability, however, is bought with a loss in artistry.

Upon the completion of *Annabel Lee*, MacLane commenced a seven-year period of wandering residence in Greenwich Village; Rockland, Massachusetts; and the Florida resort town of St. Augustine. Accounts of these years usually celebrate a romantically bohemian life. Cutting family ties, in New York she associated with artists, actresses, bohemians, and anarchists, indulged in café life and haute couture, attended prize fights, and gambled away her earnings from *The Story*.[64] She claimed during this period to have "known" over one thousand men and to have refused an opium pipe from Evelyn Thaw.[65] Yet despite the apparent whirlwind of gaiety, during this period MacLane was often financially desperate and under physical and psychological duress. Having quickly run through the fortune *The Story* made her, she thereafter eked out her living from irregular freelance income and money that her family, the Monroes, and Stone sent her. The Newberry Library houses a poignant series of letters, spanning three years, in which MacLane demands from Stone the thousand dollars still owed her from *The Story* (the publisher had gone out of business in 1905). After each letter, Stone sent a small sum he called alimony on which MacLane subsisted until in need of more.[66] The tone of her letters, at first jaunty, steadily darkened:

> Have you forgotten little Mary? Well, then, little Mary has by no means forgotten you. For one thing you still owe little Mary some money (money is—so—nice!!) which she would very much like to have.—What with "matching" and playing rouge-et-noir I have managed to eke out 3 square's per day, and one or two blue tailor-made suits a year. . . . I am now living in penury and want—in want, at least, of a Good Time.
>
> For the last eight days I have lived chiefly upon eggs. . . . I boil them hard and I boil them soft. . . . They are very good eggs but they grow very, very tiresome, and they leave one with a languid feeling. I heat water and drink it and pretend it's coffee.
>
> I have enough money to live perhaps four days in Boston. After that, if I receive no money from you, I shall be entirely destitute, and I think it likely that I may commit suicide. . . . I can't wait another year, nor any longer than the time I have mentioned.[67]

Harriet Monroe and MacLane's stepfather eventually concurred, "Mary can not manage her own affairs and should not be left alone . . . anywhere."[68]

To interject briefly into this biographical account issues of genre (which are taken up again at chapter's end), these letters highlight how MacLane's interest in writing about her body diverges from the tendency in women's autobiography to pass over physical experience.[69] Virginia Woolf maintained of the two "adventures of [her] professional life" that "the first—killing the Angel in the House—I think I solved. She died. But the second, telling the truth about my own experiences as a body, I do not think I solved."[70] In contrast, MacLane never lets her readers forget about her body, although the differences between its representation in her published texts and in her private letters make an interesting contrast. The body in *The Story of Mary MacLane* has a feline sensuality. It sleeps in the sun, wanders the plains, relishes its food. The text is underwritten by repressed sexuality as MacLane yearns for the devil and the absent Fanny. By referring to her frontispiece photo, she calls readers' attention to her body and to the fact that she represents it. In an age she detested for its references to a woman's "shape" and "limbs," MacLane goes so far as to describe her excellently functioning internal organs and to proclaim "a spasm of pleasure seizes me when I think in some acute moment of the buoyant health and vitality of this fine young body that is feminine in every fiber" (22).

Yet, as we have seen, MacLane paints a very different portrait in her personal correspondence. Her body, just as salient a fact, is now a continual source of woe rather than joy. Her body in her letters is most notably a starving one that she struggles to feed. It is suffused with desire not for sexual deliverance but for food. It is a burden she must clothe. It is a potential source of income through prostitution.[71] MacLane takes particular interest in considering the ways it responds to its experience of privation and disease, dwelling almost with pleasure on the way her hair was unable to regenerate itself to its former splendor of "Canadian curliness." Her letters to Stone demanding payment are entirely a list of travail and desire; her body works as a source of reproach that (she hopes) cannot be overlooked. The letters complete the story left unfinished by her youthful portrait in asserting that life is fundamentally lived at a physical level, in dire circumstances as much as in comfortable ones.

The letters also offer context for the homoerotic strain in MacLane's work, which has particularly interested contemporary readers. A more than usually desperate plea to Stone, for example, was for money to resolve a case of blackmail at the hand of a wealthy woman.[72] MacLane's account of the affair suggests that the woman was a former lover, although she never names as lovers the women with whom she shared lodging and moved back and forth between Florida, Massachusetts, and New York.[73] In her writing, MacLane covers her sexuality with the thinnest of veils. She proclaims in "The Borrower of Two-Dollar Bills — and Other Women" (1910) that "the women I have known and loved have been the crucial incidents in my life, the real and informing events. . . . Women have always been . . . more interesting to me than men, because they're more complex, more subtle, fuller of delicate incongruities and illusions, harder to understand. Two-thirds of all the women in the world, some consciously and some unconsciously, have the same feeling toward their own kind."[74] She also wrote unabashed love letters to Harriet Monroe, apparently a poor choice for her affections given Monroe's tendency to languish over much older, unavailable men.[75] By 1917 MacLane had come to wield the word lesbian and to figure love between women as irresistibly "demoniac"—an intriguing choice of words in light of her earlier focus on the devil:

> I have lightly kissed and been kissed by Lesbian lips in a way which filled my throat with a sudden subtle pagan blood-flavored wistfulness, ruinous and contraband: breath of bewildering demoniac winds smothering mine. . . . Not only so with me: so with millions whose stars have jangled. . . . The deep-dyed Lesbian woman is a creature whose sensibilities are over-balanced: whose imagination moves on mad low-flying wings; whose brain is good: whose predilections are warped: who lives always in unrest: whose inner walls are streaked with garish heathen pigments: whose copious love-instincts are an odd mixture of mirth, malice and *luxure.* (*IMM*, 277–78)[76]

Wonderful Aridness

Contrasting Butte to New York, lesbian paradise, MacLane hints at the isolation she felt from other women after finally returning to Montana: "I sit on the shaded front veranda in the summer noon day and look away south at the blue Highlands, ever snow-peaked: or east at the near towering splendid grim wall of the arid Rockies which separate this Butte from New York, from London, —the Spain-castles—the Pyramids—the Isle of Lesbos" (*IMM*, 13–14). Hand-delivered by her step-father, who also forced Stone to honor his debt, MacLane had returned to Butte in 1909 after an absence of seven years. The move was meant to avail her writing along with her finances: while living in Butte, she explained, she hoped she could produce "so big a thing that I can come back and not merely look at this New York thing but *live in it.*"[77] As opposed to the claim of 1902, that MacLane needed the literary influences of the East, MacLane herself contended that Butte's privations, its lack of intimacy and warmth, made for an enhanced artistic sensibility: "There is nothing benign, nothing enlightening—no gentleness, no pity in its barren beauty. But its hard chaste influence on the sensitive spirit is beyond any analytical power to gauge. . . . Its wonderful aridness starves human nerve-soil till the sad wide eyes of the soul grow bright . . . from denial and unconscious prayer" (*IMM*, 287).

Reversing standard notions of big city and small town life, she also contrasts New York's "quality of deep and intimate human-ness. . . the subtle freemasonry among the millions" with the people of Butte, "as shy as wild sea-fowl with each other, and absolutely dead-locked in iron-bound personal isolation."[78] We might speculate that Butte, as the site of such isolation, fostered MacLane's self-preoccupation. On her return she initially had been eager to complete her book about the women of New York, which was to reflect the city as a site of multiple, shifting, and emotionally intense human communities, "seething with po-etry."[79] It is telling that, after she was interrupted by illness, MacLane abandoned the project and wrote *I, Mary MacLane* in-stead. She had returned not only to Butte but also to an exclu-sively inward gaze.

The near-fatal bout of scarlet fever MacLane suffered shortly after her return permanently broke her health. She represented her illness as the consequence of her dissolute New York lifestyle compounded by the Montana altitude: "I had the tiredness of two or three years in me, and the altitude but quickened my heart-beats and wrought up my frazzled nerves the more."[80] After-wards she parlayed some of the material for her New York book into Sunday feature articles for the *Butte Evening News*. Some of these articles were syndicated and ran in midwestern and eastern newspapers, reviving interest in *The Story* and leading to a 1912 new edition with an afterword "showing how the leopard had changed her spots."[81] Just as in New York MacLane had written her impressions of the East as one having come from the West, so on returning to Butte she wrote her impressions of the West as one having long dwelt in the East. She was now in a position to per-ceive her home regionally: "Butte is sordid, beastly and time-serving—but withal full of romance and poetry and the wideness of the West."[82]

During her years in Butte, MacLane's main project was her fi-nal book, *I, Mary MacLane*. As in her first book, again in her third she portrays a woman of superior sensibility misplaced in the provinces. Whereas in *The Story* MacLane had represented herself as a youngster desperate to commandeer money, adventure, and fame, in *I, Mary MacLane* she is a jaded cosmopolitan eager for respite. Despite the efforts of her publisher, Frederick A. Stokes, and the endorsement of Harriet Monroe, the book met with little success.[83] *I, Mary MacLane* was received with at most guarded praise as a reworking of *The Story*, a not inaccurate assessment. *I, Mary MacLane* may lack the fascination of how *The Story* became a self-fulfilling prophecy. It does, however, reveal a writer in greater command of her prose; less repetitious and sentimental, and more consistent. It also reveals MacLane's obsession with sounding the depths of her nature as a lifelong vocation rather than mere adolescent phase, the danger of which she recognized: "I am lithe but fragile from constant involuntary self-analysis. One may analyze one's life and life-emotion till physical tissues at times grow frail, gossamer-thin. It is then as if—at a word, a whispered thought, a beat of the heart—one's Soul might flutter through the Veil, join light hands with the death-angel and flee away" (*IMM*, 16).

After the publication of *I, Mary MacLane*, MacLane repeated her exodus of fifteen years earlier, again leaving Butte for Chicago subsequent to publishing a book about herself. This time, however, she went to Chicago to make a silent film inspired by and named after her article, "Men Who Have Made Love to Me." The article, syndicated in Chicago, had attracted the attention of George K. Spohr, producer for Essanay studios. Playing a comic vamp who rejects her male lovers one by one—the "Callow Youth," "Literary Man," "Younger Son," "Prize Fighter," "Bank Clerk," and "Husband of Another"—MacLane both wrote the screenplay for and starred in the film, making more literal the compelling theatricality of her first production, *The Story of Mary MacLane*. James McQuade remarked in *Motion Picture World*, "It is the first time in my remembrance that I have seen on the screen author and actress concentrated in the same person. . . . The author appears as her very self."[84]

MacLane's film was lavish, and despite its titillating title and promotion, a relatively serious production. A trade magazine counseled,

> If you are running a house that appeals to a high-class crowd, you ought to please your patrons much with this. . . . There still is some magic in Mary's name. The public that read Mary's book, however, is not as well represented as might be in the clientels of "pop" houses. . . . The cast is so excellent that one suspects that Miss MacLane had a hand in selecting the players. They certainly put the story actress in fine shape. Even the bit parts are ad-

mirably played. Miss MacLane herself is a capable actress who has personality and screens well. . . . Play for high-class trade where possible.[85]

Concurring with such praise, the film's director, Arthur Berthelet, compared MacLane to Sarah Bernhardt and stated he had never seen "personality score such a triumph over unfamiliar scenes and undertakings."[86] Despite the respect that MacLane and her film won from the industry, however, they were panned by the general press. Again representing Butte as a site that through its desolation potentially protects the artist, the response of the *Chicago Daily Tribune* was typical: "Poor Mary MacLane! Was it for this you left your Butte fastnesses? . . . 'I, Mary' on the screen is eloquently expressed by the minus sign."[87] A series of MacLane films had been planned, but the project was abandoned after the market failure of the first.

MacLane disappeared shortly after the release of "Men Who Have Made Love to Me," leaving in her apartment only a display of fan letters; such a testimonial to past fame would later compose her death scene, too.[88] She was discovered by detectives in Chicago the following year and arrested for absconding with the elaborate gowns used in the film. Hinting at prostitution, a newspaper account described MacLane on her arrest as dressed in a kimono and a feathered hat, claiming less than a dollar to her name.[89]

Despite her destitution and her family's wishes, MacLane never returned to Butte. Instead, she settled in Chicago in one of the few white hotels in a district her obituaries dubbed as "Black and Tan," having apparently chosen the area to be near her companion Lucille Williams, an African American artist and photographer who specialized in miniatures. Williams later explained to the press, "She was my friend, and she was ill and needed me. That is why she lived where she did, to be close to me."[90] During this period, MacLane's identity as an erstwhile celebrity was unknown. Her family claimed that she held a responsible position in an advertising company; others contended she lived in near penury. Regardless, MacLane's final letter to Monroe indicates that her last years were not happy:

Dear Harriet—I would be such a poor luncheon companion that I'm asking to be let off from your invitation for Sunday. Except for

Lucille I have lived so long friendless and solitary that I feel more
like a ghost than a human being. And I shrink more from friendship, especially such as yours which brings back the feel of too
many loved memories, than from enmity. I know that I'm over-
morbid, physically and mentally, but I hate emotions and I'm not
always strong enough to combat them.[91]

MacLane was found dead in August 1929, along with the display
of clippings. Reports of the cause of death are contradictory. She
had been planning an abdominal operation and it is unclear
whether she died before or afterwards; there were also rumors of
suicide. MacLane's landlady, denying a suggestion of tuberculo-
sis, allegedly "shook her head and said: 'No—loneliness and a
broken heart.'"[92] Continuing the seamlessness between her texts
and life, MacLane's final isolation and obscurity seem an eerie re-
alization of the fate she had fearfully envisioned in *The Story*'s
conclusion:

None of them, nor any one, can know the feeling made of relief and
pain and despair that comes over me at the thought of sending all
this to the wise wide world. It is bits of my wooden heart broken
off and given away. It is strings of amber beads taken from the fair
neck of my soul. It is shining little gold coins from out of my mind's
red leather purse. It is my little old life-tragedy. It means everything to me. Do you see?—it means *everything* to me. It will amuse
you. It will arouse your interest. It will stir your curiosity. Some
sorts of persons will find it ridiculous. It will puzzle you. But am I
to suppose that it will also awaken compassion in cool, indifferent
hearts? And will the sand and barrenness look so unspeakably
gray and dreary to coldly critical eyes as to mine? And shall my bitter little story fall easily and comfortably upon undisturbed ears,
and linger for an hour, and be forgotten? Will the wise wide world
itself give me in my outstretched hand a stone? (124)

Although MacLane had requested that she be buried in Chicago,
her mother had the body taken to MacLane's birthplace of Fergus
Falls, Minnesota, where her father James MacLane was also
buried.[93] This final dispute epitomizes MacLane's life of conflict
between the urban and the provincial, "East" and "West" (the
proximity of Illinois and Minnesota notwithstanding), solitude
and family life, transciency and rootedness.

Women's Autobiography?

The conflict in MacLane's life is mirrored in the conflict that pressures her texts. The arrogant posturing in her autobiographies might lead one to overlook their strain, as they seek to incorporate at once a discourse of feminism and of femininity, to paint a portrait of both rebel and maiden. Rachel DuPlessis suggests that a claim to genius such as hers, instead of resolving the conflict between femininity and feminism, actually contributes to it: "'Women of genius' sets in motion . . . conventional notions of womanhood. . . . Genius theory is a particular exaggeration of bourgeois individualism."[94] MacLane's choice of genre intensifies the strain. Female autobiographers have historically run the risk of being judged unwomanly,[95] and perhaps MacLane's sense of this risk accounts for the defensive vein running through her texts, the vein that Mencken mocks in describing her as "A Puritan wooed and tortured by the leers of beauty."[96] Even as she protests the debilitating effects of bourgeois norms on young women, MacLane insists throughout on her middle-class virtue: her refined sensibilities, her sure sense of propriety, and, most important, her chastity. Referring primly to her "maid-senses" so easily repulsed and her desire for "Badness," she makes clear that her sexual fantasies about the devil are only fantasies, and that her body, "feminine in every fiber," remains inviolate. She further works to demonstrate her superiority through defining herself against inferior ethnic others.

Writing at the end of the nineteenth century and the beginning of the twentieth, MacLane is positioned at an important transition period in women's autobiography, when women were beginning to explore constructions of gender roles and identity more explicitly. Yet although women were becoming more assured and self-consciously feminist in writing about themselves, the dominant traditions of women's autobiography, in keeping with still current ideals of womanly silence and modesty, continued to strike a muted note. (Georgi-Findlay notes that at this time women's western writing also remained primarily a discourse of femininity rather than feminism.[97]) The tension in MacLane's text attests to the friction between a nineteenth-century mode of writing women's autobiography, and a more modern one.[98]

Despite MacLane's insistence on feminine purity, her egotism and claims to genius make her very different from other women autobiographers of the time. The texts of her contemporaries, in Heilbrun's words, document "exciting lives" with "narrative flatness," or "fail directly to emphasize their [authors'] importance" despite "dazzling accomplishments."[99] They rarely highlight their bodily experiences, either. Accordingly, MacLane does not fit with influential theories about women's autobiography, such as those developed by Mary G. Mason, Susan Stanford Friedman, and Margo Culley, that are based on the premise that "the female autobiographer has lacked the sense of radical individuality . . . that empowered Augustine and Henry Adams to write their representative lives large."[100] Mason, as Smith and Watson summarize, contends that "women's life writing involved the postulation of an 'other' toward, through, and by whom women come to write themselves."[101] Friedman builds upon Mason's theory to claim that a woman's "autobiographical self often does not oppose herself to all others . . . but [feels] very much with others in an interdependent existence."[102] Culley argues that "the dominant tradition of American women's autobiography has roots in Puritan beliefs about the self"; women thus write autobiography in order to be "useful to others."[103]

These theories, as valid as they may be for some women's texts, seem simply to not apply to what MacLane is up to in hers. In MacLane's work, family and community are grounds for rejection and disassociation; her affiliations are all of the imagination. Likewise, although she clearly writes her books with an eye towards utility, she means them to be useful to herself rather than anyone else. MacLane rarely places herself within or directs her text towards a community of women, even though she found an ardent audience among them.

Mason asserts that Rousseau's *Confessions* "finds no echo in women's writing about their lives."[104] To the modern reader looking backwards, however, Rousseau sounds entirely "marymaclaneish":

> I have resolved on an enterprise which has no precedent and which, once complete, will have no imitator. . . . I am made unlike anyone I have ever met: I will even venture to say that I am like no one in the whole world. I may be no better, but at least I am differ-

ent. Whether Nature did well or ill in breaking the mold in which
she formed me, is a question which can only be resolved after the
reading of my book. . . . So let the numberless legion of my fellow
men gather around me, and hear my confessions.[105]

Because MacLane's autobiographies differ so greatly from those
of her female contemporaries, it is worth asking whether and how
they may resemble those of her male ones. Or, to put it another
way, do we hear the echo of Rousseau's *Confessions* in the texts of
turn-of-the-century American men? We might consider not only
how MacLane breaks with dominant traditions in women's autobiography, but also how she breaks with dominant traditions in
American autobiography as a whole. It is true that men have often spoken in a "detached, autonomous, and self-consciously au-
thoritative" voice largely unavailable to women.[106] They also, as
in Henry Adams's case, are more readily seen as a "representative
of the time, a mirror of [their] era." Nevertheless, as Lawrence
Buell and Susanna Egan argue, and indeed as the description of
Adams suggests, throughout the nineteenth century American
men as a rule produced texts that downplayed their personal
lives in order to suggest an edifying universality. They thus more
resemble Culley's formulation of women's autobiography than
Karl Weintraub's oft-cited formulation of modern (male) autobiography as a genre that "celebrates individuality and eschews
conventional norms of personality."[107]

In "Autobiography in the American Renaissance," Buell discusses how antebellum literature is marked by a proliferation of
autobiographical writing and the development of "an 'I' that explicitly or implicitly proclaims its boundlessness."[108] Yet he contends that despite — or because — of this, the period "was not particularly rich in the kind of developed autobiography that one
most immediately associates with the term since Rousseau."[109]
Citing the work of Emerson, Fuller, Thoreau, and Whitman, he
concludes that mid-nineteenth-century American autobiography
continued to be characterized by the colonial practice of "objecti-
fying the self either through its effacement in favor of a narrative
of events . . . or through the subordination of the 'I's unique-
ness to shared, communal models of the self."[110] Egan, in "'Self'-
Conscious History: American Autobiography after the Civil War,"
makes similar claims for autobiography into the Progressive era:

that in contrast to renowned autobiographers such as Rousseau, Goethe, De Quincey, Gorky, and Proust, American men and women's autobiographies alike continued to subordinate the "I" in the service of universality, representativeness, and utility. Pointing to the odd absence of names that characterizes the titles of notable autobiographies of the time, and that crosses lines of both gender and race, she contends,

> Titles like *Life of the Mississippi* (1882), *An Indian Boyhood* (1902), *Twenty Years at Hull House* (1911), *The Making of an American* (1901), *Up from Slavery* (1901), *A New England Girlhood* (1889), and *The Souls of Black Folk* (1903) . . . enforce connection between the one life and all others that it may represent. They enforce attention also to place as the context that serves in part to justify autobiography.[111]

In contrast, consider the insistent naming in *The Story of Mary MacLane* and *I, Mary MacLane*, as well as in their successor *The Story of Opal*. Via Bashkirtseff, MacLane works against "the nine-teenth-century backlash to the tell-all stance of Rousseau,"[112] bridging the ocean and the century to bring to renewed prominence a Continental model invigorated by her gender politics.

Despite the fact that MacLane breaks from the paradigm of representativeness that Buell and Egan document, perhaps the dominance of this paradigm contributed to her contemporaries' insistence on viewing her as the typical girl, adolescent, or young woman. As the following chapter discusses, it may also have contributed to a similar inclination of readers to perceive little girl writers as the representative child, their precociousness in producing publishable texts notwithstanding. And, in noting that the era's autobiographies "enforce attention . . . to place as the context that serves in part to justify autobiography,"[113] Egan may also indicate why MacLane and Whiteley became so renowned as Montana and Oregon girls.

MacLane's geographical location profoundly influenced her literary career in ways that went beyond the personal. We cannot know if MacLane's Montana home was the deciding factor in the acceptance of *The Story*, but certainly it was a crucial one. The "western female aesthetic" in the air, so to speak, confirmed MacLane's depiction of her self as a genius sui generis, a child of nature whose matchless prose sprang from a communion with the barren plains around her, enabling a degree of "nakedness" unavailable in less wild vales. Yet Montana served not only to buttress MacLane's assertions of genius, but also to render her a representative small-town girl. MacLane herself drew parallels between her experiences in Butte and other women's in towns such as Waco and Kalamazoo. Montana made MacLane appear both more exotic and more familiar, more outlandish and more parochial. As the following two chapters discuss, for Opal Whiteley as well western origins provided a double identity as a child of the provinces and a child of the wild.

3

Little Girls and Their "Explores"

Tell her that she should appreciate the kindness of your mother to her when she was not her own child. Tell her its hard for most people to be kind to a child that isn't their own. . . . Tell her that you and the family feel that before she lets any of this diary be published she ought to let you all read it.

Opal Whiteley, anonymous letter to her family

Just as *The Story of Mary MacLane* was one of the most notorious books of 1902, *The Story Of Opal* was one of the most notorious of 1920. While MacLane's readers were startled by the "confessions" of a passionate young woman, Whiteley's were enchanted—at least before challenges to the text's authenticity arose—by the whimsy and melancholic yearnings of a nature-loving young girl. Whiteley claimed that *The Story of Opal*, which she published at the age of twenty, was a reconstruction of a diary she had kept as a child of six and seven. The text is a record of her sense of kinship with the natural world and alienation from the human, and centers around her "longings to go on exploration trips" in the Oregon woods pitted against her mother's determination to keep her working indoors. Its setting neatly divided between the Whiteley household and the woods surrounding it, *The Story of Opal* details Whiteley's interactions with her animal companions and adult friends, her private games and rituals, and her mishaps at home. Whiteley is at home only under duress, and when at home, she is usually at work: "All day the mamma did have more works for me to do. . . . And all the time, all day long, I did have longings to go on exploration trips" (219). These longings permeate the text: "I did have thinks to go explores [*sic*]. . . . But the mamma had not thinks like my thinks. She did tell me of the many works she did have for me to do, and I did go to do them" (276). So intent is her mother on keeping the child at home, she once actually ties her to the house. This enforced domesticity generates Whiteley's textual production, in that she writes only when housebound: "The mamma is gone for a visit away. Before her going, she did set me to mind the baby. I do so. In between times, I print" (208); "I printed this sitting on the wood-box, where the mamma put me after she spanked me" (107); "Now I hear the mamma say, 'I wonder where Opal is.' She has forgets. I'm still under the bed where she did put me, quite a time ago. And all this nice longtime, light is come to here from the lamp on the kitchen table — light enough so I can print prints" (146). In contrast, when left to her own devices, Whiteley chooses not to write but to roam.

Whiteley resembles many women writers in her chafing against domestic confinement and expectations of a domestic identity. Her text, though, does not investigate the consequences of gender, any more than it discusses her degree of satisfaction with her life. Whiteley simply describes various events and their emotional impact on her, focusing on her relationship with her woodland surroundings and its teeming inhabitants. *The Story of Opal*, a reconstruction from fragments (it was allegedly ripped up by a jealous sister), does not purport to record the passing of time with dated entries. Like *The Story of Mary MacLane*, the diary develops through the accumulation and repetition of detail rather than through narrative movement, and Whiteley's world remains constant. Even though the text is arranged so that it ends just prior to her move into town, conceivably a calamitous change, the potential drama of the move is precluded both by the child's nonchalant response and by Whiteley's reassuring afterword that she soon returned to rural life.

The story that drives the text is not one that it tells, but rather one to which it only refers: Whiteley's myth of family. Through her pioneering grandparents, Whiteley might have drawn on a western pioneer heritage.[1] Like MacLane, however, she was uninterested in exploring the imaginative possibilities of such a family history, despite her era's penchant for "Frontier Days" and the like.[2] Instead, as a child and young adult Whiteley invented a European genealogy for herself, claiming that she was really Princess Françoise D' Orléans, the unrecognized daughter of the French naturalist and explorer Henri D' Orléans de Bourbon, great-grandson of the "Last King of France," Louis Philippe. D' Orléans died while on an exploring expedition in India when Whiteley would have been four; Whiteley claimed that her mother then left with her for America. Her mother drowned during the voyage and "Françoise" was brought to Oregon, where the Whiteleys adopted her and renamed her Opal as a replacement for their own recently deceased daughter Opal Whiteley. Throughout the text, Whiteley distinguishes between "the mamma" and "the papa"— the Whiteleys—and "Angel Mother" and "Angel Father," her French parents. She yearns for the latter, describing in the diary the messages she writes on leaves for their souls to read and her intent study of the two books she claims they left her. Her real identity is known only to the trees, grass, rain, and wind, which call to "petite Françoise" to come exploring.

The Wonder Child

The Story of Opal was first serialized in the *Atlantic Monthly*. Readers found the circumstances surrounding the text as compelling as the text itself: the diary's incredible child authorship; the mystery of its French phrases, classical allusions, and references to the "Angel Parents"; its romantic discovery and painstaking reconstruction from a mass of fragments rushed from L.A.[3] In 1919, Whiteley had approached the *Atlantic*'s editor, Ellery Sedgwick, with her manuscript of *The Fairyland Around Us*, an educational children's book about nature.[4] As the story goes, Sedgwick rejected *The Fairyland*, but was intrigued by Whiteley herself. In his oft-repeated description of their first meeting, he recalls,

> [*The Fairyland*] was quaintly embellished with colored pictures, pasted in by hand, and bore a hundred marks of special loving care. Yet about it there seemed little to tempt a publisher. But about Opal Whiteley herself there was something to attract the attention even of a man of business—something very young and eager and fluttering, like a bird in a thicket.

Coupled with her personal appeal, Whiteley's Oregon origins sealed Sedgwick's interest. After learning that Whiteley had lived in nineteen different logging camps, he maintained,

> It was hard not to be interested now. One close question followed another regarding the surroundings of her girlhood. The answers were so detailed, so sharply remembered, that the next question was natural. "If you remember like that, you must have kept a diary." Her eyes opened wide. "Yes, always, I do still." "Then it is not this book I want, but the diary."[5]

This account reveals both the commercial possibilities perceived in the diaries of young women, particularly women of seemingly far-flung origins, and the importance in this genre of the author's personality over her writing itself. By 1919, publishers would have been quick, after the success of texts such as Bashkirtseff's and MacLane's, to perceive a young woman's diary as potentially profitable. Indeed, the title of *The Story of Opal* may well have been modeled upon that of MacLane's first book.[6] It is telling that Sedgwick asked after Whiteley's diary even after seeing other work that did not impress him. What piqued his interest was not Whiteley's writing, but Whiteley herself, alluring enough to attract "even a man of business." The charisma for which Whiteley is always noted offset the dubious charms of her manuscript. Significant as well is Sedgwick's claim that Whiteley's vivid description of the "surroundings of her girlhood" led to his guess that she had kept a diary in childhood, and to his desire for it.[7] Factors of genre, region, and personality conspired to make Sedgwick want not only a text he had never read, but a text that arguably did not yet exist — at the time only a hatboxful of shredded scraps stowed in a Los Angeles warehouse.

When Sedgwick took over the *Atlantic Monthly* in 1909, its circulation was on the wane. Building on the work of his predecessors, Walter Hines Page and Bliss Perry,[8] he established a wider readership for the magazine through publishing more human interest features and a broader range of literary selections. Within ten years, he increased the *Atlantic's* annual circulation from 17,000 to almost 100,000; the serialization of Whiteley's text alone resulted in a spike of subscriptions.[9] In soliciting Whiteley's diary, Sedgwick saw himself as overturning the policy of Horace E. Scudder, a prominent past editor, who allegedly proclaimed, "I

have never invited a contribution to the Atlantic. If it is offered, I
receive it. If it is good, I print it."[10] The late-nineteenth-century
magazine boom in the U.S. had resulted in fierce competition for
readership, and by Sedgwick's time, editors were casting their
nets increasingly wide in hopes of catching stories that would attract new readers while retaining the old.

Whiteley's diary was no anomaly among Sedgwick's selections. In recalling his long tenure as editor of the *Atlantic*, he
mused, "It was to women then that my thoughts oftenest turned,
and a score of lonely, self-dependent histories were woven into
the texture of the Atlantic."[11] The editor's self-professed credo
was to find texts that not only followed "Harvard['s] . . . sover-
eign recipe [of] clearness, force, elegance" but that also possessed
an indefinable "interest":

> The simple essential ingredient which leavens any mass is interest,
> inherent, inescapable interest. . . . If interest is the nub of it, how
> can interest be gauged? Pick up a book. . . . [I]f children cease to
> distract and the dinner bell to interrupt, and you two, the Book and
> you, are alone in a timeless world, then the interest is real.[12]

Sedgwick's characterization of a book of interest as able to van-
quish the domestic scene of children and dinner bells is telling in
regard to the "lonely, self-dependent" women's texts he elected to
publish. In discussing his pursuit of interest, moreover, Sedgwick
is moved to present himself as pioneer: "If only interest were
there, and personality, I could stake out an original Atlantic claim
in the pleasantest of all the outlying territories of Literature."[13]
The *Atlantic*, bastion of New England high literary tradition,
turns to middle-brow texts and western metaphor. Sedgwick here
points to the literal connection he made between "interest" and
"outlying territories": he found particularly compelling the writings of women who were geographically as well as ideologically
or racially outside mainstream channels. Under Sedgwick, the *Atlantic* published not just Whiteley and Harrison's work, but also,
among others, Austin's southwestern writings; autobiographical
texts by Eleanor Pruitt Stewart and other pioneers such as Hilda
Rose and Annie Pike Greenwood; excerpts from the autobiography of the Russian Jewish immigrant, Mary Antin; writings on
Shintoism and Buddhism by the expatriate nun, L. Adams Beck;

and an account by Eleanor Risley of her journey on foot through Alabama.

The Story of Opal, first written by a child but reconstructed by an adult, could be considered to have almost a double author-ship. The text reads like a recipe for 1920 commercial success: as much as the haunting quality of the diary itself, the era's interest in both young women's diaries and regional writing contributed to Whiteley's renown. Just as significant, *The Story of Opal* tapped into the 1920s' vogue for texts by child authors.

The ardent response to the 1904 reprinting of Marjorie Flem-ing's diary (as in, for example, Mark Twain's "Marjorie Fleming, the Wonder Child") is an early sign of this vogue for children's writing.[14] By 1920 it had hit its peak with the extraordinary amount of attention accorded three child writers, Whiteley, Daisy Ashford, and Hilda Conkling. Commenting on this phenomenon, William Kavanaugh Doty remarked, "Since 1918 a dozen vol-umes, at least, have appeared from the pens of child authors. Per-haps there are many more, if a complete record were had. Literary expression by children is by no means new, but it may well be doubted that any period has witnessed the publication of half so many books by these precocious artists as that between 1918 and 1923."[15] Child writers were portrayed as so numerous as to have grown unremarkable: "If they do not excite wonder," the *Bookman* commented, "it is because the world has became [*sic*] callous to-ward unusual discovery."[16]

The period's three most successful child writers range across genres, but were seen as essentially akin to each other. Daisy Ash-ford's novel, *The Young Visiters,* chronicling the anxious entrance into upper-class society of Ethel Monicue and Mr. Salteena, "not quite a gentleman but you would hardly notice it but it cant be helped anyhow," was an even bigger seller than *The Story of Opal.*[17] Published by Ashford after she reached adulthood, the book was praised for its humor and its child author for her com-manding presence. Conkling, a poet, wrote over the course of her childhood in rural Massachusetts and took nature and middle-class, domestic scenes as her subject. She published first in maga-zines including *Poetry* and *Good Housekeeping* before her work was compiled into *Poems by a Little Girl,* prefaced by "For you, Mother": "I have a dream for you, Mother / Like a soft thick fringe to hide your eye. I have a surprise for you, Mother, / Shaped like a strange butterfly."[18] Classed together in statements such as "The Atlantic Monthly has its Opal Whiteley, while Hilda Conkling and Daisy Ashford have taken their places beside precocious Margaret [*sic*] Fleming of other days,"[19] the success of these three young authors encouraged many children—or rather, their parents—to attempt publication. J. M. Barrie, who introduced Ashford's text, later complained, "the whole affair has been something of a trial for me . . . as hordes of parents here keep sending me their children's works, and now they are doing it from America. I have to employ a secretary."[20]

A variety of converging factors contributed to the surge of American and British interest in children's writings, as well as in children in general. The early twentieth century saw increasing investigation of what was and was not typical behavior for a particular age group, coinciding with the burgeoning of the study of child psychology and child development.[21] The child was emerging as more and more a distinct figure, and James R. Kincaid argues that the late-nineteenth-century development of an opposition between "adult" and "child" led to a desire to locate and capture the essence of childhood.[22] The enthusiasm for Barrie's Peter Pan, the boy who won't grow up, speaks to the era's fetish for the child figure.

We might conjecture that at this time, more books by children were published simply because children wrote more books, due to a rise in public education and literacy.[23] However, the numerous instances in which children's texts were published years after they were written show that plenty of them existed long before the 1920s. Carolyn Steedman argues that it was less the new skills of children than the new desires of adults that accounted for the trend in reading children's texts as part of "a much wider social assumption that children might be used as soothing, artless and innocent figures of relaxation and spiritual refreshment by adults."[24] The development lay in the commodification of the texts, with Whiteley's diary a particularly remarkable instance of the transformation of a child's private document into a best-selling public one.[25]

The popularity of children's writings is closely bound with the turn-of-the-century avidity for "naked-soul lady" texts, which revealed their authors' innermost passions and desires. The publication of these texts laid the groundwork for published children's texts, most of which were diaries written by little girls.[26] As discussed, the "naked-soul lady" genre emphasizes extraordinariness. In this respect, the mere fact that child authors wrote so young aligned them with their older counterparts. The notion of adolescence was relatively recent, moreover, and thus there was little to separate diarists such as Bashkirtseff and Emily Shore, who both began writing at fourteen, from the realm of childhood. MacLane herself was an early participant in the girls' diary genre, contributing to the *Butte Evening News* her adult-written "Autobiography of the Kid Primitive" (1910). When pushed to its furthest extreme one or two decades later, interest in the interiority and sexuality of young women, and hence in their diaries, led to an interest in the interiority and incipient sexuality of little girls and *their* diaries. Sedgwick identifies the qualities found attractive in girl authors when he admires Whiteley as a "young and eager and fluttering . . . bird in a thicket."

Just like young women diarists, child writers were regarded as both representative of their age group and gender, and disturbingly iconoclastic by virtue of having circulated texts that displayed themselves. Yet writings by little girls were often taken more seriously than those of their older counterparts. Discussions of child writers are remarkable for their implication that the little girl writer is more interesting than the adult woman she has or will become. "Little tempted" by Whiteley's *Fairyland,* Sedgwick instead inquired after her girlhood diary rather than other books she may have written as an adult. Barrie regrets the loss of the child Daisy to the young woman: "There is no doubt that 'The Young Visiters' . . . is a scrumptious affair. . . . I find myself turning back to it for advice, instruction, and amusement, and mourning the melancholy case of an authoress who could do this when she was nine and is now occupied in putting up her hair or something of the kind."[27] Little girls and their "scrumptious" productions are more delectable than adult women and their vanities. Although he speaks lightly here, Barrie nevertheless suggests that even the most compelling of little girls necessarily pursue the trivial once they leave childhood. The future of girl writers is not one of growth.

That the vogue for children's texts builds upon the vogue for "naked-soul lady" texts—texts characterized by avowals of desire—points to the prurient interest with which some readers may have turned to little girls' diaries. Even as they extolled the purity of little girlhood, readers often searched girls' texts for signs of incipient sexuality and considered their authors in sexualized terms.[28] Like Barrie, various reviewers of the 1920s adopted a gallant tone towards little girl writers. They both perceived their texts as "luscious reading" and perceived the authors themselves as tempting to the appetite—"sweet delicious little soul[s]."[29] An elderly fan of Whiteley wrote to the *Atlantic* to urge the publication of an Opal book: "I have read for years . . . until my eyes are almost gone, but like Milton, if I go blind, I must have Opal!" and "I lend my Atlantics over and over, but I want my Opal all in one piece to have and to hold till death do us part."[30] (Struck by the selling power of these words, the *Atlantic* quoted them in an advertisement for *The Story of Opal*.) A reviewer of another child's manuscript, making this same conflation of text with child author, commends its "neat pile of little fat copy books—as satisfying to hold as the little girl who wrote it [*sic*]."[31] Two decades later, *Mademoiselle* magazine depicted Bashkirtseff as "at twelve, a delicious brat," imagining,

> Late on an August night in Paris in the year 1874, a girl was writing in a little white book. The girl's skin was white, even against the white of her robe, and her thick, pale-gold hair fell to her thighs. When she glanced up from her writing, she saw her own image reflected from every angle of the mirrored walls. The room seemed to be full of girls, all white-robed and golden-haired, all of them busily writing in little white books.[32]

The mirrors that multiply delicious Bashkirtseffs serve as an apt metaphor for child publication. Publication mass-replicates the text that is seen as synonymous with the girl child, allowing readers to bestow the bounty of the girl upon grateful friends and relatives to lend her "over and over." And the little girls who get circulated in this way are those who strike readers as somehow representative of girlhood to begin with, mirrored endlessly in real life as well as on paper.

The Spirit of Childhood

When I began work on *The Story of Opal*, my interest lay in Whiteley's conflicting investments in indoors and out rather than any signs of nascent sexuality. I was, though, tempted to treat this allegedly child-written text differently than I did those by adults. As R. M. Malcolmson remarks of *The Young Visiters*, "It was difficult to write about the book. . . . There was no yardstick by which to judge it."[33] Children's writing, both then and now, strikes readers as such an exotic and intractable genre that our instinct is to subdue it: we pay so much attention to the author's child status that her actual text becomes secondary. The circumstances surrounding the text are thoroughly and often skeptically investigated: how it came to be written, edited, and published as well as how it first came to light, whether in an attic or drawer or obscure library shelf, or by virtue of less literal discoveries (such as Sedgwick's of Whiteley's text: "If you remember like that, you must have kept a diary").[34]

Discussions of children's texts, along with the circumstances of their discovery and the motives of all parties concerned, often portray the text as an artifact: the "neat pile of little fat copybooks," Bashkirtseff's "hundred white books,"[35] Whiteley's ravaged manuscript. Sedgwick gave the story of the arrival of the diary's fragments, mixed with "an indescribable quantity of old books, papers, clothing, nature studies,"[36] a prominent place in his introduction to *The Story of Opal*:

> We telegraphed for them and they came — hundreds, thousands, one might almost say millions of them. Some few were large as a half-sheet of notepaper; more, scarce big enough to hold a letter of the alphabet. The paper was of all shades, sorts, and sizes: butcher's bags pressed and sliced in two, wrapping-paper, the backs of envelopes — anything and everything that could hold writing. The early years of the diary are printed in letters so close that, when the sheets are fitted, not another letter can be squeezed in. In later passages the characters are written with childish clumsiness, and later still one sees the gradually forming adult hand. The labor of piecing the diary together may fairly be described as enormous. For nine months almost continually the diarist has labored, piecing it together sheet by sheet, each page

a kind of picture-puzzle, lettered, for frugality (the store was precious), on both sides of the paper.[37]

Relatively speaking, at least, we invest adult-written texts with organic, self-generated properties. The process by which they came into being and became public is not nearly so exhaustively probed.

A child-written text, read *as* a child's text and *because* it is one, is primarily examined in terms of the degree to which it does or does not adhere to the reader's concept of childhood. The publication of children's texts could be perceived as a way for children to make their voices heard, to enter into the public sphere from which they are usually excluded. Despite publication, though, their voices may still be ignored. Child authors are often read as "subjects in process," soon to be worth listening to, but not quite yet.

In a 1920 discussion of *The Story of Opal* that is dense with the conflicting attitudes held towards children's publications, the *Bookman* critic, Annie Carroll Moore, commented that many

> look upon [Whiteley's] literary and historical allusions . . . as far-fetched and unnatural for a child. To those who are bored by "The Story of Opal" . . . I have only this to say: leave it alone unless you can approach it in a mood born of some close and vivid association with childhood. . . . The truest thing about the journal to my own mind is its truth of emotion—it is the absolute record of a child's emotion. "She was a queer girl," said a child of nine who had been reading the story aloud to her mother. . . . Had this journal come to us from France, Russia, or Serbia it would have seemed less strange. We think we know about what to expect of the children of America or of England. But how little we really do know![38]

In this passage, Moore's phrase "the absolute record of a child's emotion" evokes the essential child, and yet it is embedded within an effort to move readers beyond their narrow understanding of American and English children. Moore notes, too, the tendency to perceive children's writing as "far-fetched and unnatural," as "strange" and perhaps even disturbing. However, she also alludes to a central motive for reading children's texts, that of being moved by them towards "a mood born of some close and vivid association with childhood." These last words support

Steedman's assertion that children's texts were often read in order that the world-weary adult could somehow "penetrat[e] the very heart of childhood, in order to live 'child-life' anew." Steedman cites the introduction to Mary Paxon's diary: "Once in a long time an authentic bit of childhood is captured and held within the pages of a book, so that other children in spirit, whether old or young, may enjoy it."[39]

Attesting to the fact that late-twentieth-century critics are little different from their predecessors — except, perhaps, in their more explicit references to the self-interest of their reading — Laurel Holliday contends of her diary anthology, "I have selected these ten girls for their incredible ability to make me laugh and cry and see parts of myself through their mirror."[40] Benjamin Hoff, Whiteley's most recent biographer, likewise remarks that *The Story of Opal* struck him "as though it had been written especially for me."[41] These modern-day champions, like earlier readers of girls' texts, assert their private relationship with these texts ("to have and to hold till death do us part") even as they seek to replicate their private experience for as many readers as possible to gain them renewed readership. This impulse at once to possess and to share girl writers is linked to a perception of these girls as both rare subjects who lend themselves to intense relationships with kindred readers, and ordinary children who represent and can be shared by the masses.

Considering the totemic power of children's writing, then and now, it is essential that readers feel confident that the book they turn to is, indeed, the work of a child. When these texts fall under suspicion of adult authorship, readers may reject them as fervently as they first embraced them. (In Whiteley's case, furious readers returned their books to the publisher and recalled those they had given as gifts). Consequently, the question of authenticity is seldom absent from discussions of children's texts, and the child's words in published texts do not stand alone. Instead, much as slave narratives have been presented, they are usually introduced by some document, like Reverend John A. Hutton's foreword to *The Elfin Pedlar,* which "stand[s] sponsor for its *bona fides.*"[42] These introductions are often written by adults like Hutton or Barrie who are considered to have a special understanding of children and childhood.[43] The 1994 edition of *The Story of Opal* goes so far as to promote Hoff as a spirit kindred to his child subject: "As a child he, like Opal, preferred to spend his time out-doors, observing animals, insects, and plants. From an early age he, too, loved to write. He is the author of the best-selling *The Tao of Pooh* and *The Te of Piglet*." These authorities with an "insider's" understanding serve both to interpret the child to a larger and po-tentially grosser audience, and to testify that the work is, indeed, the genuine production of a real child.

Marguerite Wilkinson, the 1920 *New York Times* reviewer of Whiteley, stated, "The question asked with regard to 'The Young Visiters' is being repeated in connection with the present book — 'Could a child really write it?' Only a child could have written 'The Story of Opal.' No adult could put into language such inno-cent and spontaneous grace combined with such freshness of per-ception."[44] Doty likewise claimed of Harriss that "her diction is that of a child, and hence is unstereotyped; it is the diction of a child, and so is intensive rather than extensive; it is the diction of a child, and is, consequently, contemporary instead of archaic."[45] These statements suggest that the child's text testifies to its own authenticity by confirming the reader's understanding of "child." A text that fails to do so is more likely to be labeled, if not "inau-thentic," then at least "precocious," a common charge. Seeking to preempt such a response, the *Atlantic* explained that in publish-ing Whiteley's text "the spelling—with the exception of occa-sional characteristic examples of the diarist's individual style—has been amended, lest the journal seem precocious, rather than beautifully natural and interpretive of the Spirit of Childhood."[46]

What is this "Spirit of Childhood" that Whiteley is said to in-terpret so beautifully? The phrase appears frequently in accounts of children's texts, but without definition or discussion. Those who wield it assume its connotations are clear: innocence, kinship to nature, nascent but not overt sexuality. Existing outside of his-tory (which lends her writing a "time-arresting quality"[47]), the child is held to possess a holistic understanding of humankind and reality, instinctively discerning deep forces at play despite be-ing unable to comprehend details or articulate what she knows.

As the *Atlantic's* parry of the charge of precocity indicates, the perception of a child's text as "beautifully natural and interpre-tive of the Spirit of Childhood" exists in tension with the percep-tion of the unnatural or even grotesque aspect of a child penetrating adult territory in producing a publishable text in the first place. These texts may reveal the nature of childhood, but they are not a result of children acting naturally. Readers seek to reconcile this paradox by insisting that the child wrote her text without thought or effort: in other words, she wrote it "naturally." Likewise, in his somewhat tongue-in-cheek introduction to Ashford's text—revealing, perhaps, his discomfort with discussing a child writer seriously—Barrie states,

> The "owner of the copyright" guarantees that "The Young Visiters" is the unaided effort in fiction of an authoress of nine years. "Effort," however, is an absurd word to use, as you may see by studying the triumphant countenance of the child herself . . . it has an air of careless power; there is a complacency about it that by the severe might perhaps be called smugness. It needed no effort for that face to knock off a masterpiece.[48]

It would be "absurd" to assume that a child writes in the same way as an adult, Barrie maintains, with conscious effort and thought. Rather than Ashford's mind, the face displaying the girl's carelessness, power, triumph, and complacency writes a text that encodes the instinctive physical and emotional knowledge of a child. Likewise, Wilkinson admired Ashford's "spontaneous grace" and "freshness of perception," and in remarkably similar language—suggesting that successful child writers could appear cast from a similar mold—praised Conkling's poetry for its "freshness of imagery and spontaneously graceful phrasing," adding that it was natural it should be so since its author was a child.[49] Amy Lowell avowed that "the only possible explanation" of Conkling's work "is that the poems are perfectly instinctive. . . . When the feeling is strong, it speaks for itself. . . . She probably hardly thought at all, so natural was it."[50] She went so far as to assert that the writing was "subconscious": "How comes a child of eight to prick and point with the rapier of irony? . . . Did she quite grasp its meaning herself? We may doubt it. In this poem, the subconscious is very much on the job."[51] Lowell is typical of readers in dwelling on the apparent gap between what the child observes and records and what she actually understands, the gap that generates the humor of Ashford's text or the pathos of Whiteley's.[52] Children generally are not read as writing with sophisticated intent. Instead, their texts are seen as a spontaneous overflowing of the "Spirit of Childhood" that somehow gets translated to the page.

At the same time, "childhood" precludes full aesthetic success, to the relief of some readers. "Where childhood betrays genius," Lowell remarks of Conkling, "is in the mounting up of detail. Inadequate lines not infrequently jar a total effect. . . . This is the perennial child, thinking as children think; and we are glad of it. It makes the whole more healthy, more sure of development."[53] Among child writers, this passage suggests, a "betray[al of] genius" is welcomed. Even those celebrated as geniuses are faulted when they fail to appear childlike and hence not "healthy." A reviewer complained of Ashford's second book that, unlike her first, "it g[ave] the effect of a burlesque of a 'grown-up's novel' more than of a spontaneous efflorescence of childhood."[54] Conkling's work was praised because it did not "smack of the exotic and consciously clever."[55] Helen Douglas Adam's editor promised that she was "entirely free from self-consciousness or any thought of posing. . . . There is nothing of the prodigy encouraged in her young mind."[56]

Thus, even as Whiteley is declared "magical"[57] or the claim is made of Conkling that "one has stumbled upon that flash of personality which we call genius,"[58] those who promote the girls insist that they are ordinary and even representative children. Tellingly, Conkling's volume of poetry is entitled *Poems by a Little Girl*. Likewise, the preliminary title for Whiteley's text, *The Diary of a Child*, shows Sedgwick's intention to market Whiteley as the essential child.[59] The many imitations that texts such as Whiteley's and MacLane's inspired point to the central paradox of children's and "naked-soul lady" texts alike: a display of genius or conviction of it causes readers to marvel over their own or others' likeness. In her introduction to *My Brilliant Career*, Carmen Callil maintains, "One can hardly restrain oneself from leaping back in time to tell Miles Franklin, 'Sybylla is me'"; she "could be any girl in any country, any place, at any time."[60] In the most extreme manifestation of this phenomenon, readers sent letters to the publishers of the recent MacLane anthology contending that they were MacLane in a previous life. Reading her work caused them to exclaim not only "she's just like me" but also "she *is* me" (or rather, I was she).[61]

To study the reception of children's writing is to discover a series of contradictions. The categories that construct readings of
children's texts seem always to be opposed, undermining each
other and threatening collapse. First and foremost, the unnatural
fact of a child having written a text that speaks to adults generates
an uneasy sense that this child writer is not a real child at all. To
create too sophisticated a text suggests precocity rather than the
"spirit of childhood" that readers seek; it may even point to an
adult writer posing as a child. The child's text must amuse, but
the child herself must not consciously attempt humor. The child's
text must educate, but the child herself must appear innocent.
Readers fetishize the figure of the child-author, but often ignore
what she actually says. They valorize those words that confirm
their perceptions of childhood, while they denounce as unnatural
those that challenge them. The child writer offers a private experience—she appears to speak just to you—but she must also
speak to everyone. Last, and most impossibly, the child writer
must appear strikingly rare and yet reassuringly representative.
She is at once perfectly ordinary and utterly extraordinary.

Reading *The Story of Opal*

Due to the very success of her text, Whiteley was unable to maintain this precarious balance for long. Her fame prompted investigations into her past that revealed the tenuousness of her royal
orphan claim and cast doubts on the text's child authorship.
Whiteley's belief that she was a D'Orléans was almost certainly a
delusion, prefiguring the mental illness for which she was institutionalized the last forty-four years of her life.[62] Friends and family testified that she was born into the Whiteley family; "before"
and "after" pictures show the same child; she bore a strong re-
semblance to Edward Whiteley, "the papa," and an even stronger
one to her younger sister Pearl. Certainly authentic, however, was
Whiteley's sense of estrangement from her family and her desire
for compensation. This alienation and craving lie at the heart of
The Story of Opal.

In her text, Whiteley constructs alternative families—both animal and human—in order to reject her real blood relatives. In part,
she appears motivated by sheer personal antipathy, especially

towards her mother. But another ground for her rejection is that of class: the lumbering Whiteleys are unfit for the princess she conceives herself to be. In contrast to the learned "Angel Mother" and "Angel Father," the Whiteley family does not read; nor does it "appreciate" nature, much less the prodigy it shelters.

In *The Story of Opal*, Whiteley never refers to members of the Whiteley family by name, nor does she use "my." Instead, without exception she names them as "the mamma," "the papa," "the baby," "the grandpa," "the grandma," "the aunt"; her home is "the house that we live in." She calls her sister merely "the little girl"—as in "she told me to get the mush for the little girl's breakfast" (218). She distances herself even from the family cats by referring to them as "that gray cat" and "that big black cat." In marked and startling contrast, Whiteley names just about everything else she sees, whether plant, animal, or human. Her dog is "Brave Horatius"; a horse, "William Shakespeare"; a mouse, "Felix Mendelssohn"; a cow, "Elizabeth Barrett Browning"; and Browning's calf carries the name "Mathilde Platagenet." She designates favorite pine trees "Michael Raphael," "Charlemagne," and "Byron." She renames an entire flock of sheep along with their shepherd. In plotting her surroundings, she borrows from sites in France the names of woods, streams, and gardens.[63] Whiteley evinces a virtual obsession with names, and the glossary at the beginning of *The Story of Opal* lists over ninety of them.

Whiteley declares of her animal companions, "I did feel a big amount of satisfaction that I have such a nice family" (257); "I am getting quite a big family, now" (225). Her interactions with this family all revolve around some kind of language activity; Whiteley's communion with nature is not a silent one. She recites poetry to her animals, sings to them, says prayers over them, and lectures them on geology. She marks, in their company, the deaths of historical figures with hymns; she writes messages to deceased pets; she conducts lengthy "conversations." Hardly a paragraph in the text lacks a reference to language or the voices she hears:

> My work was to pick up the potatoes they got out of the ground.
> I picked them up, and piled them in piles. Some of them were
> very plump. Some of them were not big. All of them wore brown
> dresses. When they were in piles, I did stop to take looks at them.

> I walked up close; I looked them all over. I walked off and took a
> long look at them. Potatoes are very interesting folks. . . . And
> all the times I was picking up potatoes, I did have conversations
> with them. . . . I have thinks these potatoes growing here did have
> knowings of star-songs. I have kept watch in the field at night, and
> I have seen the stars look kindness down upon them. And I have
> walked between the rows of potatoes, and I have watched the
> star-gleams on their leaves. And I have heard the wind ask of
> them the star-songs the star-gleams did tell in shadow on their
> leaves. And as the wind did go walking in the field talking to the
> earth-voices there, I did follow her down the rows. (120–21)

As we see here, Whiteley anthropomorphizes not just large animals and large trees, but everything she comes into contact with.
A litter of caterpillars needs the christening robes she provides
for it; bushes dance and pussy willows speak; a road longs to go
over a river. Whiteley animates everything so consistently that
her world view begins to persuade the reader: it seems plausible
that her dog feels lonesome for the company of the pig and that
"William Shakespeare has likes for poems" (164). After reading
The Story of Opal, one may perceive not Whiteley, but rather the
skeptics like her grandmother as deluded: "She used to tell awful
lies when she was little about what the toads and birds and snakes
said to her, just as if toads and bugs could talk."[64]

With such a vast circle of intimates, Whiteley is continually
under the sway of emotion: compulsion to name and to mother,
joy in the company of her "family," sorrow at its members' deaths.
It is sorrow that dominates *The Story of Opal.* Whiteley suffers
repeated losses, which come at closer intervals as the text progresses. She has so much empathy that she lives her life at a
painful pitch, herself "feeling dead" when her horse dies or when
her favorite tree is felled. Her companions' emotions become her
own, or rather, she attributes her own emotions to them and then
presents their feelings as stimulating her to a similar response.
Her discussion of the "cheese longings" of "Felix Mendelssohn"
shows how much of the misery that she accords the mouse comes
from out of her own store of loneliness and desire: "It was then he
did give his squeaks. He began, and went on, and did continue so.
I just couldn't keep from crying. His cheese longings are like my
longings for Angel Mother and Angel Father" (128).

Whiteley's record of the death of "Peter Paul Rubens" is at once wrenching and comic:

> We had not gone far, when we heard an awful squeal—so differ-
> ent from the way pigs squeal when they want their supper. I felt
> cold all over. Then I did have knowings why the mamma had let
> me start away to the woods without scolding. And I ran a quick
> run to save my dear Peter Paul Rubens—but already he was dy-
> ing. And he died with his head in my lap. I sat there feeling dead,
> too, until my knees were all wet with the blood from the throat of
> my dear Peter Paul Rubens. After I changed my clothes and put
> the bloody ones in the rain-barrel, I did go to the woods to look for
> the soul of Peter Paul Rubens. I didn't find it. . . . When I was come
> back from the woods, they made me grind sausage. And every
> time I did turn the handle, I could hear that little pain squeal Pe-
> ter Paul Rubens always gave when he did want me to come where
> he was at once. (156)

One might concur with a contemporary reviewer, who remarks "I couldn't help recalling Oscar Wilde's comment on the death of Little Nell—that one would have to have a heart of stone to read it without laughing."[65] In its day as well, *The Story of Opal* evoked complaints of sentimentality, especially from British reviewers.[66] The sentimentality, the seeming excess of the emotions that Whiteley describes, however, serves a function in her text, mak-ing it a protest against a relentless economy in which horses are worked to death, trees are dismembered for firewood, and a crow is "nothing but a crow" (295). Whiteley perceives the adults around her as in fundamental opposition to the natural world they inhabit. She does not mourn natural deaths such as that of her friend Lola. Instead, it is always some form of what she sees as murder that her violent grief protests.[67]

Whiteley can be quite playful in her resistance to the adults who rule her world, making for the text's sly humor. On being asked to stack firewood, for example, she recalls "I did wonder how I would feel, if I was a very little piece of wood that got chopped out of a very big tree. . . . I felt of the feelings of the wood. . . . Just when I was getting that topmost stick a bit wet with sympathy tears, then the mamma did come up behind me with a switch." In response to her mother's command to "Stop your meditations!" Whiteley explains "I did hum a little song—it was a good-bye song to the sticks in the wood-box" (142). Her protest usually takes place on this domestic level as she revamps common practice to accord with her own beliefs—dipping chickens in a vat of dye to experience the ornamentation of bluing, uprooting a tomato plant so that it can enjoy "dabbling its toes in the brook" (244, 282). Underneath the text's depiction of a comic, almost slapstick, struggle between mother and daughter, however, lies a representation of the family as literally deadly, hostile to everything Whiteley cares about.

The era's published children's texts usually reflect child- and book-centered families; "especially favored and often described by editors were isolated and mildly eccentric middle-class households, where the romance of bourgeois individualism was played out and highly intelligent children might 'dodge the governess and let the rest of the world go hang.'"[68] Descriptions of child authors paint warm family scenes that spotlight the writing child and, often, her mother: Ashford composing at the kitchen table and occasionally asking for a word; Conkling's mother covertly writing down the poetry that her daughter recites before her; Fleming's cousin, her "little mother," making spelling corrections in the diary even as Fleming fondly quotes her in it. As Lowell describes the Conkling's New England household,

> On rainy days, there are books and Mrs. Conkling's piano, which is not just a piano, for Mrs. Conkling is a musician, and we may imagine that the children hear a special music as they certainly read a special literature. . . . just that sort of reading that a person who passionately loves books would most want to introduce her children to. And here I think we have the answer to the why of Hilda. She and her sister have been their mother's close companions ever since they were born.[69]

In contrast, Whiteley's family, due both to its remoteness from urban centers and its working-class status, little lends itself to such scenes. Whiteley asserts that unlike her lost family, her foster family has no pretensions to book culture: "There are no rows and rows and rows of books in this house, like Angel Mother and Angel Father had. There is only three books here. One is a cookbook, and one is a doctor-book, and one is a almanac. They all are on top of the cupboards, most against the top of the house. They have not interest names on their backs" (134). Whiteley represents her writing as entirely of her own agency and conducted in secret; the Whiteleys actively discouraged their prodigy's efforts, to the extent, she later claimed, of destroying her manuscripts.[70] *The Story of Opal*, then, sprang from the family bosom just as surely as did any Conkling verse: as an act of resistance against and aggression towards it.

The diary portrays "the mamma" as Opal's most dangerous enemy,[71] unloving and violent, blind to her intentions and indifferent to her needs; this portrayal, along with Whiteley's claim to the French aristocracy, caused a permanent rift between Whiteley and her family.[72] She depicts her mother, whom she later praised as "a very clean housekeeper — often the most neat one in all the camp,"[73] as assigning her endless domestic work. According to one typical passage, "After that, all day the mamma did have more works for me to do. There was more wood to bring in. There was steps to scrub. There was cream to be shaked into butter. There was raking to do in the yard. There was carpet-strings to sew together. Inbetween times, there was the baby to tend. And all the time, all day long, I did have longings to go on exploration trips" (219). Many chores may be common for rural children, but Whiteley claims she also endured frequent beatings at her mother's hand, of which the diary describes over twenty: "The mamma reached over for me. She jerked me. She spanked me with her hand, and the hair-brush, and the pancake-turner. Then she shoved me out the door. She said for me to get out, and stay out of her way" (219).[74] In *The Story of Opal*, the home is the site of danger; the outdoors, nurture. Not surprisingly, in all the variations of her outdoor play, Whiteley never once plays "house." Instead, in the reverse move, when forced to stay in the house she literally tries to recreate the outside indoors: "I had longs to go to the forêt de Chantilly, and adown by Nonette. I did have thinks more about it. I took some of the wood out of the wood-box. I stood it up for trees. I called them all forêt de Chantilly. We went a walk between them, Lucian Horace Ovid Virgil and I did. Then I took the dipper full of water, and I let it pour in little pours a riviere on the kitchen floor. That was for Nonette. Then all of us went a walk by Nonette. We went in little steps to make the time go longer" (136).[75]

An American Adam?

Mrs. Whiteley, like Mrs. MacLane, served as the model against which her daughter rebelled. The narrators of their daughters' texts long for the love of mothers who regard them as untenably odd while at the same time seeing in their way of life that which they need to escape. As MacLane wrote, "This house is comfortably furnished. My mother spends her life in the adornment of it."[76] The mothers she and Whitely describe are consumed with domestic concerns and turn their backs on the world beyond the house, coming into bitter conflict with the daughters who refuse their example.[77]

Such texts hinging on mother-daughter conflict belie expectations of the western text as plotting the progress of the orphaned male in the West. It is perhaps Whiteley's claim of literal orphanhood, however, that led Blake Allmendinger to read *The Story of Opal* as "one of the most oddly typical stories in western American literature."[78] In his "Anastasia of Oregon" (1995), Allmendinger contends that Whiteley, typical of immigrants to the West, works to recreate in the wilderness the civilized spaces she has left behind, in her case the "domestic realm." She inhabits a world "unconflicted, timeless, and tame," according to Allmendinger, in which she "creat[es] an alter ego who, by virtue of her youth and unknown origins, exists outside time and history."[79] Yet this reading is most persuasive when turned around 180 degrees. Whiteley's text demonstrates that she inhabits a deeply violent world: the hungry axes that Allmendinger claims leave her equilibrium if not the trees intact are in actuality represented as a source of anguish, leading Whiteley to attempt reformation as much as recreation. In doing so, she thickly invests her surroundings with history, turning to the Old World. For Allmendinger, Whiteley's status as both child and westerner overshadows her identity as female. Placing her in a genre defined by the presence of the questing male, he compares Whiteley to Natty Bumppo to claim her as one of R. W. B. Lewis's "new American Adams."[80] This conflation of Whiteley with Adam accords with Kolodny's argument about the difficulties nineteenth-century women writers faced in laying their claims to the West:

> The image that has taken hold as the figure whom most Americans associated with the frontiers, was "the solitary, Indian-like hunter

of the deep woods.". . . . The problem facing the domestic fictionists when they took up their western relocation stories, therefore, was that the terrain into which they wanted to insert a domesticating Eve was the same terrain already imaginatively appropriated by the "most significant, most emotionally compelling myth-hero" of American culture, the isolate American Adam.[81]

The Story of Opal may at first appear as support for Kolodny's own argument, that western women settlers imagined their homes as gardens. Consider, for example, Whiteley's description of her "Jardin des Tuileries":

> I did go ways to look for Jardin des Tuileries. I found it not. Sadie McKibben did say there is none such here. Then, being needs for it, and it being not, I did have it so. And in it I have put statues of hiver and all the others, and here I do plant plants and little trees. And every little tree that I did plant, it was for someone that was. And on their borning days, I do hold services by the trees I have so planted for them. (126)

However, Whiteley differs from Kolodny's nineteenth-century writers, in that she has no desire to extend the domain of private domesticity. As with all of the other spaces she designs, including a cathedral, nursery, hospital, abbey, and an entire "ville," the "Jardin des Tuileries" is of the public, not private, sphere. Whiteley explicitly contrasts her desire for this public French space of her own creation with her mere forbearance of her household's garden: "Then the mamma did have me to weed onions. There were an awful lot of weeds trying to grow up around those onions. It took a long time to pull all the weeds, and my back did get some tired feels; but I did get those weeds pulled out. . . . From the onion garden, I did go to the Jardin des Tuileries. I so did go to have a little service there, for this is the borning day of Charles de Valois in 1270, and the going-away day of Saint Gregoire I, in 604" (213–14).

We usually associate a penchant for the outdoors with a regional "sense of place."[82] Yet for Whiteley, the outdoors is an arena where she recreates distant sites, imaginatively locating herself far elsewhere. Each one of her namings and rituals takes place out of doors, and each, Whiteley claimed, was taken from the two "angel books" that her French parents had left her. With her games, Whiteley tries to recreate the world in the image of her books, a world saturated with history, literature, and religion. Giving Oregon's birds, beasts, and places names from classical and European history, Whiteley renders her new world as old as possible. Indigenous Oregon culture, either native or folk, has no place in this attempt. Instead, the culture that Whiteley chooses to replicate consistently appears far-flung, incongruous to the place. Although she records the songs she hears her neighbors singing—"Rock-a-by baby" (214), "Gallop-a-trot, Gallop-a-trot, This is the way the gentlemen ride" (140), and "There little girl, don't cry—I'll come back and marry you, by-and-by" (105)—she herself chants Latin hymns, recites verses from the King James Bible, and quotes English poetry. The names she gives her pets are not in use in her community, with the exception of that of a single piglet, Solomon Grundy, which Whiteley borrows from the rhyme her (Oregon) grandfather sang (216). This exception points out in even greater relief Whiteley's general rejection of her cultural surroundings—except in her habit of diary writing itself, then so common among little girls. Yet this writing, too, Whiteley locates literally outside, hiding her manuscript in a log in the woods. Indeed, just as she works to make the house a forest, she works to make the forest a book: "This day—it was a lonely day. I did have longings all its hours, for Angel Mother and Angel Father. In-between times all day at school, I did print messages for them on gray leaves I did gather on the way to school. I did tell on the leaves the longings I was having" (191). She then ties the leaf messages back on to the trees.

Whiteley takes all of the familiar motifs and themes that we have come to think of as western, civilization versus wilderness, new versus old, individual versus society, Adam versus Eve, and turns them on their heads. In doing so, she illustrates both the pervasiveness of these motifs and the flexibility of the ways in which they can be employed, often contrary to our expectations. Whiteley, along with many of her female contemporaries, will not turn the pages of the western book that we all know so well.

4

The Disappearing Region

The previous chapters investigate the sources of the avid reception of Whiteley's book. The beginning of the twentieth century is notable for a surge of American interest in the publication, reading, and public discussion of women's autobiography, particularly autobiographies written in diary form. This interest produced a cluster of related literary vogues: young women describing their inmost desires, little girls recording their innocent impressions, eccentric women describing remote regions and distant philosophies. Writers like Bashkirtseff, MacLane, and Whiteley both tapped into this interest and fostered a readership for the lives of unusual women, and thus, for texts that ranged far from traditional autobiography: the birth-to-death chronicle of the life of an eminent figure, usually male. *The Story of Opal* at once profited from interest in young women's diaries, little girls' diaries, and the diaries of so-called faraway women.

This development in literary history, then, helps us account for Whiteley's fame. More difficult to explain, however, are the contradictions in the role that region played in her book's success. Considering how essential Whiteley's regional image and subject matter were to her book's publication and impressive sales, and considering our prevalent understanding of what early-twentieth-century readers wanted from regional literature, it is startling that writer, editor, and readers all work to "edit" details of place out of Whiteley, to minimize the role of her childhood home in her life, character formation, and memoir. An investigation into the production and reception of Whiteley's text sheds light on how region — the West, the Pacific Northwest, Oregon —

existed in the imagination of 1920s' Americans, and reveals how often regional identity is erased. Whiteley was dubbed "Oregon's wild rambler rose."[1] Yet while central to her allure, readers nevertheless seem to will her home away from Whiteley's text and life, substituting instead a generic pastoral realm specific only to the realm of childhood.

In the readings that follow, I consider how the phenomenon of *The Story of Opal* challenges some common beliefs regarding how region worked in early-twentieth-century literary markets. At the same time, I examine the role that region played or did not play in one woman's "fiction of selfhood." The American West figured prominently in Whiteley's larger-than-life persona. Even while inventing for herself other families and homes located elsewhere, Whiteley used the West as a point of departure. This chapter devoted to Whiteley and her reception begins by suggesting some foundation for her seemingly sudden emergence as an author of national repute: Whiteley's youthful history of fashioning for herself an array of different identities, often in quite literal ways, through costumes and photography. Whiteley took on conventional female roles in order to act in a decidedly unconventional manner. Following this "pre-context" for the text, I turn to "post-context": a discussion of the reception of *The Story of Opal* and the insights it offers into how region may have been conceived by Whiteley's contemporaries. The chapter concludes by outlining Whiteley's life after publication and the ways in which her later years correspond with her youthful diary. As with other mavericks, the study of this writer's life enhances the study of her text.

The Little Housemaid

Although the diary gained Whiteley national and international attention, her fame was new only in degree, not kind. From early childhood she had been in the public eye. Whiteley was renowned locally for having begun to write at the age of three and for talking as an adult at six, as well as for her ability to recite from the Bible.[2] At the age of thirteen, she began lecturing for Junior Christian Endeavour, a Christian youth group, and through it holding outdoor religious services and nature classes for groups of rapt children. Of her speech four years later at the Christian

Endeavour's state convention, its president declared, "She was a knockout. She captured the convention. Every delegate and every one in Eugene sat up and took notice of this little mountain girl who had such perfect self possession."[3] As a former acquaintance told Sedgwick, "It would be hard for me to tell you the effect the child had upon me at that time. . . . the sense of her unusualness haunted one so that I tried in vain to explain it to my self."[4]

Arguably, Whiteley's youthful success as a Christian crusader is even more remarkable than her success as a best-selling writer. Once elected at seventeen as the Junior Christian Endeavour's state superintendent, Whiteley caused the organization's growth to explode: the number of its branches in Oregon increased from fifteen to one hundred during the course of her two-year administration, with a gain of over three thousand members.[5] The Senior Christians even began to worry that the junior ones were becoming too prominent. During 1916–17, as superintendent Whiteley traveled 2,000 miles and sent out 1,600 letters.[6] As if modeling westering conquest, she took on one small Oregon town after another, lecturing and recruiting in Springfield, Hillsboro, Brownsville, Salem, Albany, Dorena, Roseburg, and others. In her Manifest Christian endeavor, Whiteley seemed bent on making the entire state her own. After her mother's death, however, she slipped off this evangelical costume as quickly as she had donned it, devoting herself instead to nature study and her attempts to establish an acting and writing career.

As a student at the University of Oregon, Whiteley continued to attract attention. Her charismatic brilliance and forest origins—which seemed exotic even in a city less than twenty-five miles from her home—were as enthralling as they were later to be on the publication of *The Story of Opal*. Describing her first visit to the university, the Eugene *Daily Guard* reported,

> Tutored by nature, a tiny seventeen-year-old mountain girl, her hair down her back, has opened the eyes of the Eugene teaching profession and left it gasping for breath. Educated by herself in the forests of the Cascade Mountains, she has made a college education appear artificial and insignificant, university officials admit. In three days, she became the talk of the faculty of three educational institutions. Entrance rules have been cast aside; scholarships are proposed; a home was found for her in Eugene— everything has been done to keep her here.[7]

Whiteley actively promoted her conspicuousness. During her one and a half years' Eugene residence, she achieved renown for "almost finish[ing] the library,"[8] falling out of a tree in a trance, singing to earthworms, amassing a massive nature collection, and planning a children's nature museum.[9] She also accumulated enough incompletes to lose her scholarship. To earn tuition money she conducted a series of nature lectures around the state ("In the Woods," "Nearer to the Heart of Nature"), one of which had an audience of over three thousand.[10] Her hobbies at the time included the study of eugenics and genealogy—and self-portraiture.

After the publication of her book, widely circulated publicity photos included one of Whiteley dressed in a buckskin costume holding a string of fish at Crater Lake and another of her in a white dress, hair tumbling down her back, gazing raptly at butterflies perched on her hands. Yet these posed portraits preceded her fame: while still a university student, Whiteley had had both friends and professionals take countless pictures of her. One of her professors recalled her "walking along the halls like a princess with a group of photographers walking about snapping pictures of her."[11] Her school notes include a list of planned shots:

 on bed with pillow
 sobbing
 curls kept back with comb
 arms full of flowers
 hand at side of face
 thoughtful look
 in rocking chair, pouring tea
 in cap and boudoir robe, in big armchair with books and holding
  curls at throat
 Evangeline
 Greek Costume, Greek tunic
 Peasant girl[12]

Ostensibly, Whiteley had herself photographed in order to assemble the portfolio needed for an upcoming Hollywood attempt. The extent of her interest, though, suggests commitment running at a much deeper level than that of utility. The portraits both planned and executed are remarkable for their stylized poses of femininity, insisting on their subject's sweet girlishness (and in everyday life, too, Whiteley had a penchant for ruffles). There are no portraits of Whiteley dressed as other less cloying types—as adventurer or seductress, for example—and certainly none of her in masculine guise. Yet the self-assertion inherent in having herself so frequently photographed works against the costumes' bid for demureness. So too does Whiteley's fierce ambition. Whiteley perceived herself as a model of conservatism, remarking in her teen-aged "Recollections of Childhood" that "Papa really don't mind my being old fashioned."[13] Throughout her public career, she was to maintain a deft balance between old-fashioned guises and modern triumphs. As with her costumes and their literal poses of femininity, she sought to try on a variety of public female roles, including those of temperance advocate, missionary, teacher, lecturer, movie star, and author.

The slippage between Opal Whiteley, paragon of feminine virtue, and Opal Whiteley, eccentric with a raging will to power, takes place at the site of the house, that testing arena of female worth. A central tension in her text, as discussed, is that between her resistance to housekeeping and her explicit endorsement of it. And, just as in the diary, so in life Whiteley appeared to bungle household chores despite unwavering self-confidence. In a burbling letter to her Christian Endeavour mentor, she reported, "I am going to keep house while going to school. I have four rooms here. . . . I've earned my little housekeeping outfit with my nature work. I am fixing the rooms so that they will be homelike."[14] However, after Whiteley's publishing success several Eugene women somewhat maliciously recalled her ineptness: "Incidentally, for one who has been doing the family washing and housework since the early age of six years, Opal is jolly awkward. After two or three days, I remember, we firmly refused any help from her in our household duties."[15] Another described the mad tea parties Whiteley hosted in her small house, her guests local notables: "The menage was the scene of a series of open-houses and tea-less teas. . . . [Guests] were expected to mill about, examining the natural history specimens while the hostess darted about, talking constantly in a high voice. . . . [T]he house . . . [was like] a child's play house, with Opal showing off her toys."[16]

Just as Whiteley's notion of proper housekeeping differed from that of these matrons, so too did it differ from the earnest endeavor modeled for her in her early childhood reading. The same archive that houses records of Whiteley's housekeeping attempts and failures includes a small collection of her childhood books: fiction, textbooks, and how-to books on publishing. By far the oldest among them is an oversized picture-book, *The Little House-maid and Other Stories*, presented to Whiteley in 1903 as a gift from her aunt. At the time Whiteley would have been five, just short of when she claimed to have begun her diary. In *The Little Housemaid*, an adult greets two little girls:

> What have you been doing all day, Lizzie?—I have been playing.
> And what have you been doing, Agnes?—I have been helping mother.
> Helping mother! That is right; but can a little girl like you be of any use?
> Oh yes. I can take care of baby while mother is at work. I can bring water from the well. I can hang out the clothes to dry. And I can dust the room.
> Mother says I must learn to do all the things that she does.
> Your mother is right; that is the best way of helping her.
> When your mother sweeps the room, you must learn to sweep the room as she does. . . . When your mother washes your clothes, you must learn to wash too; when she starches the clothes, you must learn to starch them; when she irons them, you must learn to iron; and so be able to help mother. When your mother mends your clothes, or darns your stockings, you must learn to mend clothes and to darn stockings. You will soon be able to mend your own clothes and those of your little brothers and sisters; and that will be a great help to mother. You must learn to knit; and by-and-by you will be able to take some of that work off mother's hands; and that will really be helping mother.[17]

Even from the perspective of an adult, the tone of this passage is oppressive. The array of tasks the girl is expected to master multiplies into her future, until presumably she becomes a mother herself. With its emphasis on marital titles, the book's inscription of "To Miss Opal Whiteley From your Auntie Mrs. Anna Rearsen" seems to reinforce the message of proper female behavior. Yet the book's ideology is challenged by what is literally tucked inside it: a tail that at first appears to be that of a squirrel. Closer examination reveals its feathers: an untidy, somewhat grotesque trophy of the outdoors that has been wedged inside *The Little House-maid* for almost all of the twentieth century. The tail, aggressively

signaling outdoor play and plunder, counters the text's endorsement of hard-working, dutiful housebound girlhood. So, too, do
some moments in the text itself: during hay season the girl pro-
tagonist is allowed to engage in outdoor work that, in contrast
to the sheer duty of her inside work, incorporates play and sensual pleasure. This outdoor work/play includes racial mutabil-
ity as the "little haymaker" exclaims, "How brown [the sun] will
make my face! I shall soon look like a little gypsy!" The gypsy
haymaker, evoking India and Europe, reminds us of the domains
Whiteley staked claims to as an adult.

The resistance she displayed as a child by inserting the feathered tail in *The Little Housemaid* prefigures the ways in which
Whiteley negotiated her way through girls' texts as an adolescent
and young adult. Whiteley reveled in Christian novels and traditional girls' fare. Sounding much like *The Little Housemaid*'s heroine, she wrote in a letter to a younger friend:

> Have you read "The Shepherd of the Hills" and "Their Yesterdays"
> by Harold Bell Wright? Also "Freckles" by Jean Stratton Porter
> [*sic*], "Stepping Heavenward," "The Christian Secret of a Happy
> Life," "Black Rock," and "The Sky Pilot" by Ralph Connon? These
> are among my favorite books and I have gained much from these.
> What are your favorite books?
>
> I am busy helping mother keep house and take care of the chil-
> dren. I have three younger sisters and a dear little baby brother
> eight weeks old. I am sixteen years old and have dark hair and
> dark brown eyes. I wear my hair in two braids down my back.
>
> Let us always close our letters with a Bible verse. I believe we
> will both enjoy this.
> Your loving Sister in Christ,
> Opal I. Whiteley
> "A Friend Loveth at all Times." Proverbs 17:17[18]

Whiteley's pleasure in girls' novels might be contrasted to
MacLane's resentment of them: "I am not that quaint conceit, a
girl: the sort of person that Laura E. Richards writes about, and
Nora Perry, and Louisa M. Alcott. . . . [or] a heroine — of the kind
you read about." Whiteley's letter suggests that she endorsed the
"quaint conceit[s]" of girl and heroine, and demonstrates the
seamless connections she made between her identity as reader,
her identity as mother's helper, and her identity as an exhorter of

Christian values. After she entered the University of Oregon, she continued to supplement her wide-ranging study of geology, botany, and biology with an avid consumption of girls' books, and was said to have gone through 10,582 pages of library books in only four months. In the University of Oregon's library newsletter, Inez Fortt later argued that "the total impact [of Whiteley's reading] on any young girl blessed with a lively imagination must have been numbing. Evidently in order, she read: Rebecca of Sunnybrook Farm, The Rosary, Girl of the Limberlost, Knight of the Cumberland, Old Rose and Silver, That Printer of Udill's, Patty at the Circus, My Lady of the South, Corporal Cameron, Anne of Green Gables, Red Pepper Burns, Just Patty, Daddy Long Legs, The Garden of Allah, The Awakening of Helen Ritchie, and the Iron Woman. This steady diet of sugar and corn must have contributed to her later excursions into never-never land."[19]

Fortt is surely right in perceiving the powerful influence of these books on Whiteley, but perhaps not in her judgment of their perniciousness. The conflict in girls' texts, with their bids for freedom set in opposition to models of obedience and passivity, is mirrored by the conflict in Whiteley's text, which portrays a child's furious discomfort in her would-be allegiance to traditional female culture.[20] With their valorization of conventional femininity embedded in the standard plot of girls' novels — "the story of a young girl who is deprived of the supports she had rightly or wrongly depended on to sustain her throughout life"[21] — these books might have offered Whiteley models for acting out her powerful egotism and ambition in ways acceptable to her "old fashioned" nature. Whiteley's reading activities support Barbara Sicherman's contention that rather than affording mere escapist entertainment, the culture of girls' and women's reading, so prominent in the 1880s and 1890s, encouraged "dreams of female heroism."[22]

More directly, Whiteley's girlhood reading may also have provided her with models for her own work. Tellingly, she persuaded several girls' novelists, including Mary Roberts Rhinehart and Eleanor Porter, to write endorsements for *The Fairyland Around Us*. A British reviewer suggested that Whiteley's market success was due to her reworking of themes ubiquitous in popular girls' novels: "There is everything in it that is in an American best-seller. It is the least common denominator of 'Daddy Long Legs,' 'A Girl of the Limberlost,' and 'The Rosary.'[23] Whiteley uncannily resembles the heroine of *A Girl of the Limberlost:* Eleanora, an impoverished nature lover foiled by her hostile, ignorant mother, who raises money for school by harvesting swamp specimens moths and arrowheads alike—to sell all over the world. Whiteley also resembles the author of *Limberlost*—Gene Stratton-Porter, a prolific writer who was tremendously successful in the marketplace. Through the character of the woman who links suppliers and buyers of swamp goods, Stratton-Porter dramatizes her own use of the Indiana swamp in specifying its potential for both literary and literal harvest: "We Limberlost people must not be selfish with the wonders God has given to us. We must share with those poor cooped-up city people the best we can. To send them a beautiful book, that is the way, is it not?"[24] "This way" is that of both sharing a place and escaping it.

In February of 1918, Whiteley left the University of Oregon for southern California, where she continued lecturing and teaching. Her motive for the move, which she made the month after the national release of MacLane's "Men Who Have Made Love to Me," was to break into the movies, ostensibly in order to raise funds for publishing the series of nature books she had planned. In Hollywood, she visited agencies and studios with her portfolio of herself in the various costumed poses. As an actress, Whiteley wanted, essentially, to play the role of her own self, that of the "misunderstood waif" who talked to animals.[25] At the same time, she was able to perceive this identity as something that could be sold.

While in Pasadena, Whiteley stayed for a time with Charles Fletcher Lummis of Arroyo culture fame; the two ended on bad terms.[26] She also was taken in by a theosophy group, purportedly at the point of emaciation.[27] By 1898, Pasadena had already been dubbed home to "more sanctified cranks to the acre than in any other town in America,"[28] and Whiteley's experience there reads like a parody of southern California New Thought culture: "Mrs. McMillan says that . . . it was a very beautiful and inspiring experience to see Opal and Dr. Turnbull together in the parks; that they both saw fairies and wood-nymphs and talked freely to each other about them. . . . proof positive . . . that Opal has the marvelous clairvoyant power."[29] In April 1919, the group made arrangements for Whiteley to travel to Boston, there to solicit the

Atlantic with *The Fairyland*. It was as a result of this attempt that the diary came to light.

Figs from Thistles and Grapes from Thorns

Selections from *The Story of Opal* were first published serially in the *Atlantic Monthly* in the spring of 1920. They caused a dramatic increase in subscriptions, particularly in the Northwest:[30] with each "successive installment ... interest rose to a high pitch.'"[31] After the sixth excerpt had appeared, the recently established Atlantic Monthly Press released *The Story of Opal* in a standard two-dollar edition along with a deluxe $6.50 one.[32] The diary, extolled by one reader as "the revelation of the imaginal life of a feminine Peter Pan of the Oregon wilderness—so innocent, so intimate, so haunting that I should not know where in all literature to look for a counterpart,"[33] went through three American editions and fifteen thousand copies in less than a year, earning Whiteley between five and eight thousand dollars.[34] There were also two brisk-selling British editions of 5,000 copies each.[35] The book spent two weeks on Boston's best-seller list for nonfiction and generated avid interest among the general reading public as well as professionals of all kinds: "scientists, editors, ministers, psychologists, psychics, men of letters, nature lovers and literary critics of every magazine of consequence in America and England."[36]

The diarist's disclosure of her private self, as in the case of Bashkirtseff and MacLane, became a matter for enthusiastic public discussion via the dialogue and debate both in national newspapers and literary magazines and in more local forums including schools, reading societies, women's clubs, antiquarian societies, and even businesses. *The Story of Opal* received its most frequent hearing, though, within the family circle. Whiteley's status as a child writer made readers perceive her as endorsing the family, despite the fact that she actually portrays it as a claustrophobic, violent site. Letters to Sedgwick describe the pleasure parents found in reading the book aloud to their captivated children, and their desire to pass it along to friends. Readers imagined Whiteley as part of their own family: "We cannot let this child, Opal, go at seven years, without knowing more about her.

To know no more of what befalls her, will make the many of us who love her, feel almost as if there had been deaths in our families. . . . I have simply *devoured* her words."[37]

Given such appetite for more access to Whiteley, together with Whiteley's previous efforts in Hollywood, it might be expected that after *The Story of Opal* she would have followed a public career similar to MacLane's, promoting products, writing for newspapers, and perhaps even realizing her ambition to make movies. Indeed, unlike MacLane, Whiteley had already begun a highly visible lecturing and teaching career long before she published her book. The doubt cast on her claim to child authorship, however, closed this route. Such doubt first arose when her claim to the French aristocracy was investigated and debated among Oregon newspapers; the issue was quickly taken up nationwide. As it became increasingly clear that Opal was a Whiteley by blood, her claim to have written the diary as a child was also challenged. Whiteley was not only a liar, it appeared; she was also just an ordinary American girl. That Whiteley wrote the diary in such seemingly remote, unknowable parts contributed to undermining her credibility. Bede recalled, "Could a girl reared in such an environment have developed the mental gifts necessary for the evolvement of something of such beauty . . . ? That question was asked a thousand times."[38] Readers debated both what it was possible for a child and what it was possible for a rural Oregonian to know.

The controversy was so intense that to escape the press Whiteley family members changed their names and moved.[39] Yet as much as the debate gripped the public, it killed interest in the text itself; after ten months of brisk trade, sales of *The Story* abruptly ceased.[40] This child's text only had value so long as it appeared authentic.

A later anthologizer well captures the typical reaction to the text: "How could it be written by a child? How could it *not* be written by a child!"[41] Certainly, even now the first question the reader is likely to put to *The Story* is whether it really was written by Whiteley as a child, and, if so, the extent to which the diary was rewritten as it underwent reconstruction. One needs a book to discuss all the evidence for and against the text's child authorship, and indeed, Bede, Bradburne, and Hoff organize their biographies around the issue. Perhaps the most persuasive argument for the diary's child authorship is simply the question of why the adult Whiteley would have gone to the trouble of writing a manuscript of a quarter-million words in multi-colored crayons on assorted scraps of paper, in handwriting that gradually evolves from childish printing into a more adult hand, ripping the scraps into tiny pieces and storing them in Los Angeles, approaching a Boston editor without the text itself and without mentioning it unprompted, and then painstakingly piecing the scraps together in an intensive labor of nine months.[42] I proceed from the assumption that the text is based on a real childhood diary and the fragments it became, but that this diary was transformed into *The Story of Opal* by two adults: Opal Whiteley as adult writer and the *Atlantic*'s Ellery Sedgwick as editor. Together, the two created a "regional" text in which "region" itself is decidedly absent.

From the onset, Sedgwick was a central player in the text's production—indeed, according to his own account, he was responsible for bringing the text to light. In response to the furor Whiteley aroused, he declared in his preface to the diary, "the authorship does not matter, nor the life from which it came. There the book is. Nothing else is like it, nor apt to be."[43] Sedgwick was not just being disingenuous: his extensive correspondence with and about Whiteley over decades demonstrates his desire that the more sensational aspects of Whiteley and her text be overlooked in favor of close attention to the text itself, and attests to his belief in the text's authenticity despite his bewilderment over much about it. Sedgwick conducted his own investigations in an attempt to plumb the mystery of *The Story of Opal*, and even readers who thought it a hoax believed in his innocence, especially since he had a reputation for gullibility.

Nevertheless, Sedgwick did admit not only to suppressing various rumors about Whiteley, but also to extensive cutting of some of the diary's less credible elements.[44] It would be an understatement to say that Sedgwick had more than the usual editorial control over the text: under his guidance it was put together literally word by word. After the fragments were reassembled, Sedgwick chose which of them to publish and decided upon their order. His choices were motivated, of course, not merely by the desire to produce a text that readers would believe, but also by the desire to produce a text that readers would buy. He finally included in the published book only about a quarter of Whiteley's childhood diary.

Sedgwick's criteria for selection are telling. Stating that "the mass of material available presents a very interesting problem of selection,"[45] he chose to solve this problem by using only those portions of the text that located Whiteley's traumatic emotional experiences in a woodland idyll largely bereft of geographic and historical specificity. A London newspaper described Whiteley's story as "one which would have formed a fit subject for the author of the 'Luck of Roaring Camp.'"[46] Oregon logging camps may vie with California gold camps for picturesque appeal. Yet Whiteley's diary is quite unlike Bret Harte's stories in that much of the potential "local color" has been not highlighted, but systematically eliminated.

A prominent argument about regionalist texts, according to Richard Brodhead, is that they perform "cultural elegy: the work of memorializing a cultural order passing from life at that moment, and of fabricating, in the literary realm, a mentally possessable version of a loved thing lost in reality."[47] The nature of Sedgwick's editorial manipulations illuminates this argument in interesting ways. Sedgwick excised from *The Story of Opal* most of those elements that would have marked its setting as local, particular to one time and one place. In working towards portraying a world far removed from urban and cultural centers—a child's domain, Sedgwick clearly emphasized the regional identity of Whiteley's home. At the same time, however, he satisfied the public's nostalgia for lost community in the broadest way possible— by stripping the area of all specificity he made it especially "possessable." His ministrations, coupled with the self-absorbed nature of Whiteley's childhood writing, served to create a text featuring a kind of generic rural community. Just as Whiteley became the embodiment of childhood, her home became the embodiment of region.

Although Whiteley kept her diary between the ages of six and twelve, Sedgwick chose for publication only material from the first two years, when Whiteley was least aware of the complexities of the community around her and most preoccupied with her imaginary life.[48] Significantly, although Sedgwick had originally planned to include in the published text photographs of a mill and "donkey engine," in the end he decided not to.[49] Whiteley and Sedgwick's correspondence cites various diary passages that are remarkable for their difference from anything found in the published text, and *The Story of Opal* hardly reflects Whiteley's reminiscences:

> School being out we carried warm dinners to the logging men in the woods and stopped to watch them bucking trees and snaking logs. Then "we went across the river on the chute when the cable was slack." We stood near the railway to watch the send-up man and the sky hooker.... Our house was very close to the mill-pond—some fifty feet from it. The chute ran through our back yard. The railroad track was fourteen feet from our front steps. To the right of our front door were two more houses exactly like ours and very near unto us. Across the track and to the left was a house like ours.[50]

This account, in contrast to the sense of rustic isolation that the published text usually conveys, shows the Whiteley family living in almost inconceivably close contact with the industrial—a proximity that the children, moreover, find attractive.

Sedgwick promoted the diary in the same way that he edited it, as reflecting an isolated, pre-modern community. Suggesting the license he may have taken, a reader remarked on "the town where Opal's parents . . . live—that 'little western lumber camp' which in reality is a sizable village on the main line of the S. P. from Portland to San Francisco." Similarly, an Oregon resident protested that an advertisement for the diary represented Whiteley's childhood camp as cruder than it actually was. [51] By her day the town of Cottage Grove—located less than three miles from her allegedly wilderness home and only twenty-two miles from the University of Oregon in Eugene—had a population of about 2,000 and was typical of many small American communities.[52]

Signs of modernity are by no means absent from the text, as in the following description of train tracks: "they stretch away and away, like a silver ribbon that came from the moon in the night" (8). The tracks, though, certainly do not appear to be a mere fourteen feet from Whiteley's front door, and the fanciful description is scant preparation for Whiteley's allusions to the brand-name products, including "Castoria," "Menthol," "Vaseline," and "Bon Ami," that the railroad brought even to communities as seemingly remote as hers. Such allusions, along with those to the "China-Mending Glue—Guaranteed to Stick" and the "blue dish that came as a premium in the box of mush" (130, 152), are jarring. Signs of Cottage Grove's participation in a nationwide economy of consumption, they rend a text that usually depicts a community represented by Whiteley's imaginative activities as "cultured" and Old World, not market-oriented and New. They are so disruptive that some readers saw them as evidence that the diary was written long after Whiteley's childhood had passed, prompting the following response to one such skeptic:

> Apparently you are suspicious of Opal Whiteley. Just as many people were of the author of "Young Visitors." Bon Ami was probably not on sale in 1895. . . . Are you not mistaken however in supposing that Opal Whiteley wrote 25 years ago? My impression is that she is . . . now 21 years old which would bring her use of Bon Ami well with the bonds of reasonable probability. Yours very truly. THE BON AMI COMPANY.[53]

As discussed, specific details of place appear to have been kept out of the text. However, the fact that Whiteley wrote as a child made her home seem all the more "regional"—not as a particularized place, but rather, as remote from the metropolitan centers where "real life" is understood to happen. Like nature, region, too, is perceived as having a special relationship to childhood.[54] Jim Wayne Miller argues that often, "Reading 'regional' fiction . . . is like going to grandmother's house, where we feel like children no matter how old we are."[55] And it is significant that in asserting the identification of region with childhood, Miller invokes grandmother's rather than grandfather's house: his metaphor reflects prevailing representations of region as the locus of not just children but of women, too. "Views of place," Doreen Massey argues, "which reverberate with nostalgia . . . , are coded female."[56] The West of action and adventure and growth, land of cowboys and Indians and the westerns that portray them, is, of course, closely associated with masculine youth ("Go West, Young Man, to grow up with the country"). Yet when such frontier associations are absent, western landscapes can revert to a condition of feminine regional identity. Her little girl status fetishized, Whiteley seemed to have overshadowed her home even as she represented it.

The early-twentieth-century Pacific Northwest was particularly susceptible to such overshadowing, due in part to the paucity of prominent Northwest writers and narratives, especially contemporary ones. Whiteley was said to have shared her status as a nationally known writer from the Northwest only with Mary Carolyn Davies.[57] (Bede claimed, "Opal has received more personal publicity . . . than all other Oregon authors combined."[58]) Moreover, because it lacked the ranching and mining associations of a Wyoming, Montana, or California, Oregon was not mythologized as the wild West. Readers' response to *The Story of Opal* reflected this relative absence of mythic resonance. Although readers would have had access to images of the Pacific Northwest as an agricultural paradise or lumber frontier, these images do not appear in their reactions to the text. Few other widely held images of Whiteley's home vie with those in *The Story of Opal:* the nature of readers' allusions to the place more or less reflected Whiteley's portrayal. In contrast to the plethora of images generated by MacLane's Butte, in readers' responses to her text, Whiteley's Oregon home, although always mentioned, was vaguely imagined. At most it was simply associated with forests and mountains.

The most salient image of Oregon territory, said to have "loomed in the national psyche as the ultimate in newness,"[59] seemed long to have been that of the childishly blank slate. This perception led Sarah Orne Jewett to dub it "unworn surroundings"[60] and Laura Ingalls Wilder to represent it as beyond the reach even of houses. In ironic contrast to Whiteley's depiction of her housebound girlhood, Wilder represents Oregon as a place where girls could escape the demands of domesticity:

> "Gosh!" Lena spoke that wicked word boldly. "I'm glad this summer's over! I hate houses." She swung the milk pail and chanted. "No more cooking, no more dishes, no more washing, no more scrubbing! Whoop-ee!" Then she said, "Well, good-by. I guess you're going to stay right here as long as you live."
>
> "I guess so," Laura said miserably. She was sure that Lena was going out West. Maybe even to Oregon. "Well, good-by."[61]

Of course the Dakotas (and California, New Mexico, Montana, all western sites) struck eastern readers as remote, but Oregon figured as especially so, perhaps due to its both western *and* far northern location.

It could have been the perception of northwestern blankness that led one critic to perceive Whiteley's text as "reproducing" the woods of colonial New England, in the nineteenth century so richly imagined:

> In the "Story of Opal" we find a more or less exact, sometimes improved upon, occasionally deformed, reproduction of a certain precocious child invented and boldly written up by Hawthorne in the "Scarlet Letter," published some 75 years ago; and the child of his brain is just about as reasonable, or unreasonable, as the story of our Opal. The latter has a sister Pearl in real life in Oregon; and in the old novel she finds a deformed pattern for herself by that name. But as that foundling was born in 1645, some 275 years ago, perhaps this Opal is a reincarnation of that selfsame spirit of the Massachusetts colony. In fact, Opal Whiteley is there right now, in the vicinity of Boston, where the original precocious Yankee child was. She seems to have just naturally drifted back to the scenes of her "first appearance in America."[62]

This conjecture about Whiteley's use of Hawthorne, picked up by the Associated Press, gained some credence, far-fetched as it may seem. Perhaps it was endorsed because it provided such a generically unclassifiable text with the familiar axes of fiction and the East, province of the "precocious" child. The easy sighting of Hawthorne's forest in Whiteley's also suggests that the almost generic pastoral aspect of *The Story of Opal* contributed to making its actual setting indistinct. Such a nature effects the partial disappearance of "Oregon," "the Pacific Northwest," and even "the West." Instead, the place appears as the locus of children and nature: outside of both region and history.

Consequently, in contrast to claims made for Cather, Austin, and MacLane, Whiteley was read as a child of nature instead of a child of her region: "She has practically grown up just like 'Topsy' of old, a child of Nature right from the beginning"; "She seemed a part of nature . . . like a human fairy"; "[*The Story of Opal*] is the revealed spirit of the true child of nature, perfectly tuned. . . . No country-loving child could imagine Opal's story being other than the spirit of childhood 'left wild' as nature itself."[63] With her Oregon woods functioning as a substitute for anyone's rural paradise, Whiteley's world appears as a mythic one: she "lived in the woods, and had such relations with the trees and the living creatures as folks in general might have had if Adam and Eve had never been evicted from Paradise. Perhaps St. Francis of Assisi attained to relations something like them."[64] Indeed, Whiteley comes not only to represent other children, but to evoke the childhood of all humanity: "[the diary] often made me think of our literature that portrays the childhood of the race, the time when animals lived in the folk tale."[65]

With its headline "Child's Story of Her Life in Lumberland,"[66] a London review alludes to the unreal, fairy-tale quality of Whiteley's book, with its enchanted forest, wicked adults, and friendly birds and beasts. Bradburne points out its class dimensions: "Here was the authentic Fairy Story: the Princess brought up by the Woodcutter."[67] In their reception of *The Story of Opal*, American and British readers closely associated class with place. Since they assumed the barbarism of the Whiteleys and all the other lumber camp residents, they accepted Whiteley's purported refinement as proof that she must be from elsewhere. At least before reports about inconsistencies in Whiteley's story became widespread, readers embraced her claims to royal ancestry, declaring *The Story* "a marvelous study in heredity as opposed to environment"[68] and "[a] powerful revelation of the apparently unknown fact these days — that a child is first of all the child of its parents."[69] One reader remarked, "Not only is it impossible to gather 'figs from thistles and grapes from thorns', but Miss Whiteley gives every evidence of having been born not only of parents of so called good birth, but of unusual culture and education."[70]

Steedman suggests that the publication of Whiteley's text during an era that emphasized heredity contributed to the initial acceptance of Whiteley's foster family story.[71] More precisely, the early enthusiastic — almost defiant — support given it reflects an assumption both of the limitations of native westerners and of the negligible impact of environment. Readers were eager to concur with Whiteley's disassociation of herself from rural America. It was not Whiteley's bucolic upbringing that was perceived as the source of her affinity with nature, but rather the aristocratic blood in her veins, blood brewed in the capitals of Europe.

Part of the public's fascination with Whiteley, as with that of MacLane, the "Butte Bashkirtseff," arose from the incongruity of a cultured, urban, aristocratic Continental sensibility appearing to infiltrate a raw, provincial, working-class American environment.

(This fascination continues into the present—Allmendinger's "Anastasia of Oregon" is remarkably akin to "Butte Bashkirt-seff.") Yet while Oregonians themselves may have perceived Whiteley as a native literary daughter—hence the local protest over her account of her origins[72] —others did not. The letters written to Sedgwick in response to *The Story of Opal* are striking for their lack of desire to claim Whiteley even as an American, much less as a westerner. On the contrary, readers expressed outrage and betrayal when Whiteley was found to be homegrown after all.

Challenging the "familiar account" of the function of regional literature, Whiteley's readers did not reveal nostalgia for Whiteley's rural childhood, but rather satisfaction that she escaped it.[73] And throughout her life, Whiteley herself evinced no nostalgia for the sites of her youth. Sedgwick dramatically structured *The Story of Opal* by opening it with her move to a new lumber camp and closing it with her move from the camp into town. Since the text portrays Whiteley's deep love for the woods, one expects that she will find the prospect of leaving devastating. She reveals, however, that she is eager to go, speculating, "Maybe in the fields over on the other side of the mill town—maybe there will be *etourneau,* and *ortolan,* and *draine,* and *durbec,* and *loriot,* and *verdier,* and *rossignol,* and *pinson,* and *pivoine.* When I am come to the mill town, I will go explores to see" (281–82).

Ironically enough, it is in revealing the ease with which she leaves the camp that Whiteley's narrative seems most in harmony with western or frontier ideas. This early painless departure and eagerness to explore new sites foreshadow her lifelong lack of attachment to place—or perhaps her superabundance of attachment, in that she makes each place she inhabits a deeply felt home. There is only one record of Whiteley espousing patriotic sentiment, her statement that, although she had once aspired to be a missionary in India, she soon realized "Our own dear homeland . . . needs and is calling for teachers and leaders."[74] Later, however, Whiteley definitively chose India over the homeland just as, despite her Indian princess costumes, she accounted for her dark complexion by claiming French and subcontinental Indian ancestry instead of "the papa's" actual French-Canadian and Native American stock.[75] Like so many western writers, Whiteley made racial claims to account for where she belonged.

Whiteley styled herself as a historian and naturalist unaffiliated with any one place. Although her Oregon upbringing enabled her immersion in empirical nature study, she perceived her residence in the lumber camps, along with the Whiteleys she held responsible for it, as having cut her off from naturalist pursuits. In a letter to a sister in which she pretended to be one of her former guardians, Whiteley declared "Of course we had always intended that she should always stay in the lumber camps but she slipped us up on that and got out and continued her studies of the out of doors. Your mother we know did her best to put a stop to her foolish nature studies but the girl is too much like that French father of hers in her desire for knowledge of the out doors."[76] Claiming that the Whiteleys found her nature study "a disgrace to the family,"[77] Whiteley, like her readers, perceived her love of nature as arising not from environment, but from blood.

Whiteley had no wish to be a "western writer." After the publication of the diary, she never again wrote about Oregon or any other western sites. While many of her literary predecessors and contemporaries argued for their right to represent the West, Whiteley, born and bred in the area she depicted, preferred to invent herself as an outsider even as she demonstrated her intimate knowledge of the birthplace she renounced. Indeed, she put herself at a double remove, claiming to be an exiled member of a royal family that was itself exiled.

Whiteley's adult wanderings led her farther and farther from her actual origins but closer to her fantasized ones, "out of a more or less commonplace environment," as one acquaintance put it, "into the far distant environment of her particular fancy."[78] After breaking with Sedgwick and the *Atlantic*,[79] Whiteley left Boston for New York City and Washington, D.C., where she was "petted and patronized" by prominent figures and independently published a book of stories and poetry.[80] In 1923 she left the United States for England under the sponsorship of Edward Grey, never to return to the United States again. Until 1935, this period included prolonged residence in London and Oxford (where she converted to Catholicism), a year in India, two years in an imperial convent in Vienna, and visits to Paris and Rome. As in the United States, the rich, powerful, and titled continued to befriend her, and she was a frequent guest at their homes, parties, and, in France, various historical and naturalist organizations.[81] At least in England, some accepted Whiteley's claim of high birth, as the following newspaper account reveals:

> A beautiful young Frenchwoman who is the most direct descendant of Louis Philippe, the Last King of France, has just arrived in London. She is the Princess of Bourbon-Orléans, the daughter of that Prince Henry of Orléans who was born at Ham, near Richmond, after his father, the Duke of Chartres, had fled over to England as a boy with King Louis Philippe. The Princess is very dark and has lovely brown eyes. She told me that the only country she has not visited recently is France, for she has been a great traveller. When I remarked on her faultless English she told me that she spoke English better than any other language.[82]

Whiteley, in all the countries in which she lived or traveled, claimed her right to the territory through family connections and early childhood associations. Home was wherever she chose to locate her family and her past. Through Henri D'Orléans, she was able to claim both France and England.[83] On occasion she referred to being born in Italy, and variously named her mother as D'Orléans's French cousin, Marie, as the archduchess of Austria, Alice of Tuscany, and as the granddaughter of the Indian maharaja of Udaipur. Whiteley also claimed to have been found as a child in a gypsy caravan,[84] and hinted at Russian connections as well.[85]

Of her imagined childhood home in Austria, she maintained, "It was such a dear old historic house . . . filled with the shadows of the past, memories of the whole Empire."[86] In the same way that as a child she invested the New World forests of Oregon with Old World culture, throughout her life Whiteley aged her own lineage, crediting herself with a host of ancient pedigrees. She also was drawn to rich historical sites, in both imagination and practice. After extensive travel in India, for example, she fixed on Udaipur for her residence, dubbed the "Indian Venice"; she lived there for ten months at the palace of the Udaipur royal family.[87] For the trip, which British newspapers announced beforehand, Whiteley received assistance from Grey and D'Orléans's mother.[88] Along with researching D'Orléans's death and her own genealogy, part of Whiteley's professed motivation for the journey was to complete D'Orléans's book about his discoveries in India, following "'in the footsteps of my father.'"[89] As with her explanation that her interest in nature was a family inheritance, Whiteley presented everything that she did—writing, exploration, sojourn, travel—as repetition of what came before her.

Just as its origin in Montana was a significant if not deciding factor in the publication of *The Story of Mary MacLane,* so too was Oregon central to the publication of *The Story of Opal.* As Sedgwick recalled, after hearing Whiteley had spent her childhood in Oregon lumber camps, "it was hard not to be interested now." In addition to her status as child prodigy, Whiteley's seemingly remote origins secured her celebrity. Yet through Whiteley American readers renounced, as it were, American regions, declaring them impossible of producing the cultured brilliance *The Story of Opal* displayed, and attributing it instead to Whiteley's French blood and inheritances.

The Story of Opal enabled Whiteley herself to relinquish region. The book stands as an elegy of Whiteley's rapport with the spaces of her childhood in that the same text that records her kinship with northwestern woods launched her permanent separation from them. In wending her way from the western to the eastern United States, to Europe, and to the oldest kingdom in India, Whiteley could be said to have pursued a "counter-pioneer" trajectory back to its ultimate Old World, eastern destination. Whiteley never returned to her western roots, either literally or in her writing. She devoted her energies to her more distant past in researching the genealogy she claimed for herself. And yet, there is less disjunction between her western childhood and her peripatetic adulthood than may first appear. As one journalist wondered, "Did other imaginings lead her to 'go on explores' back to the realm of babyhood and find a parentage of greater refinement than one in the lumber camps of Lane county?"[90] Whiteley's travels and research are a version writ large of her early forest rambles.

5

"Betwixt and Between"

Southerner, Californian, European?

A Burma Lady said to me at Darjeeling you are just betwixt and between. one minute you have a fine time with the lowest cast next minute with the highest Hindoo. one minute you wear a blue suit next minute a dress of 2 cent a yard crape then a little velvet dress with diamond ear rings how can we tell. one minute you stay in a hotel at $5.00 a day then go to a restaurant and have a 5 cent meal. youre betwixt and between.
Juanita Harrison, *My Great, Wide, Beautiful World*

MacLane and Whiteley's beginnings as writers were linked to leisurely roaming in western realms peculiarly their own. As white writers, through describing their ties to Montana and Oregon landscapes, they earned themselves western child-poet fame. They were perceived as the "Charlotte Brontë" of Montana and the "mountain maid" of Oregon, distinct from their fellow westerners through their kinship with outdoor spaces. Yet the texts declaring their affinity with the West enabled them to leave it, and their champions sent them eastward posthaste. MacLane left the West for seven years; Whiteley, forever. MacLane and Whiteley are distinguished by their utter lack of nostalgia for their western homes and childhoods. We expect veins of longing and regret from writers hailing from places seen as regional, so much so that their lack of sentimentality may disturb. MacLane and Whiteley's departures coincided with a severance of family ties that appears just as extreme; neither did they attempt to replicate the family life left behind. Their lives could be read as ending tragically, but neither woman ever doubted the necessity of her exodus.

Because MacLane and Whiteley wrote about local western experiences, they were able to travel. The reverse holds true for Juanita Harrison, who represented her travels as pressing upon her the identity of writer, and who as a result of her mobility was able to choose among a range of experiences in the West. Raised in Mississippi's South, she moved in the urban milieu of Los Angeles while working as a domestic laborer. She visited the Rocky Mountains of Colorado as a tourist and, after publishing her book, established a home in Hawaii, at once the country's most western point and a site highly resistant to being named "Western."

In the U.S. marketplace, Harrison's self-proclaimed identity as a Californian afforded her no intrigue. As a black woman, Harrison was perceived in terms of the Mississippi of her childhood upbringing rather than the California of her adult choice. The South and the West, Harrison's American reception suggests, stand as mutually exclusive categories, with the former but not the latter seen as home to black women. Yet as a world traveler, Harrison could range outside of black/white polarities. Abroad, beyond claiming Hollywood for the sophistication it suggested, she manipulated a host of racial, ethnic, and national identifications. "Betwixt and between," she appeared as not only Californian, but also as Japanese, French, Arabian, Cuban, Moorish, Indian, Jewish, Argentinean, and Greek, among others. Harrison's class status also appeared variable, and often determined how she was perceived ethnically. Thus, her travels can be read as similar to Whiteley's project: she claimed multiple homes through claiming multiple identities. In Harrison's case, though, the enterprise appeared to have been kept under control: she played the trickster but duped only others, not herself. She also took the opposite tack from Whiteley in that she negotiated not through family claims and a preoccupation with the past, but through a remarkable abandonment of both.

There has been little discussion of working-class American women's travel literature *as* travel literature. The texts that are widely known fall under the rubrics of slave narratives or captivity narratives; formal classification of women's sojourns as "travel" is reserved for upper- or middle-class white activity. In contrast to texts chronicling the wanderings of white working-class men, which are prominent in an American canon that privileges male quests, first-person texts written by working women traveling for pleasure or experience are largely invisible.[1]

Harrison's description of her very first destination challenges widely-held assumptions about the socioeconomic class of women travel writers: "The first look at London I liked it. It was a beautiful morning the maids in their neat blue dresses and white caps was cleaning the brass whiting the door steps and scrubbing the sidewalks" (4). This portrayal of servants contributing to the appealing quaintness of a foreign scene seems very familiar.[2] Yet in the next sentence, Harrison challenges the pleasure we may have found in the scene by continuing, "I promised myself when I Looked For a job not to get in a house with such work but instead a apartment." Harrison, no longer the detached observer, puts herself in the place of these women, reminding us both that their labor is not just an aesthetic matter and that the traveler is a potential laborer. Harry A. Franck avowed in his preface to *A Vagabond Journey around the World* (1910) that "a man *can* girdle the globe without money, weapons, or baggage."[3] Harrison's text demonstrates that in the 1930s a woman could, too.

Beyond the realm of class, as a travel writer Harrison also challenges readers' expectations regarding race. First and foremost, she is a black woman who travels, by her own choice and for her own pleasure. Rather than participating in black protest traditions, she joins Zora Neale Hurston and other twentieth-century writers in a lesser known African American literary tradition that Nellie Y. McKay describes as specific to black women. This tradition focuses on individual development and possibility rather than racial identity and the state of "My People, My People," to borrow an exasperated Hurston's term, thereby "free[ing] black autobiography from the ideological supremacy of race."[4] Harrison's text thereby constitutes an important addition to what is as yet a relatively small pool of discussed texts.

Harrison's work contends that travel can dismantle race. Contributing to the rich literature of racial passing, she represents herself not as deceiving others concerning her "true" identity, but as possessing multiple identities that vary according to her location and economic state. Just as she crosses national boundaries, so she crosses racial ones. With its portrayal of the transformative power of travel, her text makes explicit what so many travel narratives imply, that international movement engenders a fluidity of class, racial, and national identification. Henry Louis Gates Jr. points out that although "race, as a meaningful criterion within the biological sciences, has long been recognized to be a fiction," it nevertheless is invoked daily.[5] Questioning the belief that race is "natural, absolute, essential,"[6] Harrison shows that through travel, race can unravel in life as well as in theory. And in the process of making salient the close ties between geographic, economic, and racial configurations, she undercuts a widely held perception of African American women as static, bound by race into immobility.[7]

Despite having published her text in the 1930s, Harrison is very much MacLane and Whiteley's contemporary—born only five years after the former, and indeed eleven years before the latter, with whom she had an editor in common. It is certainly debatable, though, whether Harrison, a world traveler from Mississippi, belongs in a book entitled *Maverick Autobiographies: Women Writers and the American West*. What is Harrison doing in a study of western writers?

As I will discuss, Harrison, too, reinvented herself through mobility in a decidedly "western" fashion. Her travels and travel narrative temporarily undo class and race markers fixed in her birthplace and transform her into an aristocrat of the road. The following discussion emphasizes Harrison's self-professed southern California origins, and the way she used Los Angeles and Hawaii as urban bases. More relevant, though, may be her exuberant reinventions of self, through which she entirely liberates a practice central to "westering" from matters of geography. Indeed, Harrison's travels really began with her movement eastward, in which she completed Whiteley's counter-pioneer trajectory. Like Whiteley, the relative wealth of southern California provided her with the means to travel to the east coast; from there she traveled to Europe (her book begins with her departure from Hoboken to Great Britain), and from Europe to Asia. In Harrison's case, however, the wanderer continued on from Asia to reach—from the East—the western edge of United States territory. Written by an African American woman of southern origins, Harrison's urban-centered celebration of mobility helps us to consider ways in which the notion of "western literature" can be enlarged.

My Great, Wide, Beautiful World, for the most part composed in on-the-scene present tense, consists of approximately two hundred and twenty journal entries and letter excerpts highlighting Harrison's new locations, jobs, and experiences as she slowly circles the globe. She challenges the ideal of feminine vulnerability by using the same to ease her travels: "I being a poor lonely woman of course that lonely look helps me a great deal but there never were one less lonely than I am" (282). Most of her entries describe the first three years of her trip, 1927 to 1930, during which she traveled and worked in Great Britain, western and eastern Europe, the Middle East, and India. There are no entries between 1930 and 1934, when Harrison worked in southern France augmenting her funds as she waited for a more opportune time to visit China. This period may also have been when she assembled, with outside assistance, her text. The last sixth of the diary covers her final and most rapid year of travel in Germany, Scandinavia, Russia, China, Japan, and the Philippines, and its epilogue describes the Hawaiian home she established after completing the journey.

Born in Columbus, Mississippi in 1887, Harrison quit school as a child to begin full-time domestic labor. At thirty, during the peak of the "Great Migration" of southern blacks, she left Mississippi and embarked on a series of service jobs in Alabama, Michigan, Illinois, Indiana, Iowa, New Jersey, Pennsylvania, New York City, Florida, the Colorado Rockies, Los Angeles, Texas, Kansas, Canada, and Cuba.[8] When she could, she also enrolled in YWCA or night school classes where she studied languages and the ways of "an accomplished lady's maid" (ix). George and Myra Dickinson, her employers in Los Angeles, invested her slowly accumulated savings to yield an annual income of two hundred dollars. By 1927, at the age of forty, Harrison had the means to leave North America and travel while supplementing her funds with intermittent employment as a maid, cook, companion, or nurse.

Shortly after leaving the United States, she worked for an American family in Paris that encouraged her to record her travels, to the end of producing a book. The daughter of the family, Mildred Morris, eventually served as Harrison's editor in selecting and arranging her writings. Harrison's dedication of the book suggests that her text may have been partially compiled from letters she had written to her L.A. sponsor: "To Mrs. Myra K. Dickinson: Your great kindness to me have made my traveling much happier if You hadnt been interested in me I never would have tryed to explain my trips also your True and Kindness encourage me and made me more anxious to tell you the way I spent my time."

Along with the official record of the Morrises as instigators of the text (as given by Mildred Morris herself in her preface), this dedication, with the image of a benevolent Dickinson extending her interest and encouragement to an otherwise reticent and even uncommunicative traveler, suggests that Harrison's publication and even writing itself were due primarily to the efforts of white patrons. In the actual text, though, Harrison tells a different story, one that highlights her own agency. She writes of the Morrises, "one of the Daughters is a writer and the mother said my travellers [sic] should be put into a Book. I told her I would come back [to Paris] after my trip to India and work for nothing if Miss Mildred, the Daughter would help me" (16). She also describes herself looking up the Morrises on her return. (243) It is impossible to know how seriously the elder Morris intended her words, but one can certainly envision her making the idle, admiring comment so often proffered travelers—"you should write a book!"—and her surprise that it should lead to Harrison's arrival on her doorstep to barter cooking and cleaning for her daughter's editorial skills. Typically, Harrison profits by exchanging her domestic desirability, along with her sexual desirability her main asset, in exchange not for money but other prizes. (And it is interesting to note where literary production fell in Harrison's hierarchy: not worth usurping a trip to India for.)

Harrison's resistance to conventions of formal writing, coupled with her loosely organized impressionistic style, may make her appear an unlikely author. How did such a person ever come to write a book, must less publish it? Sidonie Smith addresses this question in arguing that as a genre, autobiography invites "culturally marginalized peoples" into print, those who "are assigned inauthentic voices by the dominant culture." Its flexibility and proliferation of forms, coupled with the opportunity to tell one's own story, make autobiography accessible and appealing.[9] Yet more specifically, Harrison's text also implies that travel itself demands writing and that writing is an organic component of travel. The simple logistics of travel immerse Harrison in a world

of writing. She depends upon travel guides and YWCA direc-
tories to negotiate her way (naming "Bradshaws Continental
guide" as "the book that means everything to me" [50]). She fre-
quents public libraries and buys newspapers, magazines, and
books about the places she visits. She sues by mail for compensation from a railroad accident. She reads and places advertisements for jobs in English language newspapers and on employment agency bulletin boards; she also collects written references,
not for utility, but because "the memories of the writer are sweet"
(244). Perhaps most important, her travels lead to extensive correspondence with patrons, past employers, and new friends.

This last suggests that there is a link more profound than the
merely utilitarian between travel and writing. As in the case of
western American overland accounts, which constitute one of
the largest body of writings by ordinary people, the belief that
one is engaged in "outlandish" experience either historical or personal compels non-writers to write.[10] Even those who previously
wrote little, correspond with friends, family, and new acquaintances once they are on the road; they may also attend assiduously to journals. Harrison's dedication to Dickinson suggests
that the pleasure of travel is augmented by writing about it:
"Your great kindness to me have made my traveling much happier if You hadnt been interested in me I never would have tryed
to explain my trips." Moreover, writing links new places to old.
Referring to Indian workers moving to a nearby town, Harrison
marvels "they don't read or write so its just like a person was dying no way of getting in touch with them" (65). As the narrative
progresses, writing increasingly becomes a means for her to make
connections between different places and her experiences there,
as well as to relive past events. Writing may have helped Harrison
not only to reinvent identity but also to establish a continuity in
her life.

Distracted by its idiosyncratic spelling and grammar, the
reader might initially miss the creative richness of Harrison's
prose. Harrison manipulates language in unlikely ways, and her
fused sentences typically build towards climactic moments that
determine their end. To select a few examples:

> I never go with a Lady because you must pay her carfare they like
> to stop and have a cup of tea another stop in the Publice House for

a glass of beer and another at the W. C. and the time have pass and your little change. (6)

I visited the Famous Painter Wiertz's Musee the most and best of his pictures are such horrod thoughts. (264)

the Moon is bright and the houses on the many mountains seem to be touching the sky the snow covered mountains are like pearl just below my cottage are a floor of white Clouds. the darkness of the tall fir trees and tea plants on the mountain sides beside the snow white clouds far below are to wonderful. up and down are the thousand of light as this is a City above and below mountains and clouds the lights seem to mix with the stars. (140)

We are now on the Sea or I do not know just how to say it as Holland are the Sea itself. While the men were conquring the Sea they also made the parts that they conqued beautiful so nelected the style of their women. (272)

a red room with cream curtains are pretty but when I awoke this morning looked like I was in a great blaze no more red rooms. (236)

Describing a shipboard meal, Harrison recounts, "We had a wounderful dinner each had a stuffed gosslin I don't know if it is spelled right. but it is the geese's babies Our Pleasant but not very hansom Captain name is Gosslin" (3). Her speculation here over whether her language is "right" makes for a rare moment in the text. Considering her plethora of grammar and spelling mistakes, this instance of self-doubt indicates just how confident a writer she usually is, especially since she moves on to make a play on words. Indeed, in describing her response to the Taj Mahal, Harrison shows that in the more significant matter of representation rather than protocol her language use is superb. She opens by making the conventional gesture of so many travelers confronted with a celebrated spectacle: words fail her. Signaling what a good tourist she is in feeling appropriately moved, she states, "It thrilled me through as the beauty cannot be painted" (133) and again, "It cannot be described eyes must see it" (134). Yet she continues, "As we left [my companion] asked me how it impressed me. the night was getting dark the dew was falling heavy and I said, 'I would just like to put a glass over it I feel I must cover it over.' He said, 'That's beautiful.'" (133) Harrison suggests, in recording the praise, that she offers access to the spectacle through her accurate representation of the emotion it prompts.

Harrison is much more likely to discuss speech than writing. Unlike so many autobiographers, prior to the epilogue she does not dramatize her own production of the text, which occurs invisibly as a seemingly natural outgrowth of travel. Neither does she participate in the text's framing; her editor alone provides the supporting materials including the preface, an occasional footnote, and an explanation for the gap in entries. Yet tellingly, in her very first entry Harrison dramatizes her agency as a writer:

> A beautiful June Morning. I arrived at 9 A.M. with my two suit cases the larger one with 2 blue dresses 2 white dresses and one black aprons caps and references. The smaller one with my dress up cloths. and 2 jars of sour cucumber pikles which is so good to keep from being sea sick. Our cabins looked good. I always want a upper berth I don't want anybody making it down on me. I went to the 1st and 2nd Class. Their towels looked more linnen so I took two, the soap smelt sweeter so I took 2 cakes. I went up to the writing room and the paper was the kind you love to touch so I took much and tuked it away in my bunk. (1)

In the same way that she secures the upper berth and steals the towels and soap reserved for the flusher travelers, so does she steal the writing paper she finds so sensuous. As a writer, Harrison appropriates the materials of the classes above her, and the use to which she puts the stolen paper amplifies her mischief: she writes with a blithe disregard of convention not only in form but also content, inventing a shifting self that does not fit her readers' expectations and deters them from "making it down" on her. Travel leads to writing. And as African American literary traditions in particular attest, writing, perhaps even more so than travel, is itself a means of self-transformation.[11]

Wherever Harrison sojourns she insists on a private room, declaring "my room is my personal self" (122). She refuses to let anyone enter even to clean it, turns down appealing jobs if they entail shared quarters, and makes it a policy not to have "Lady Friends" because, unlike men, they would expect to be entertained in her room. Harrison's fond descriptions of many of her rooms are often more developed than those of the sights she visits, and she describes herself spending blissful days alone in them, sometimes in bed. Such pleasure partially stems from the very public nature of travel, which makes a room a more than usual retreat. Yet although Harrison never explicitly discusses the process of writing and certainly not its preconditions, perhaps too this "room of her own" fosters her writing and so accounts for her zealous defense. A note of caution, though: Harrison discomfits the critic who would make too earnest an analysis of her relationship to writing, through assertions like "when I think of the good things I can get to eat for what the stamp cost I just stick these letters in my case" (293).

Presumably as a result of Harrison's persistence and Morris's savvy, Ellery Sedgwick, Whiteley's former editor, agreed to include two excerpts of Harrison's text in the *Atlantic Monthly.* These appeared in the fall of 1935, about six months before Harrison completed the journey that, according to Morris, itself was inspired by a magazine travel article.[12] In 1936 MacMillan compiled Harrison's accounts into *My Great, Wide, Beautiful World,* heralded by the announcement "The clamorous demand for 'More!' which followed publication in Atlantic Monthly last Autumn of condensed portions, is now met with the complete diary."[13] The full text too seemed to have inspired a demand for "More!" and went through nine editions in ten months. Introduced by Adele Logan Alexander, it was recently reprinted in a series edited by Gates and Jennifer Burton on African American women writers, 1910–1940.[14]

My Great, Wide, Beautiful World, long before its incarnation in this series, was put forth as a text written by an African American woman: editors, publishers, and reviewers all emphasized Harrison's race. Perhaps most significantly, the decision to leave Harrison's spelling and grammar untouched, along with the framing of her text by an editorial voice attesting to veracity, served to signal the extent of the writer's difference from a white, middle-class readership. In the preface to both the *Atlantic* selections and the book, Morris reinforced this sense of difference by opening with a familiar scenario of black Southern poverty: "Juanita Harrison is an American colored woman. . . . Born in Mississippi, she had a few months of schooling before she was ten. Then began an endless round of cooking, washing and ironing" (ix). Following suit, the text was advertised as "the hilarious but penetrating diary of an American negress," and reviews invariably labeled Harrison in their first paragraph as colored or negro.

The reminiscences of Sedgwick, arguably the pivotal figure in securing Harrison a national readership and fondly named by Harrison as her "unseen sweetheart," are dismaying.[15] In his description of Harrison, Sedgwick quite literally as well as metaphorically redomesticates the transgressive figure of an African American woman unfixed by race, class, or place. Dubbing Harrison a "Black Pearl among Servants," he states that his thoughts turn to her whenever he has troubles with his maid or cook. Harrison's narrative of the joys of travel, he asserts, provokes white readers to covet her—their desire taking the form, bizarrely enough, of not envy of her freedom and adventures, but jealousy of her services. Reading Harrison's book, he contends, makes readers long to have Harrison working for them, to get her off the road and into their kitchens.

Sedgwick is also committed to rendering this self-named westerner a southerner, no matter how far West he may find her. In describing meeting Harrison in Waikiki, he recalls,

> As I approached her tent, there was a mighty commotion within. "Sakes alive!" I heard in a syrupy gurgle. "I ain't got a mortal thing on me." But things were found, the tent flap parted, and out came Juanita, her teeth shining under a carmine bandana, her big eyes bright as blobs of Mississippi molasses. "Gord's sake," she cried, "did ever nigger see the like of this!" and she bent double under the weight of her laughter.[16]

In both text and life Harrison dramatized her freedom and mobility, but in his official memoir of his professional life Sedgwick pins her fast. (The contrast to his thoughtful and sympathetic descriptions of Whiteley is striking.) Sedgwick cannot look beyond Harrison's body. Figured by sugar and topped by the stereotypical bandana, it dominates his account as he notes her unseen nudity, shiny teeth, bright head and eyes, and laughter so viscous that it has weight. With his invocation of "Mississippi molasses" (distinct from the molasses of other states?), Sedgwick returns Harrison, a world traveler who claimed California for her past and Hawaii for her future and countless places in between, back to the South of her birth where he perceived her as belonging.

To be a servant, to be a southerner, and to be black are all of a piece. Like Morris's preface, Sedgwick's account supports Robert Stepto's contention that in African American literature, "artist and authenticator (editor, publisher, guarantor, patron) [compete] for control of a fiction,"[17] that of the author's identity. Sedgwick's portrait of Harrison is impossible to reconcile with the Harrison of the text.

Yet despite the widespread reception and representation of Harrison as a black woman, the text itself reveals that Harrison was difficult to fix racially, repeatedly portraying the confusion the question of her identity generated. Morris first introduces Harrison as racially ambiguous. Although she calls Harrison simply a "colored woman" and does not comment on the origins of her Spanish name, she provides a careful physical description that implies mixed blood. Morris's choice of verb is telling in her description of Harrison's difficult Mississippi childhood as "the sordid life that colored her early years" (xi), suggesting that region and poverty themselves contribute to rendering a woman "colored."

More important, Harrison herself avoids the expectations set up by others' emphases on her race by not defining herself as an African American—of any shade—and not making her text a record of African American experience. In this respect, *My Great, Wide, Beautiful World* is very different from the travel narratives of Harrison's near contemporaries, like James Weldon Johnson's fictional *The Autobiography of an Ex-Colored Man*, Zora Neale Hurston's *Dust Tracks on a Road*, Eslanda Goode Robeson's *African Journey*, or Fay McKeene Hershaw and Flaurience Sengstacke Collins's *Around the World with Hershaw and Collins*. Harrison is Californian or European, but never "black," nor, for that matter, "white." She does not refer to herself as colored, Negro, African, much less as (according to Sedgwick) a nigger. She does not claim a "people"; she does not discuss American racism or suggest that she went abroad to escape it. Her book contains remarkably few references to life before travel, and her single allusion to past discrimination lies in her comment about Nice: "I always get a comfortable and Home like place to stay for here you never think of your color" (21). Speaking more generally, leaving America, it seems, enabled Harrison to cease to "think of [her] color" and shuck the monochromatic identity of a young, unprivileged, uneducated African American woman in Jim Crow Mississippi. Writing and publishing the text allowed her to continue the journey.

Most readers will perceive Harrison's achievement of cosmopolitanism that few approach as a triumph over race and gender prejudice. This former child laborer, quite possibly the descendent of slaves, claims the world and names it beautiful. Margo Culley remarks that Euro-American women autobiographers generally announce gender in their titles (*Memories of a Catholic Girlhood, Wyoming Wife*). In contrast, African American women usually signal race, race and gender both (*A Colored Woman in a Black World*), or, more rarely, gender alone.[18] Only a few exceptions indicate neither; Hurston's peripatetic *Dust Tracks on a Road* is one and Harrison's book is, of course, another. Harrison's title, "My Great, Wide, Beautiful World," elides markers of identity in favor of proclaiming the world her own. Nor does the actual text provide an overt narrative of triumph over adversity; Harrison does not recount her own history.

What she wants most to reflect upon is not race but travel. *My Great, Wide, Beautiful World* is both a paean to the joys of travel and a guide to traveling well. Harrison proposes that it is her own practice that renders "her" world so appealing. Even for those raised in a society where their labor is possessed by others, traveling right leads to possession of their own. In contrast to the "race movies" of the black bourgeoisie that encouraged the formation of rural Southerners into "Black Babbitts,"[19] Harrison asserts that for those of any race, accruing wealth and status is an empty ambition. As she concludes, "Well you have bring out your moth ball smelling cloths and no doubt feel very pleased with the world to be in a caged up Building looking out on others more caged up. I have gone through the same and how greatful I am to myself" (318). Through asserting the superiority of her own choices and offering readers a model of action, Harrison eschews the stance of the "minority autobiographer."[20]

My Great, Wide, Beautiful World makes an argument about what makes a good traveler rather than a superficial tourist. Its central premise is that the traveler must incorporate local attentiveness within global ambition, observing individual places closely even while ranging as widely as possible: "I spend a day in a town as though I was going to spend my life there this is for my own consciance" (75). Harrison contends that to travel well one must concentrate on a country's peoples rather than its sights, through working, playing, eating, drinking, dancing, and flirting with them. She suggests that successful travel also includes getting gratis even that which one could otherwise afford, in her case, often from amorous males whose expectations of sexual exchange she—"manproof"—disappoints. She makes clear that traveling well very much means eating well and rarely neglects to describe the foods that distinguish a new place. It also means traveling light: she carries her few possessions in her pockets, gloating that she is less encumbered than even a man; she makes it a principle to dislodge travel companions no matter how agreeable, since "when you find the Places alone you enjoy it better" (6). Perhaps most significantly, she models traveling light as being unburdened by loneliness, homesickness, nostalgia, or even a past.

In a sense, though, Harrison's childhood and young adult past of incessant labor is made present in the text by the intensity of the delight with which she embraces leisure and her ability to choose when, where, and how much she wants to work—in the United States, for all but a privileged minority, work had long been "part of the definition of what it meant to be a black woman."[21] For Harrison abroad, work is a means of learning about other cultures through close living. She shows even the job search as a way to explore new terrain, on arrival sallying forth "to enjoy some interviews" (27). Work also offers her stability and simple relief from leisure, and Harrison demonstrates that staving off satiation through alternating travel with work augments the enjoyment of both. She portrays herself as an awesomely competent worker ("I can teach a Spanish maid more in a minute than she can teach me in a week" [175]), implored by employer after employer to stay on, and clearly takes pride in her skill and desirability. She does not, however, show labor as having value in and of itself, and is little interested in describing her day-to-day tasks. There is nothing of the Protestant work ethic in her text: "I always get a job when I go out to get one but never feel any to glad no matter how good it is. Its when I am ready to give it up that I have the grand feeling" (253).

Surprisingly, perhaps, considering her description of her pleasure in excess, her text also makes a "less is more" argument. Within her celebratory narrative of glut—the surfeit of a traveler's pleasure—Harrison folds a celebratory narrative of asceticism—the travel's minimalism. A small room or a tent, she shows, can be eminently pleasing. A single dress and coat meet her needs better than a cumbersome wardrobe; and when the weather turns warm, she plans to give the coat away. Harrison prides herself on her ability to make bountiful meals out of humble ingredients, bought cheap at local markets. The objects whose use she highlights are similarly indigenous—a Spanish cooking pot, an Indian veil. Maintaining that satisfaction depends on meeting one's appetite "just right," Harrison asserts the superiority of her own taste through demonstrating her moderation. That she owns little shows just how particular she is.

To repeat, Harrison's primary concern is travel, not race. Yet although she does not tackle race explicitly, her text emphasizes that her racial identity was a constant factor in her travels. Throughout the text she shows how her dark but not obviously African looks made her racially and ethnically unreadable, and how she used these looks to her advantage just as she used her status as lone female. In the text's preface, Morris notes that Harrison's looks masked her age: "Her slight form, fresh olive complexion, long hair braided about her head, made her appear younger than her years" (xi). What Morris does not remark upon but what Harrison's text clearly reveals, is that these signs were also deceptive racially. The hair and skin marked Harrison as not white but did not mark her as black, a gap others' imaginations worked to fill. "Betwixt and between," Harrison confounded people across the world as they griped "how can we tell" and groped for clues.

Harrison replicates this confusion in her text itself, choosing not to define her ethnic identity to the reader and instead emphasizing how she puzzled others. She takes pleasure in recording mistaken guesses, which pepper the book. In Italy she notes that she was thought Chinese, Japanese, or Spanish; in Turkey, French; and in Spain, Argentinean or Moorish. An Egyptian thought her English, although approvingly "not the cold English type" (96). In Syria, she writes, "At Aleppo they thought I was Chinese. Here they think I am Aribian I have no trouble getting into every little nuck and corner" (65); in Hungary, "they think I am Italian and am makeing believe when I say I am American I just leave it to them" (53).

Harrison belies this last assertion, that she "just leave[s] it to them," through demonstrating that she chooses to be perceived as whatever best suits her ends. In Israel: "I have a very Oriental looking scarf I ware most of the time on my head everyone thinks I am Arabian but are puzzled to see me with such a short french dress and the first thing they ask my Friend If I am Arabian then when I ware my little French cap they take me for Jewish. I am willing to be what ever I can get the best treatments at being" (75). The inverse of this last statement holds true as well, in that Harrison is not willing to be what will not procure her good treatment, as in Nice: "I no longer own up to be American but are a Cuban" (24), she states, since "the French have not time for [the Americans and English] only to make them pay well for everything and I agree with the French" (24).

Harrison's ambiguous appearance and indeterminate social standing facilitates her travels, in that her possession of, and willingness to deploy, a slippery persona gratify her desire to "[get] into every little nuck and corner" without forfeiting the privileges of the American or European traveler. Harrison actively manipulates her appearance by her dress, as when she learns where not to wear a hat: "If I go out without a hat the Italians do not take any notice of me and always talk right along with me. But if I have on a hat they call me a Chinese or Japanese. You can get along so good if you are not dressed up" (38); in India, "I started through the quarters with my hat on but found I was out of place so went back and got my Vail then everything went lovely" (94). She takes even greater efforts in Boulogne, boasting "I looked so much like one of the Fishman wives that even the coustom offices refused to look through my baggage. most of the women have long hair and dress it in two brads as I do all I laked was ear rings. I had 2 pairs in my case Mme. gave me. Well I put on my correll ear rings and was a perfect Boulognesser" (14). Harrison's disguises are good enough to work too well, as when she looks so "auful casty" on an Indian train — "about as low cast as a European can look" (110) — that an upper-caste woman wants her ejected.

Traveling stamps Harrison as middle class even as it exposes her as an outsider. Ironically, although Harrison does not come from a middle-class background, she has to dress in costumes designed to deceive in order not to appear that she does. In native clothing, she regains the working-class identity she "naturally" possessed in the United States. In Djibouti, she recounts, "in just a few seconds after suluting a few women I has swams around me first they thought I came from Greece after a while they decide I was Chinese as many as could get to me I had to shake hand it was very pleasant. then a woman came up to beg and another let her know she were not to beg me" (161). Just as in England her identity as a servant prevents her from being regarded as a boorish American ("of course they always talk to me as a maid and not as an American" [26]), so in Asia her sociability and lack of affluence prevent her from being "begged." For Harrison as a traveler, working-class status opens rather than closes doors. Of course, on occasion being a lady can be useful too, and in India she successfully applied for a job as "a nurse companion . . . open for a European lady only" (114–15). She explains, "I don't mind being a high cast but I want to be a low cast too" (110).

As the surprise of an Israeli acquaintance indicates ("This young man have met wealthy American women traveling alone but I am the poorest girl that ever traveled alone" [74–75]), the difficulty in classifying Harrison results from the mixed messages sent not only by her looks and dress, but also by her behavior. Harrison is a cipher: a single female traveler of independent income who sporadically works in service positions that she leaves as soon as she loses interest, she is neither an upper-class lady making her grand tour nor a working-class woman striving to make ends meet, nor is she an underclass "hobo" and even less a middle-class professional taking a well-earned vacation. At once both servant and jet-setter, she takes equal pleasure in living high and low. With their favorable exchange rates ("My how powerful rich one can feel in India" [145]), the Middle East and Asia in particular allow her to indulge both inclinations. Demonstrating both the range of her experiences and the vexation her plasticity provokes, she recalls "A Burma Lady said to me at Darjeeling you are just betwixt and between. one minute you have a fine time with the lowest cast next minute with the highest Hindoo. one minute you wear a blue suit next minute a dress of 2 cent a yard crape then a little velvet dress with diamond ear rings how can we tell. one minute you stay in a hotel at $5.00 a day then go to a restaurant and have a 5 cent meal. youre betwixt and between" (141).

As we have seen, Harrison unselfconsciously refers to herself as "European" when distinguishing herself from the inhabitants of Asian countries. European, Euro-American, and African American travelers can all be classified by the umbrella term "European," since divisions between and within western nations become less important in the face of the more significant division between native residents and the travelers among them. Yet although it is in Asia that Harrison conceives of herself most broadly—she is simply a European (or sometimes a Christian as opposed to a Hindu or Muslim)—it is also where she takes the most pleasure in noting nuances of physical difference in other women. For example, women in Burma, she notes, make "a beautiful picture a few fair Europeans the Anglo Burmases girls in their cool short frocks some fair some light and some dark. the Burmases Ladies in their bright silk cloth wrapped around their suple bodys then short white waist bracelets of gold bare feet in sandles their black hair slick as an eil and like a black crown on their heads and their soft yellow skin" (150–51). Similarly, she remarks in Madras that "the Anglo-Indian Girls are . . . not as good looking down here as in Bombay and Calcutta. at Calcutta they dress good and pretty have the cleanest teeth and finger nails Bombay come next. Rangoon they have more pleasure and are lovely but not as good dressers and you can see a little trace of that Burma-Chinese blood so are not as good looking as the Indians Anglos. I have had much joy noticing the difference" (153–54). Speaking as a European, Harrison displaces discussions of her own "blood" onto these variegated exotics. Even while she attests to joy in noticing the physical differences of other women, she never discusses her own racial makeup or even admits a racial identity. What she does instead is provide an endless succession of snapshots of how others saw her.

The range of these snapshots calls to mind the statement of a contemporary African American writer, Shirlee Taylor Haizlip: "I have been called Egyptian, Italian, Jewish, French, Iranian, Armenian, Syrian, Spanish, Portuguese and Greek." Yet, unlike Harrison, Haizlip goes on to state "I have also been called black and Peola and nigger and high yellow and bright."[22] Although Harrison repeatedly notes when she was mistakenly identified, what is one to make of her silence about the presumably numerous instances in which she was recognized as African American? As implied by the almost ethnographic nomenclature of "now no body

can cook cabbage to beat the Irish of Cork not even the American
Colored Southerners" (8), in her text Harrison does not align herself with southern African Americans or with African Americans
in general. Indeed, she does not name any group with which she
does align herself. From her narrative alone, we cannot know
how Harrison "really" identifies herself. What we do know is that
she enjoys her ambiguity and her status as a world citizen.
MacLane and Whiteley's texts were trumpeted as offering an un-
mediated view of the authentic young woman and authentic
child. Yet their texts undermine this claim of transparency by
making their subjects appear all the more mysterious, as does the
behavior of these women after publication. Harrison even more
explicitly proffers a series of masquerades.

In thinking about these masquerades, it is useful to turn to
Smith's discussion of the ways in which Hurston "sought to di-
vert . . . the pressures of the confessional autobiographical mode"
while "in the midst of a white culture that kept her identities
as black/woman at the fore."[23] Smith builds upon Claudine Raynaud's analysis of Hurston's dealings with her white editors in
writing the autobiography they wanted from her.[24] Detailing the
various subject positions Hurston claims for herself in *Dust Tracks*
(including "a wanderer, an artist, a collector of tales, a teller of
tales, a child, a philosopher, a young girl, a woman, an American,
a Negro, an individual, and an inhabitant of the globe"), Smith
states that Hurston "fills her narrative with allusions to 'lies' and
'lying'. . . . She will not let [readers] fix the autobiographical subject, 'Zora Neale Hurston,' as a unified subject of autobiography."[25] We do not as yet have records of Harrison's dealings with
her white editors and publishers, but Harrison, too, may have
been playing the trickster in order to satisfy both others and herself. The canny practices she describes herself engaging in
throughout the text, especially in regard to her travel "disguises,"
suggest she may have been similarly canny in constructing her
textual identity.[26]

At the same time, her *own* view of herself changed according to
where she was. Thus, whereas in Asia Harrison conceived of herself as a European, in Europe she conceived of herself as a Californian. After leaving Columbus, her four-year sojourn in Los Angeles was her longest in North America; her friendship with the
Dickinsons, with whom she remained in lifelong contact, may

partially account for her ties to the state.[27] Stray comments suggest that a genuine sense of Californian identity led her to see California as her home: "I read the names on many [of the headstones in the American Cemetery in Paris] and it were one from every state and many from Calif" (19); or, on her discovering a fellow traveler in Ireland was from Fresno, anticipating the fact to be a "joy to me" (11). At the same time, though, Harrison suggests that her choice was also motivated by a desire to shore up her personal image, in that California lent her recognition and prestige. Referring to a Spanish village she visited, she remarks "Elche have many flappers and all are Hollywood fans and all the Picture House show the Calif. Films I am glad I choosed Calif. for my home before I left as every one know it" (192). Claiming southern Californian origins appears to have facilitated sociability with other women: Harrison recalls of two English girls, "When I told them I was from Los Angeles they thought it just wonderful" (9) and later adds that in Zurich "The Girls think it so lovely I am from far away California and all are so lovely to me" (46).

Harrison uses her home state to proffer an image of Americanness familiar to all she meets. Fictionists of the 1930s, like Harrison largely outsiders to the area, often portrayed Los Angeles as a place of sham and violence, the American dream of hypermobility betrayed. In Harrison's text, though, it remains true to mythic type, "the golden land of opportunity and the fresh start."[28] The incessant image-making, lack of history, and restlessness decried by others serves Harrison well. Avowing California as her own helps her evade racial categories. California, unlike Mississippi and the South, does not connote black-white polarization, and its movies disseminate internationally an "America" that is available even to those these same movies exclude. As Michael Rogin notes, Hollywood was "important in making Americans, in giving people from diverse class, ethnic, and geographic origins a common imagined community."[29] The land of Hollywood, its racially stereotyped films notwithstanding, seems a more than fitting place of genesis for an actor like Harrison to claim.

Although Harrison makes conscious choices about how to present herself to others, it does not appear that she tries to "pass" in the sense that she works to deceive. Instead, she allows herself or helps herself to be regarded as whatever secures her the "best treatments." In one moment in the text, though, in describing her time in Paris, Harrison alludes to blackness as something best kept hidden and signals her complicated relationship to her African ancestry:

> I went out to the Garden d'Acclimatation where they are having an expostion of Central Afircanes from the French part of Africa. I climbed over the fence and got in the native village where the Plate mouthed women are. a slip is cut just wide enough in the lip to fit around the rim of a wooden plate they can hardly talk with it only the women have the plates there is about ten of them and they took a fancy to me. I think they saw I had some of their blood I couldnt fool them. the yongest wife was during the Cooking as I hung around the Camp fire she offered me some it was good and I would have accepted to save the price of my supper But the spit run out of her mouth on this plate and often droped into the pot. When I left I climbed over the fence again so it didn't cost me any- thing. (19)

This passage is a dense configuration of the way Harrison simul- taneously identifies herself with and distances herself from these African women. While Harrison may have "fooled" so many oth- ers, she cannot fool them. This is not to say that the moment is an unhappy one for Harrison: on the contrary, since her blackness allows her to claim "some of their blood," it contributes to her pleasurable perception of herself as a cosmopolitan. Harrison suggests that it is the women's recognition of their shared ances- try that leads them to "t[ake] a fancy" to her, and leaves open to speculation whether it contributes to her own attraction to them. She lingers by the fire, drawn to the women and the food they cook, and in so doing transforms a domestic scene staged for entertainment into a domestic scene affording real food and real sociability. By dodging the entrance fees, Harrison further trans- forms the interaction.

Yet although appetite and canniness make her hunger for the food the women cook, she perceives it as contaminated by the saliva that spills from their "Plate mouths." Harrison portrays these mouths as deformities inhibiting communication and clean- liness alike, and notes that they are limited to women alone. Her emphasis on the women's mouths and on the wall that contains them well represents the difference she perceives between her own experience and theirs, between that of a Californian and that of Central Africans. In contrast to these women on display, Harrison describes herself as roaming freely in unrestrained concourse with people from all over the world. She eases her travels by her exploitation of gender conventions: attracting and manipulating men and wielding the housekeeping skills she acquired as a child. While among the Africans one man has many wives, Harrison shows herself as having many men; like the African women she too labors domestically, but solely for herself, not for family or the pleasure of tourists.

On departing Paris for the south of France, she regrets that she did not have time to return to the exhibition and throw the warm coat she no longer needed over the wall to the women. Her compassion reveals her feelings of both affinity and difference. In contrast to the Africans on display as captured primitives, becoming a relatively wealthy and highly mobile traveler renders Harrison a "European," one in the position to bestow alms. Conversely, Harrison describes a wealthy white American girl who is forced to obey the whims of her mother and mother's lover as "just like a black slave" (27). As Gates asserts, "language use spell[s] out the distance between subordinate and superordinate, between bondsman and lord in terms of their 'race.'"[30] Harrison refigures blackness as a matter of power, not of bodies.

It is no coincidence that all of the "black" individuals Harrison describes are women. Throughout the text she meditates upon the varying degrees of power and freedom that the women she meets possess, without engaging in similar musings about the men. Always cognizant of the tight link between her own appearance and her agency, she is especially interested in how visual markers indicate status. Her interest intensifies when she leaves Europe for Asia and the Middle East, and women's bodies appear increasingly inscribed: veiled, tattooed, or ritually scarred faces; bejeweled necks, arms, and legs; bound feet. Harrison suggests that women of high status have less freedom than "pheasants," as in India: "I have learned that the high castes would like very much to walk and save their Rickshaus fare like I do but of course their caste wont allow it. I enjoy teaseing the Girls and ask if they Wish to be free like me to go out in the street at any hour. . . . Now they wish to be like me" (101). Harrison proposes that as one who is cultureless, or at least "nothing but a glob trotter" (294), her own freedom is unlimited. Yet her responses are not simple rejections of unfamiliar practices. She admires, for example, the bound feet of Chinese women: "the feet are just the size of your two fingers togather and they have little wooden sandles with high heels and walk only on the round heels and some have nice slender ankles not broken and they walk without a limp. Some are tall well built women" (297). Harrison goes further to show that the seeming barbarism of the aesthetic practices that western women encounter in their travels is matched by their own (142).

In discussing an African American nurse whom she encounters in Rome, Harrison comes the closest she ever does to commenting on her own transformation from a black domestic laboring in the rural South to a mobile, urban Californian/European effortlessly commanding a surfeit of adventures, jobs, men, and delicacies. Harrison enjoys whiling away the afternoon with the nurse, who has moved with her employers from Albany, New York, recalling,

> The last day in Rome I was walking through their largest park I notice setting down on one of the lower Terices a colored nurce about 40 and weigh about 200 lbs. I went and ask her if she spoke English and laughed when she answered "I say I do" She was a joly old Girl I spent the rest of the afternoon She think that the men are the most delightful of all men. She said it seem like a dream To her to have a Hansom Italian kissing Her hand. I hadnt give it much thought but when we got togather we sure did have a good time talking it over. . . . [T]he Family. . . . have 4 children she is so sweet and Gentle with them and they love her so. (36)

Harrison's experience as a black domestic worker in the United States would in many respects have resembled the other woman's, notwithstanding her transient work habits and resistance to building enduring relationships with the families she served. However, in calling the other woman a "joly old Girl" and focusing on her age, weight, and close ties to the white children she cares for—in other words, describing the woman in terms reminiscent of the mammy figure so cherished in American lore, Harrison suggests the expanse of difference that she felt separated her from the nurse. At the same time, her account also suggests the similarities of their experiences overseas, and it is telling that the Roman setting caused her to hesitate in identifying the woman as an English—presumably American—speaker.[31] In the

United States, due to her size, occupation, and disposition, the nurse would have been readily perceived by whites as a provider of nurture rather than the object of courtly attention. Yet even this most "colored" of black women, one who, unlike Harrison, does not have a "slight form, fresh olive complexion," and hair to her waist, enjoys privileges abroad that in the United States could barely be imagined. Despite the fact that, true to form, Harrison "hadnt give it much thought," a change in geography has, like "a dream," utterly changed both her and the nurse's social identity.[32]

Patricia Yaeger suggests that when the early-twentieth-century South is alluded to, racism must always spring to mind.[33] For Harrison to refer to her southernness would be to solicit a version of black identity antithetical to her self-construction as a gloriously unfettered, globe-trotting European/Californian sophisticate. Harrison's refusal to be "black" parallels her refusal to be "southern." Yet the marketing and reception of her book, which focus on the author as "Negress," worked to counter her claims. Alexander, in her introduction to the 1996 edition of Harrison's text, wonders if "editors at Macmillan . . . elect[ed] to publish Harrison's book because it so clearly proclaimed its uncelebrated black author as a 'primitive': a lovable yet somewhat clownish Aunt Jemima or latter-day Uncle Remus, whose narrative was readily acceptable to white America as part of a traditional and popular black dialect genre" (xvii).[34] Alexander suggests that white readers would have been more open to viewing Harrison as a rural southern black (a Remus or Jemima) linked through employment to white families than as an urban, racially unfixed, family-denying westerner. Harrison's reception as a "45-year-old Negro lady's-maid," a "colored domestic" with eyes like "blobs of Mississippi molasses," shows that Alexander's fear has grounds.[35] One review of Harrison is simply titled "Natural," and an advertisement declares the book "primarily a unique human document"—that is, of worth despite Harrison's race.[36] Contemporary reviews expressed sincere admiration of Harrison's vitality and sense of adventure, coupled with racist condescension.[37]

At the time, African American women writers had long used their texts to counter animalistic stereotypes of black women. It would be interesting to know the reactions of those who read Harrison's book: did they greet it with dismay? Harrison does not concern herself with addressing racial stereotypes, and she

appears indifferent to whether her text might reinforce essentialist views. She couples her interest in food and men to boast of how
she scored chicken dinners, elaborate lunches, amber paste, and
other delicacies from avid suitors; with her "snapy eye for flirting" (309) she enjoyed dalliance for its own sake, too. She repeatedly — even obsessively — features her appetites and the ways by
which she gratified them, often showing how she used her ambiguous appearance to multiply the experiences available to her.
Her omnivorousness is perhaps best represented through her
presentation of her meals, in all their endless variety: "I have enjoyed the trip I had a good lunch of boiled Chicken fried meat
balls boiled eggs radishes french rolls fried sweet potatoes co-
canuts sweets cakes oranges and a bottle of red wine" (209–10).

In such contrast to Harrison's behavior, women writers associated with the Harlem Renaissance reveal that their preoccupation
with resisting racial stereotypes could constrict their worlds.
Shortly before the start of Harrison's journey, to take one example,
Marita O. Bonner published "On Being Young — A Woman — and
Colored." Bonner regrets that the disapproval of her African
American middle-class community could render a black woman
unable even to travel alone from Washington, D.C., to New York
without crossing the line of propriety. She represents her anxious
desire to deny the perception of African American women as
"only a gross collection of desires, all uncontrolled" as motivation
to censure her own behavior.[38] Seen in comparison to Bonner,
Harrison's apparent lack of racial self-consciousness or introspection ("I hadnt give it much thought") served her well. My intention here is neither to valorize nor censure Harrison in comparison to her more political contemporaries. Rather, it is to show
how very different her text is from theirs, by virtue of the way she
attempts to make race a non-category even while reiterating its
pervasiveness.

In other words, Harrison carries out her dodge of a fixed racial
identity by making some essentialist moves of her own. Her radically various identity depends upon the invention of a backdrop
of stability and comprehension for all of the "natives" she encounters: she displaces onto others the kind of ethnic or national
essence that she will not accept for herself. Harrison repeatedly
demonstrates the ease with which she locates and comes to know
other peoples — the French, Spanish, Indians, Chinese, and so on.

Despite detailing a range of class positions, racial mixtures, and ethnic groups, she presents each nationality as united through a clearly delineated identity. The Spanish and French never remind her of Americans or Japanese, or even of Italians or Swiss. Certainly, no one resembles her own chameleon self. Harrison presents the people she meets, to borrow William Carlos Williams's term, as the world's "pure products."[39]

Just as the people she meets are "pure" and easily defined, so too is the world through which she moves culturally constant, available to the traveler independent of political and other changes. Although Harrison portrays herself visiting historical sites, in her text, history itself takes place off stage. She occasionally hears reports of disaster or upheaval, but marvels, "this time last year while I were at each place everything so peaceful" (251) or (in India), "Rioton was very bad last week and I payed so little atention" (113). Her text simply passes over the four-year period in which political upheaval checked her travels, representing it only by the editorial comment, "Because of the unsettled condition in China Juanita determined not to complete her journey around the world at this time but returned to the south of France where she remained until May 1934" (265); Harrison's narrative then resumes without comment. The book portrays a world in which events are eclipsed by the always similar routine of the traveler—moving on, finding a room and job, procuring food, entertainment, acquaintances. The scene changes, but the world does not.

Eric J. Leed asserts that the modern traveler experiences "the pervasive feeling that *real* travel. . . . is no longer possible"[40]; or as James Clifford states, "One no longer leaves home confident of finding something radically new."[41] Yet despite her very modern rendition of self, Harrison is not driven by the sense that "real travel," the authentic, the exotic, continually eludes her grasp. Although she relies on an elaborate and commodified system of travel—money exchanges, guidebooks, commercial tours—she never suggests that this network separates her from experiencing what is real. Even one of the world's most vaunted tourist attractions, the Taj Mahal, surpasses rather than fails to meet her expectations. She never laments that she has reached a place too late, after it has succumbed to western or global standardized culture; she is not driven to search out rough guides and roads less traveled; she does not rank the cultural verisimilitude of her experiences. Never disappointed, she greets moments of novelty and familiarity alike—with delight. Her travel experience can provoke the reader's deep envy: not only of her mobility, but even more of her endlessly repeated satisfaction.

Travel presupposes a home that one travels away from and returns to, and the discourse of travel often centers around an endorsement of home.[42] Harrison's emphasis on sexuality and sensuality affiliates her with Hurston and the era's blues singers in a black women's tradition different from that of writers such as Bonner.[43] She radically differs from them, however, in eliding her childhood home and an American past. Harrison never reveals any desire to return to the United States, and certainly not to Mississippi. Outside of a few hungry references to American turkey and Christmas, she expresses no nostalgia for her birthplace. As if her life began only in Hoboken when she stepped onto the ship to England, "happy that I had no one to cry for me," she makes no references to family, friends, or past events in the South.[44]

Rather than hearkening back to a single originating home, in her utopian travel text Harrison asserts that homes abound, depending simply on the traveler's adaptability: "I look so much Chinese am not at all out of Place," she states, leading her to conclude "every old Place is Home" (296); she "can't help but like the last place best" (20). Yet her repeated assertions of the continual availability of home—"each home have a new beauty and a different comfort so I never long for one of the pass" (267)—are disrupted by a wistful comment that is one of the few in which she alludes, however obliquely, to her life prior to travel. Regarding a visit to a former residence in Seville, she states, "It was just like coming home not that I have ever had a home to return to but it must be something like it" (221). Harrison's past as a disenfranchised laborer during her first thirty years in Mississippi precluded not only the ownership of an actual American home but perhaps also the metaphorical home of a stable identity, one acceptable to herself, that she could locate in America.

It is only through publication that Harrison portrays herself as securing a home on both literal and metaphorical fronts. Her epilogue, set in Waikiki at the close of her eight-year journey and entitled "NOW," opens with the statement, "that cheque from the Atlantic Monthly for my article gave joy" (315). She goes on to describe how, having received the money, she quit her job, custom built her "first and only Home" (318)—a large furnished tent—and erected it on the front yard of a Japanese family's home. While living there, Harrison planned to swim, cook, and learn to surf and hula dance.

Her choice of Hawaii for her future seems as significant as her choice of Hollywood for her past. While she associates Hollywood with the films that impress other nations, in Hawaii Harrison uses her own writing to establish a semi-private idyll. Harrison, west even of California, just barely reaches American territory. Arguably the nation's last western frontier, Hawaii continues to be a land of great ethnic variety and mixing that belies the American myth of race as either black and white, or cowboys and Indians. It seems appropriate, too, that Harrison should have arrived in Hawaii from the Far East as opposed to making the journey west so central in American history. Yet it is also on American ground that, for the first time in the text, Harrison portrays herself besting overt discrimination in a move that seems to refer to the unwritten subtext of American racism that underpins her narrative: "When I went to the American YWCA the Lady in charge of the Employment said why did you come here. I advise you to go back as the white People here want only Japanese help Well when I got through talking to her She thought very different as if any nation can keep me from getting a job and the Kind and Place and price I want" (311–12). Even as she shows herself persuading an individual woman, Harrison makes clear that the problem is rooted in "nation." This passage is also the first instance in which she wields the term "white People," absent from the rest of her text as too general to be of use.

Alexander, calling Harrison a "mystery woman," worries that Pearl Harbor may have destroyed Harrison's "carefree existence" in Hawaii, and speculates that she may have enjoyed "further odysseys." As it turns out, Harrison did, branching out to a new continent. Passport records reveal that she lived in Hawaii from 1935 to 1939, leaving before the attack on Pearl Harbor to begin a sojourn of over ten years in South America. From 1940 to 1942 she spent three to nine months each in Brazil, Uruguay, Argentina, and Chile. She then returned to Argentina, where she lived from January 1943 to 1950. In 1950, she applied for a new passport in order to travel by train in Bolivia, answering "uncertain" to the query as to when she "intend[ed] to return to the United States to reside permanently." At the age of sixty-three, then, still single and childless, Harrison continued to travel actively. Her new passport photo belies her age, showing a serene, half-smiling, broad-shouldered woman of powerful appearance wearing a black ruffled dress decorated with a single flower. In contrast to Sedgwick's remembrance of her as the "Black Pearl among servants," on the application Harrison declares her occupation as "author."[45]

Amy Kaplan's reminder in "Manifest Domesticity," that "domestic" refers not only to home but to nation, is most literally relevant to Harrison, but applies to MacLane and Whiteley as well.[46] All three conspired to leave both constrictive households and places of origins perceived as provincial for the foreign realms of New England, Europe, and Asia. In the new lives they created for themselves, they chose not to recreate bourgeois homes.

Having reached Harrison's Hawaii tent, I would like to conclude this chapter by turning briefly to the subject of housekeeping, which all three maverick autobiographers make such a salient theme. MacLane details her methods of cooking, scrubbing, and mending. Whiteley dramatizes her devotion to household chores. Perhaps most conspicuously, in her travels Harrison portrays herself as establishing a dizzying number of temporary homes with only a pot, a bed, and a garment or two. For modern readers, this emphasis on home is perhaps readily overlooked, eclipsed by MacLane's egotism, Whiteley's mysticism, or Harrison's joie de vivre. (Ann Romines shows how we miss domesticity in women's texts with her example of a Cather fan unaware that Cather wrote about cooking.)[47] We might, however, conjecture that these writers' portraits of women at home contributed to their contemporary appeal along with the more remarkable aspects of their texts.

Yet these three are remarkable for their lack of sentimentality in their home depictions and for the way their texts work against notions of home as the fount of virtue. It is as the "scene of departure" that their homes, as in so much twentieth-century American women's writing, are a site of intense narrative energy.[48] They show how ultimately the house, historically so central in women's lives, has little hold on them. Detailing her tedious existence as an adult daughter in her parents' home, MacLane may surprise readers by declaring how much she enjoys housework ("Every Friday I wash up the bath-room. Usually I like to do this. I like the feeling of the water squeezing through my fingers, and always it leaves my nails beautifully neat" [55]). Such a declaration of sensual pleasure, however, challenges convention. MacLane trivializes housework by knocking it from its pedestal of duty or even necessary labor. Whiteley, in contrast, deeply embroiled in a culture of femininity, explicitly endorses the importance of housework throughout the length of her text. She struggles to be a perfect "Little Housemaid." Yet such endorsement is undercut both by her freely admitted longing to escape outdoors and by her acts of household sabotage, which meet with beatings at her mother's hand. Whiteley invests the dull round of daily work with conflict and drama: nothing that she attempts in the house ever comes out right, in contrast to her serendipitous "explores" in the forest. Thus, she works to dissolve the boundary between inside and outside altogether by recreating the forest within the house, and her writing in the forest.

Last, as a professional domestic worker, Harrison, as we have seen, describes herself as superbly adroit in all manner of household management. And in her private quarters she does some serious nesting: arranging jealously guarded rooms out of a minimum of a traveler's accouterment, venturing out to local markets to procure bargain goods from which she conjures meal after delicious meal. In her text, glamour adheres to housekeeping via exotic locales and the makeshift innovations travel demands. Yet the sheer multiplicity of Harrison's homes is subversive. Recreating one after another after another, Harrison suggests that homes are temporary, fluid, and easily replaced. In contrast to southern ideologies of home, she deigns neither to linger with her employers in the guise of the devoted black domestic, nor to retain her own snug quarters. Neither holds enough allure to keep her from moving on to explore new terrain. Tellingly, the final home Harrison describes in her text is literally portable, a tent designed such that she can carry it on her head. The tent gives the lie to any notion that the conclusion of Harrison's book marks the conclusion of her own travel plot.

Conclusions

Questions of Genre

I have attempted in these chapters to recreate the literary milieu in which these maverick writers operated, to flesh out their single bestsellers. MacLane, Whitely, and Harrison had predecessors, descendants, contemporaries; they participated in and influenced literary trends; they enjoyed massive sales and a brief period of renown. And yet, by providing this context, I hope I have not obscured the fact that these mavericks were, after all, mavericks—strange women who wrote strange texts and lived strange lives. My challenge in writing *Maverick Autobiographies* has been to transform MacLane, Whiteley, and Harrison from fodder for anecdotes into subjects of analysis without obliterating their maverick identity and making them appear too familiar, too legible, too generic, too domestic—the last ways these writers should be seen.

This study, I hope, can serve as a precedent for studies of the multitude of mavericks whose work is passed over not out of lack of interest, but out of a sense that their maverick character precludes critical consideration. The sheer proliferation of autobiography augments the "sense of impossibility" that dogs American literary scholarship, the sense that it is impossible to do justice to all worthwhile texts.[1] That many autobiographical texts are the work of untraditional writers makes the genre appear especially daunting. In contrast to other genres, Caren Kaplan notes, the "'troubles' of autobiography seem to define it."[2]

One strategy is to see autobiography as a cultural map: "as writers or actors in their own times," Avrom Fleishmann contends, individuals "will stamp their autobiographies with the marks of the literary and other cultural movements in which they are engaged."[3] Sidonie Smith and others demonstrate, however, that the more private lives led by nineteenth- and early-twentieth-century women make them less recognizable as such "actors."[4] Certainly, the texts I discuss resist the easy interpretation of reflecting broader public movements. In what manner, for example, is the record of a dreamy, perhaps incipiently schizophrenic child who talks with plants stamped with the times?

The difficulties a text like *The Story of Opal* poses point to the special need to contextualize the work of women autobiographers. Such contextualization works from the premise that it is not just the text itself but also the text's publishing history, reception, and role in the author's life that is "stamped." Teasing out significance depends upon close readings, along with literary reviews, popular magazine and newspaper accounts, publishers' archives, personal correspondence, and artifacts. The study of autobiography, especially in the case of authors who published only autobiography, suffuses into biography and cultural studies as we move back and forth between the text and the life. Helen Buss, alluding to the autobiographer's "ritual re-enactment" of scenes from her life, suggests that autobiography is analogous to drama.[5] But Buss's drama analogy can be taken further, in that the writing, publication, and reception of the text transforms in real time the life that the text represents, especially in the case of writers for whom the publication of their autobiographies constituted a major life event.

In the early phases of efforts to legitimize women's autobiographical writing as a subject of study Joanna Russ suggested that most women's texts, not just their autobiographies, had long been seen as oddities unsuited for serious consideration. In a vicious circle, the invisibility of women's literary history made women writers appear "bizarre, extraneous," thereby justifying their continued exclusion.[6] Russ went on to assert that the most "generous" response to those women not "ignored completely" was simply

"She's wonderful but where on earth did she come from?"[7] This reaction remains a particularly likely one to MacLane, Whiteley, and Harrison, who strike readers as having come from a literary and literal nowhere.

I was surprised, in linking these writers with better known ones—to women who compared to my three could be considered near canonical, to find repeatedly that those I looked to as context were considered anomalous too. *The Story of Mary Mac-Lane* is seen as an anachronism, and yet MacLane's Russian/ Parisian forebear is herself dubbed "abnormal," her journal "ahead of its time, as the Eiffel Tower was in 1889."[8] Austin and Hurston are two of the most prominent figures to whom I refer, and yet a biography of the former is entitled *Mary Austin: Song of a Maverick,* while the latter is described as "one of the most enigmatic and elusive figures in black American literary history."[9] Other women I turn to include Jean Stafford, Georgia O'Keeffe, Laura Gilpin, Laura Ingalls Wilder, Mourning Dove, Daisy Ashford, Hilda Conkling, Gene Stratton-Porter, Dorothy Scarborough, and Willa Cather—all at the edges of critical inquiry, with Cather the salient exception that proves the rule. Making a network for MacLane, Whiteley, and Harrison becomes a matter of making a network for many more. As we have seen, a maverick autobiography might better be defined not as an anomaly, but as a text that appears to be anomalous, as standing outside of any literary traditions. Beyond just rescuing a lost voice or two, making a network of investigations into maverick autobiographies can fill in more extensive blanks in literary history, especially women's history. In the process, we revise our own critical paradigms of what it means to a "women autobiographer" or "western," "child," or "black" writer. Through analyzing MacLane, Whiteley, and Harrison together, I make a case for a network of case studies. Demonstrating the value of the case study in this relational way is especially important in this era of "post-recovery" in women's studies, in which, perhaps as a backlash to the eighties' enthusiasm for recovery and the overwhelming number of primary texts excavated, the initial fervor for forgotten voices seems to have ebbed.

Although certainly not the case for all maverick autobiographers, the maverick identity of MacLane, Whiteley, and Harrison actually contributes to a remarkable number of shared characteristics. These early-twentieth-century writers were distant from social power due to factors of gender, geography, class, or race. They were neither "new women" with professional careers nor well-connected "ladies." Instead, they fashioned themselves and their texts into packages both fitting within and serving to establish one or more of the era's burgeoning mass-market niches. Their success as a group reflects the era's interest in the self-writings of regionally and otherwise marginal women. So too does the practice of the *Atlantic Monthly*, increasingly attuned to middle-brow tastes, to publish such women's stories. Together these writers illuminate the relationships among autobiography, gender, region, and early-twentieth-century print culture and celebrity, as they participate in and revise the romance of individualism that is so prominent in American literary history.

MacLane is a particularly significant figure in the history of American autobiography, inaugurating in the United States an arguably Continental autobiographical tradition as well as a new mode for women writing about their relationship to the American West. By virtue of aggressively contesting constructions of femininity and trumpeting her accomplishments, she stands at a crossroads in women's autobiography. Widely imitated, MacLane's texts helped popularize "naked-soul lady" texts, texts that laid bare the astonishing soul of an ordinary rather than a celebrated woman.

The initial enthusiasm for Whiteley's book testifies to and augmented the era's enthusiasm for the self-writings of little girls, which is related to "naked-soul lady" enthusiasm and can involve a similar prurience. Responses to *The Story of Opal* reveal how readers defined proper girlish writing, and indeed, proper girls. They also point to a prevalent desire that American regionalists triumph over provinciality: readers were proud of Whiteley and MacLane both because these Oregon and Montana women surpassed their European/non-regional counterparts, and because in doing so they surpassed their regions themselves.

Harrison participates in a kind of innocents-abroad travel genre of the 1930s. She vied with the globe-trotting Abbe children (*Around the World in Eleven Years*) for attention from the press, matching their youthful naiveté with the naiveté that white readers perceived as a function of her race.[10] Yet Harrison herself, a strong voice in non-protest African American literature, argues against racial essentialism. She demonstrates not only how the crossing of regional and national boundaries reconfigures racial ones, but also how writing one's own story challenges others' categories.

A writer's apparent eccentricity does not forbid critical conclusions. To the contrary, my experience with these mavericks leads me to conjecture that the more out of place a once best-selling writer may appear, the more she does not fit standard renditions of literary history, then the more cultural insights her text may offer. At the same time, as the previous chapters have shown, the "worth" of a writer is not simply equivalent to the number of such insights. That these mavericks provide them may be what is needed to justify their study, but once they are through that door, I hope there is room also to enjoy the richness of their texts, their power and creativity.

Questions of Region

At the end of this book, it should be clear that these mavericks wrote about very different Wests in very different texts — different both thematically and generically — in focusing on desire, on the natural world, and on travel in confession, diary, and letter. Yet it is their discontent and their determination for change that link MacLane, Whiteley, and Harrison as writers of western autobiography. Their texts are not records of public and professional achievement, starting with birth and ending with eminence. Instead, in ways both explicit and implicit, they record their dissatisfaction with their lives as they were in their places of origin and with the futures they anticipated there.

Unlike the subjects of so much western women's history, MacLane, Whiteley, and Harrison are not women who came *to* the West, but women who came *from* it (and sometimes returned) while continuing to name the region as home in some way. Even as they left western sites — Whiteley's native Oregon, MacLane's near-native Montana, and the Los Angeles and Hawaii to which Harrison came as a roving adult — these sites remained essential to their identities, to their private and public "fictions of selfhood." Western places fostered these women's sense of superiority — the very sense, ironically enough, that reinforced their belief that they were meant for elsewhere. In more material ways as well, these places helped procure them the means to leave home. In Los Angeles, Harrison found the white sponsors unlikely in her native Mississippi, who invested her savings to provide an annual travel income. Whiteley too found sponsors in southern California, who sent her east to solicit a publisher; the renown of her diary attracted fans who helped her travel to Europe and India. MacLane's account of Montana brought about a tour of eastern urban centers, initiating a peripatetic lifestyle funded by money from the book along with the freelance assignments it led to.

All three authors, both in their texts and outside of them, used the West's stature to augment their own. In Harrison's case, the images that excited those she met abroad came from the fictions the movie industry peddled even while as an African American woman she was fixed in white American readers' minds in stereo-typical ways associated with the South rather than with the West. MacLane and Whiteley's ties to western locales, in contrast, con-jured up romantic images of the white woman alone in remark-able natural settings, despite the fact that their texts record how "impure" these settings were, and how densely—often unpleas-antly—populated. Publishers and reviewers encouraged their western images, but only in a safe, generic way. The public, sub-sequently, was intrigued by the questions of whether their texts were authentic and whether the West could foster genius. Often, readers saw these writers not so much as indigenous phenomena than as western versions of other hailing from more cultured places. The coupling of Europe and the West appeared to have been particularly powerful, charging their narrators with glam-our and helping tilt the balance of the West's dual identity as rep-resentatively prosaic and exceptionally romantic. An evocation of self in relation to place made these women's books sell.

Leaving the West and the United States stands as the act that defined MacLane, Whiteley, and Harrison as westerners. This act encourages us to look for "westernness" in the absences in their texts and lives, in what is not written about and done, as much as in what is. These women do not revel in "regeneration though violence" or a "legacy of conquest." They do not look to myths of the frontier and celebrate Manifest Destiny, the van-quishing of the wilderness, and the establishing of new homes.

The western homes they already had are those they sought to escape, and it was for more urban eastern or European spaces that they yearned.

Nevertheless, these women do inscribe in their texts and lives the glorification of the individual and individual destiny that is a hallmark of western myth—as well as of much canonical autobiography. They delineate heroines who command not the wilderness but rather the admiration of those around them, most notably men in power who under other circumstances would not even be aware of their existence. For these women, the excess of the American West that in male texts is so often incarnated by violence, instead takes the form of supreme self-confidence and devotion to self.

Such devotion unsettled many they encountered. MacLane, Whiteley, and Harrison, indifferent to politics and little concerned with others' needs, are preoccupied with their own pleasure, experiences, or sensibility in ways that sometimes feel uncomfortably close to narcissism or even mania. Yet readers tempered the extremism they found by reading it as somehow representative and their authors as cultural types—the rebellious adolescent/ young woman, the otherworldly child, the sensual black woman. They saw in these extraordinary women reflections of the ordinary individuals around them, and indeed, of their own selves.

Notes

Works Cited

Index

Notes

Preface

1. Mary MacLane, *The Story of Mary MacLane, By Herself* (Chicago: Herbert S. Stone & Co., 1902); reprint Elisabeth Pruitt, ed., *Tender Darkness: A Mary MacLane Anthology* (Belmont, Calif.: Abernathy and Brown, 1993); MacLane, *I, Mary MacLane: A Diary of Human Days* (New York: Frederick A. Stokes, 1917); Opal Whiteley, *The Story of Opal: The Journal of an Understanding Heart* (Boston: Atlantic Monthly Press, 1920); reprint, with an introduction by Benjamin Hoff, *The Singing Creek Where the Willows Grow: The Mystical Nature Diary of Opal Whiteley* (New York: Penguin, 1994); Juanita Harrison, *My Great, Wide, Beautiful World* (New York: Macmillan, 1936); reprint, with an introduction by Adele Logan Alexander (New York: G. K. Hall and Co., 1996). All citations are from reprints.

2. Sidonie Smith, *A Poetics of Women's Autobiography: Marginality and the Fictions of Self-Representation* (Bloomington: Indiana University Press, 1987), 50.

3. *Outlook* 126 (May 9, 1920): 201.

4. Patricia Meyers Spacks's discussion of MacLane is one such exception. In *The Female Imagination* (New York: Alfred A. Knopf, 1975), Spacks compares MacLane's work with the diaries of Isadora Duncan, Margaret Anderson, Marie Bashkirtseff, and others. She reads MacLane as, ultimately, "pathetic," a spinner of cobwebs who chooses "fantasy over reality" (219–31). Likewise, with "Anastasia of Oregon" Blake Allmendinger offers an important, although limited, analysis of Whiteley's text (*Arizona Quarterly* 51.1 [Spring 1995]: 111–32).

5. Judith Fetterley, "Commentary: Nineteenth-Century American Women Writers and the Politics of Recovery," *American Literary History* 69.3 (1994): 602.

6. See Suzanne L. Bunkers and Cynthia A. Huff, who argue that "diaries beg us to define what we mean by aesthetics . . . to question what the qualities and politics of literary inclusion and exclusion involve" ("Issues in Studying Women's Diaries: A Theoretical and Critical Introduction" in *Inscribing the Daily: Critical Essays on Women's Diaries,* ed. Suzanne L. Bunkers and Cynthia A. Huff [Amherst: University of Massachusetts Press, 1996], 2).

7. Fetterley, "Commentary," 606–7.

Introduction

1. See William Cronon, *Nature's Metropolis: Chicago and the Great West* (New York: Norton, 1992) and Lee Clark Mitchell, *Westerns: Making the Man in Fiction and Film* (Chicago: University of Chicago Press, 1996), 90.

2. Krista Comer, *Landscapes of the New West: Gender and Geography in Contemporary Women's Writing* (Chapel Hill: University of North Carolina Press, 1999), 28.

3. Ibid., 26.

4. Annette Kolodny, *The Land before Her: Fantasy and Experience of the American Frontiers, 1630–1860* (Chapel Hill: University of North Carolina Press, 1984), 3–13. For references to male fantasies of western landscapes, see Kolodny, *The Lay of the Land: Metaphor as Experience and History in American Life and Letters* (Chapel Hill: University of North Carolina Press, 1975).

5. See, for example, Elizabeth Ammons, *Conflicting Stories: American Women Writers at the Turn into the Twentieth Century* (New York: Oxford University Press, 1991).

6. Jean Stafford, *The Collected Stories of Jean Stafford* (New York: Farrar, Straus and Giroux, 1969), xi.

7. Brigitte Georgi-Findlay, *The Frontiers of Women's Writing: Women's Narratives and the Rhetoric of Westward Expansion* (Tucson: University of Arizona Press, 1996) and Susan J. Rosowski, *Birthing a Nation: Gender, Creativity, and the West in American Literature* (Lincoln: University of Nebraska Press, 1999). Georgi-Findlay works to dismantle romantic images of western women by demonstrating that their sex did not render them ideologically pure. She thereby provides a much needed supplement to Kolodny's work, as well as introduces other writers. She retains, though, a traditional western studies focus on frontiers and pioneers.

8. Earl S. Pomeroy, *In Search of the Golden West: The Tourist in Western America* (New York: Alfred A. Knopf, 1957), 65.

9. Georgi-Findlay, *Frontiers of Women's Writing,* 106.

10. In referring to an upcoming wilderness venture, Elizabeth Simcoe provides an eighteenth-century comment on this kind of seeming in-

congruity: "I quite enjoy the thoughts of the long journey we have before us . . . but the people here [in Lower Canada] think it as arduous & adventurous an undertaking as it was looked upon to be by my friends in England" (Helen Buss, *Mapping Our Selves: Canadian Women's Autobiography in English* [Montreal: McGill-Queen's University Press, 1993], 41).

11. Comer states, "To the extent that the urban and the postmodern (not to mention the Californian) are generally regarded in western criticism as antitheses of the 'real' West, African American peoples and cultural production habitually meet up with western geographical imaginations on the fringes of what constitutes western identity. (Might this hint at why western literary critics, unlike western historians, have written so little on black western writers?)" (*Landscapes*, 88–89.)

12. Ibid., 9.

13. Frederick Jackson Turner, *The Significance of the Frontier in American History*, 1893; reprint, ed. Harold P. Simonson (New York: Ungar, 1963), 92.

14. Regarding their aesthetic/class aspirations, my mavericks do, however, have male equivalents in upper-class white men such as Theodore Roosevelt and Owen Wister, easterners who so earnestly sought to remake themselves into cowboys.

15. These theories include the disproportionate amount of myth loaded onto the West; blindness in the face of the intense light of Turner's frontier thesis or, more recently, Wallace Stegner's "critical blueprint" (Comer, "Feminism, Women Writers, and the New Western Regionalism: Revising Critical Paradigms," in *Updating the Literary West* [Fort Worth: Texas Christian University Press, 1997], 20); the cordoning off of Native American and other so-called ethnic writers from white writers; the identity politics of squabbles over what the West is and who has the right to represent it.

16. Cited by Kathleen A. Boardman, "Western American Literature and the Canon," in *Updating the Literary West*, 66.

17. T. M. Pearce, ed., *Literary America, 1903–1934: The Mary Hunter Austin Letters* (Westport, Conn.: Greenwood, 1979), 202.

18. In his well-known study, Richard Brodhead discusses how many writers labeled regional hailed from outside the boundaries of their literary terrain, turning to region in order to launch their professional careers. *Cultures of Letters: Scenes of Reading and Writing in Nineteenth-Century America* (Chicago: University of Chicago Press, 1993).

19. Willa Cather, *The Song of the Lark* (Boston: Houghton Mifflin Co., 1915).

20. Ibid., 235.

21. Mourning Dove, *Cogewea: The Half-Blood: A Depiction of the Great Montana Cattle Range* (Boston: Four Seas Co., 1927); reprint, with an

introduction by Dexter Fisher (Lincoln: University of Nebraska Press, 1981).

22. See Patricia Nelson Limerick, *The Legacy of Conquest: The Unbroken Past of the American West* (New York: Norton, 1987).

23. Elizabeth Duvert, "With Stone, Star, and Earth: The Presence of the Archaic in the Landscape Visions of Georgia O'Keeffe, Nancy Holt, and Michelle Stuart" in *The Desert is No Lady: Southwestern Landscapes in Women's Writing and Art*, ed. Janice Monk and Vera Norwood (New Haven: Yale University Press, 1987), 201.

24. In 1891 alone, approximately 18,000 wagons crossed the Missouri River from Nebraska to Iowa (Larzer Ziff, *The American 1890s: Life and Times of a Lost Generation* [New York: Viking, 1966], 79). Howard R. Lamar states in "The Unsettling of the West: The Mobility of Defeat" that "the unsettlement of the American West appears to be an even more profound event than its initial settlement" (*Crossing Frontiers: Papers on American and Canadian Western Literature*, ed. Dick Harrison [Edmonton: University of Alberta Press, 1979], 47). Yet, so discordant with cherished notions of American history, this "unsettlement" largely has been ignored, just as has the return of U.S. immigrants to their home countries.

25. Stafford, *The Collected Stories of Jean Stafford*, 299.

26. Carl Van Doren, *Contemporary American Novelists 1900–1920* (New York: Macmillan, 1922), 153. Van Doren cites the work of Edgar Lee Masters, Sherwood Anderson, E. W. Howe, Sinclair Lewis, Zona Gale, and Floyd Dell.

27. Melody Graulich, "'O Beautiful for Spacious Guys': An Essay on the 'Legitimate Inclinations of the Sexes,'" in *The Frontier Experience and the American Dream: Essays on American Literature*, ed. David Mogen, Mark Busby, Paul Bryant (College Station: Texas A & M University Press, 1989), 189.

28. Mary Austin, *Earth Horizon: Autobiography* (Boston: Houghton Mifflin, 1932), 191, 199.

29. See my "Redefining The Frontier: Mourning Dove's *Cogewea, The Half-Blood,*" *American Indian Culture and Research Journal* 21.4 (1997): 105–24.

30. Susan J. Rosowski notes that even Cather, known for her evocations of a western past, associates only her male, not female, characters with western nostalgia. "Writing against Silences: Female Adolescent Development in the Novels of Willa Cather," *Studies in the Novel* 21.1 (Spring 1989): 62.

31. Pomeroy, *In Search of the Golden West*, 85.

1. The Devil and Desire in Butte, Montana

1. George H. Doran, *Chronicles of Barabbas: 1884–1934* (New York: Harcourt, Brace and Co., 1935), 30–31.

2. Mary MacLane, *I, Mary MacLane: A Diary of Human Days* (New York: Frederick A. Stokes, 1917), hereafter cited as *IMM*.

3. Cited by Smith, *Subjectivity, Identity, and the Body: Women's Autobiographical Practices in the Twentieth Century* (Bloomington: Indiana University Press, 1993), 84.

4. Elaine Showalter, *Sister's Choice: Tradition and Change in American Women's Writing* (Oxford: Clarendon Press, 1991), 69.

5. Helen Beal Woodward, "Dear Diary—Will Secret Scribblings Bring Fame to a New Marie Bashkirtseff or Mary MacLane?" *Mademoiselle* (April 1943): 155.

6. Her family, working against the writer's resolve to reveal her inmost self, edited the journal with the end of portraying Bashkirtseff in the most girlish light possible. They purged the diary of most of her references to her sexuality and of all to her involvement with a women's rights group; they also changed the ages so that in each entry Bashkirtseff appears two years younger than she actually was (Rozsika Parker and Griselda Pollock, introduction to *The Journal of Marie Bashkirtseff*, by Marie Bashkirtseff, trans. Mathilde Blind (London: Virago, 1985), xi–xiv.

7. Bernard Shaw, "The Womanly Woman," in *The Quintessence of Ibsenism* (New York: Brentano's, 1922), 34, 36.

8. Respectively, Parker and Pollock, introduction to *The Journal of Marie Bashkirtseff*, vii; William Gladstone, "Journal de Marie Bashkirtseff," *The Nineteenth Century* 26 (1889): 606; *New York Times*, February 26, 1922, sec. 2, 5:1. Gladstone stated, "Marie Bashkirtseff reminds me powerfully of the ruins of Selinunti, which are unlike any other ruins I ever saw. The temple is so shattered that it may be said to be reduced to a mass of single stones: but every stone by itself is majestic."

9. Parker and Pollock, introduction to *The Journal of Marie Bashkirtseff*, vii.

10. Phillipe Lejeune, "The 'Journal de Jeune Fille' in Nineteenth-Century France," trans. Martine Breillac, in *Inscribing the Daily: Critical Essays on Women's Diaries*, 115. Lejeune shows how Bashkirtseff's feminism, self-analysis, and interest in the process of writing distinguish her diary from those of her predecessors. Growing up in the midst of a culture of writing and marketing girls' diaries, however, may well have deeply influenced Bashkirtseff, in addition to the better known men's publications to which her work is usually compared.

11. H. Porter Abbott, *Diary Fiction: Writing as Action* (Ithaca: Cornell University Press, 1984), 32.

12. Cinthia Gannett, *Gender and the Journal: Diaries and Academic Discourse* (Albany: State University of New York Press, 1992), 118.

13. Woodward, "Dear Diary," 155.

14. *New York Times,* February 26, 1922, sec. 2, 5:1.

15. George Egerton, *Keynotes & Discords* (London: Elkin Mathews and John Lane, 1893, 1894); reprint, with an introduction by Martha Vicinus (London: Virago, 1983), 58.

16. Mark Twain, *Eve's Diary, translated from the original MS,* illustrated by Lester Ralph (New York: Harper and Brothers, 1906), 25. First excerpted in *Harper's Monthly Magazine* 112 (December 1905): 25–32. Reprints of the diaries of girls or young women long since dead, such as *Journal of Emily Shore* and *The Diary of Anna Green Winslow,* were also common.

17. Barry Pain, *Another Englishwoman's Love-Letters* (G. P. Putnam's Sons, 1901), v.

18. Ann L. Ardis, "Mary Cholmondeley's Red Pottage" in *Writing the Woman Artist: Essays on Poetics, Politics, and Portraiture,* ed. Suzanne W. Jones (Philadelphia: University of Pennsylvania Press, 1991), 336.

19. *St. Louis Mirror,* cited in "A Montana Marie Bashkirtseff," *Literary Digest* 25.4 (1902): 99.

20. "The Worst Yet: Here Is a Book that Makes All other Bad Books Respectable by Comparison," *Detroit Free Press,* June 7, 1902, 11.

21. Miss Morning Glory [Yone Noguchi], "The American Diary of a Japanese Girl," *Frank Leslie's Popular Monthly* 53.1 (1901), 99. In this little known text, described by Edward Marx as either "the first Japanese-American novel" or simply "the first English novel by a Japanese published in America" ("The 'Miss Morning Glory' Novels of Yone Noguchi at One Hundred," MLA conference presentation, 2001), Noguchi works to replicate the feminine self-absorption claimed of the "American Diary." Marx notes that Noguchi's allusion in his correspondence to Bashkirtseff's *Last Diary* suggests he may well have read her better-known *Journal.* The participation of this male Japanese poet points to the degree of masquerade endemic to the "naked-soul lady" genre, so contrary to its claims to naked revelation.

22. Carmen Callil, introduction to Miles Franklin, *My Brilliant Career* (London: Virago, 1981). Franklin's text opens, "MY DEAR FELLOW AUSTRALIANS, Just a few lines to tell you that this story is all about myself — for no other purpose do I write it."

23. Respectively, *Syracuse Herald,* cited in "'Our Mary' Abroad," clipping in Butte–Silver Bow Public Archives, n.d.; "A Montana Bashkirtseff," *Literary Digest* 25.4 (1902): 99; H. L. Mencken, "The Butte Bash-

kirtseff," *Prejudices: First Series* (New York: Alfred A Knopf, 1919), 124; R. V. Risley, "The Story of Mary MacLane," *The Reader: An Illustrated Monthly Magazine of Literature* 1 (November 1902): 97. "The Harvest Begun: The Story of Mary McLane [*sic*] Drives Young Girl to Suicide in Kalamazoo, Michigan," *Butte Tribune-Review,* May 17, 1902; "'The Story of Mary MacLane, By Herself': A Very Remarkable Book that Has Just Come out of Chicago — A Montana Girl Who, a la Bashkirtseff, Declares Herself a Genius," *New York World,* April 27, 1902, Sunday magazine, 1; review, *Publisher's Weekly* 61 (January–June 1902): 1349; *Academy & Literature Fiction Supplement to The Times* 63 (1902): 502; "List of New Books and Reprints," *London Times Literary Supplement,* November 7, 1902, 335; "Strangest Book Yet," *Washington Post,* May 11, 1902.

24. "Mary MacLane, Author, Found Dead," *New York Times,* August 8, 1929, 25. Similarly, Ishbel Ross casually referred to MacLane as "having written one of the early confession books" (*Ladies of the Press: The Story of Women in Journalism by an Insider* [New York: Harper and Brothers, 1936], 419) and *The Chicagoan* asserted that MacLane, "an errant daughter of literature, whose collected writings might easily be given the title Memoirs of my Libido, was the first of the self-expressionists, and also the first of the flappers" (August 31, 1929, obituary, n.t.).

25. "The Story of Mary MacLane," *The Literary World: A Monthly Review of Current Literature* 33 (1902–3): 102.

26. Barbara Miller, "'Hot as Live Embers — Cold as Hail': The Restless Soul of Butte's Mary MacLane," *Montana Magazine* (April–October 1982): 51.

27. Leslie A. Wheeler, "Montana's Shocking 'Lit'ry Lady,'" *Montana Magazine* (Summer 1977): 23.

28. Gertrude Atherton, *Adventures of a Novelist* (New York: Liveright, 1932), 491.

29. Phil Lipson, "Mary MacLane Bibliography," c. 1970s (unpublished; Butte–Silver Bow Public Archives).

30. "Butte Authoress Dies in Chicago after Operation," *Montana Standard,* August 7, 1929, 2.

31. Ziff, *The American 1890s,* 135.

32. "The success of the 'Chap Book,'" according to Gelett Burgess, "incited the little riot of Decadence, and there was a craze for odd sizes and shapes, freak illustrations, wide margins, uncut pages. . . . The movement asserted itself as a revolt against the commonplace" (Wendy Clauson Schlereth, *The Chap-Book: A Journal of American Intellectual Life in the 1890s* [Ann Arbor: University of Michigan Research Press, 1982], 5).

33. Emily Toth, *Unveiling Kate Chopin* (Jackson: University of Mississippi Press, 1999), 219; Wheeler, "Montana's Shocking 'Lit'ry Lady,'" 24.

34. Pruitt, *Tender Darkness,* 191.

35. MacLane was not pleased, stating, "I confess that I was annoyed on learning that your title for my Ms. had been retained. I do not fancy that title at all. . . . However, it is a trivial matter, and since your judgment and experience in such things must be superior to mine, I let it pass,—particularly as there is no help for it in any case" (MacLane to Herbert S. Stone & Co., April 22, 1902, Newberry).

36. "Chronicle and Comment," *Bookman* (April 1902): 115.

37. According to "A Montana Marie Bashkirtseff" and *Great Falls Daily Tribune*, May 4, 1902, 10.

38. Wallace Goldsmith's *The Foolish Dictionary* (1904) defines the devil as "An old rascal mentioned in the Bible, now reported engaged to Mary MacLane" (cited by Penelope Rosemont, "Marvelous Mary MacLane" in *Free Spirits: Annals of the Insurgent Imagination,* ed. Paul Buhle et al. [San Francisco: City Lights Books, 1982], 33).

39. MacLane responded, "Things will be real bad with little Mary MacLane when she goes on the stage. I prefer scrubbing, smelters and sand" ("Ho For New Yor-r-k! Now Says Mary MacLane: Montana Maid, Coming Here, is 'Almost Afraid,' She Doesn't Know Why," *New York World,* July 16, 1902, 2).

40. Mrs. T. D. McKown, *The Devil's Letters to Mary MacLane, By Himself* (Chicago: Interstate Book Co., 1903), incorrectly cataloged by the Library of Congress as written by MacLane herself; Robert T. Shores, *The Story of Willie Complain* (Butte: Intermountain Publishing Co., 1902); *Anaconda Standard,* May 4, 1902.

41. Newspaper clipping in Butte–Silver Bow Public Archives, n.t, n.d.

42. "Mary MacLane Busts Home Ties," *New York World,* July 8, 1903, 3; *Butte Intermountain,* May 16, 1902, 4.

43. Johann Wolfgang von Goethe, *The Sorrows of Young Werther,* trans. William Rose (London: Scholartis Press, 1929), xxxv–vi.

44. Frank Luther Mott, *Golden Multitudes: The Story of Best-Sellers in the United States* (New York: Macmillan, 1947), 183. Ziff likewise notes the era's "rage for personality" (*The American 1890s,* 135–36).

45. "Literary Chat," *Munsey's Magazine* 27 (1902): 167. We do not as yet have theories that fully account for such turn of the century fevers, making investigation of celebrity authors like MacLane all the more illustrative.

46. Ibid., 189.

47. Ibid., 167. Some books, this writer continued, even included a "detachable coupon." The era is also noted for the widespread practice of "book-booming" through quoting the praise of celebrities (282).

48. "Mary MacLane Busts Home Ties," *New York World,* July 8, 1903, 3.

49. "Mary MacLane Slips into Boston—Dodged All the Reporters

and Camera Sharps on the Trip," *New York World*, July 21, 1902, 4; Mac-
Lane to Stone, July 1902, Newberry.

50. MacLane explained, "I shall grant an interview wherever I can
see that it will be an advantage to the book, but I shall try to avoid anything like mere cheap notoriety and sensationalism which can only de-
tract from it. I think the best possible advertisement for it would be a se-
vere criticism in the 'Bookman' or 'Book-buyer' or some equally well
known reviewer. I believe if any of them could be persuaded to review
it at length, my book would be fairly started on a career of sorts. An ex-
haustive criticism and an attractive binding must need go far toward the
success of any book" (MacLane to Herbert S. Stone & Co., April 22, 1902,
Newberry). Similarly, she parceled out interviews to more reputable papers while noting, "Nothing will induce me to see a reporter from the
Post, or from any paper of that ilk" (MacLane to Stone, July 1902, Newberry). MacLane also agreed to a paperback edition of *The Story* despite
the tawdry associations paperbacks held for her (MacLane to Stone, Autumn 1902, Newberry).

51. "Echoes of Mary MacLane—More Letters from World Readers,"
New York World, October 12, 1902, 8. The *World* solicited these letters in a
survey entitled "What Do You Think of Mary MacLane?" and printed
them over the course of three Sundays, claiming, "Although it is four
weeks since the last article was published, letters are still arriving in extraordinary numbers from readers of the magazine giving their opinions
of her work and her abilities and her promise of future success. . . . These
letters are coming from every part of the United States and even from
Canada and other countries." Similar responses were published in Chicago, where "the book stores prominently display her book, specimens
of her handwriting and her photograph, while the newspapers of that
city throw open their columns for communications from their readers
discussing her ability, her character, and her future in literature" (*Butte
Intermountain*, June 12, 1902, 4).

52. "A Montana Marie Bashkirtseff," 99.

53. *Fergus Falls (Minnesota) Daily Journal*, August 14, 1929.

54. MacLane to Monroe, October 23, 1902, University of Chicago.

55. August Derleth, *Still, Small Voice: The Biography of Zona Gale* (New
York: Appleton-Century, 1940), 59 and Zona Gale, "The Real Mary
MacLane," *New York World*, August 17, 1902, Sunday magazine, 1–2.
Protesting a widespread evaluation of *The Story*, that it "reveal[ed] a
strong impress of Whitman" ("Odd Book By a Girl," *Chicago Record-
Herald*, April 26, 1902), an *Evening Post* review stated, "It is a pity that
Mr. Gladstone, who first floated Marie Bashkirtseff into notoriety, is
not living, for Mary is thus deprived of a most sympathetic supporter
and warm admirer. As for the rest of us, we must do what we can to gulp

down Mary's incoherent ramblings and try to believe that a female Whitman has arisen" (Roswell Field, "Lights and Shadows," *Evening Post*, April 26, 1902). Similarly, a poem about MacLane queried, "Have you heard about Mary MacLane?/So vain!/Who comes from Montana's dry plain/No rain!/She has written a book,/Which the same it has 'took,'/. . . . Whitman's not in it/No, not for a minute/With the toughness of Mary MacLane/Unclane!" ("Have You Heard About Mary Mac-Lane?" newspaper clipping, n.d., Newberry).

56. Hamlin Garland, *Companions on the Trail: A Literary Chronicle (1900–1914)* (New York: MacMillan, 1931), 147; H. L. Mencken, "The Cult of Dunsany," *Smart Set* (July 1917): 138.

57. Atherton, *Adventures of a Novelist*, 491. MacLane concurred with the praise: "I think my style of writing has a wonderful intimacy in it, and it is admirably suited to the creature it portrays. What sort of Portrayal of myself would I produce if I wrote with the long elaborate periods of Henry James, or with the pleasant ladylike phrasing of Howells? It would be rather like a little tin phonograph trolling out flowery poetry at breakneck speed, or like a deep-toned church organ pouring forth 'Goo-Goo Eyes' with ponderous feeling" (*The Story of Mary MacLane*, 44).

58. *Wid's Daily*, January 17, 1918, 873.

59. Mencken, "The Butte Bashkirtseff," 123.

60. "Our Peculiar Mary MacLane," *Butte Miner*, May 1, 1902, 5.

61. Lionel Johnson, "Marie Bashkirtseff," in *Post Liminium: Essays and Critical Papers by Lionel Johnson*, ed. Thomas Whittemore (London: Ellkin Mathews, 1911), 249.

62. Respectively, "The Story of Mary MacLane," *Literary World*, 102; "The Worst Yet," *Detroit Free Press*, June 7, 1902, 11; *Academy & Literature Fiction Supplement to The Times* 63 (1902): 502.

63. Mary Cass Canfield, "Mary MacLane and the Apparent Agonies of Introspective Pathology," *Vanity Fair* (June 1917). Perhaps it is remarks such as these that have led to unsubstantiated claims that MacLane influenced Gertrude Stein.

64. Peter Chapin, "The Devilish Mary MacLane," *Montana Standard*, June 6, 1981, 2.

65. John Paul [Charles Henry Webb], "A Young Messalina Out of the West?" *New York Times*, May 10, 1902, 4.

66. "Strangest Book Yet," *Washington Post*, May 11, 1902.

67. "What They Think of Mary MacLane," *New York World*, September 28, 1902, Sunday magazine, 5.

68. Paul, "A Young Messalina Out of the West," 4.

69. *Critic* 51 (1902), 7.

70. John D. Dorst, "Short Excursions," *Looking West* (Philadelphia: University of Pennsylvania Press, 1999).

71. "The Story of Mary MacLane," *Literary World*, 102.

72. "A Montana Marie Bashkirtseff," 99.

73. "The Worst Yet," *Detroit Free Press*, June 7, 1902, 11.

74. *Butte Miner*, May 1, 1902.

75. Canfield, "Mary MacLane."

76. "Cleverness," *Atlantic Monthly* (December 1902): 852. Professing concern for "our present responsiveness to an irregular and decadent cleverness," Boynton continues on to suggest that MacLane influenced the work of professionals in alluding to "later books which express a similar condition of morbid sensibility. More than one of them have appeared in well-known magazines, and are the work of experienced writers" (853).

77. Chapin, "The Devilish Mary MacLane," 2.

78. Madge Merton [pseud.], *Confessions of a Chorus Girl* (New York: Grafton Press), 14, 20.

79. "She's a Genius of Poetic Woe: New York Produces a Composer that Beats Butte's Wonder a Block," *New York World*, July 15, 1902, 5.

80. "'Our Mary' Talkative," *Butte Intermountain*, May 24, 1902, 5. Zona Gale noted that while she interviewed MacLane at the "Anemone Lady's" home in Cambridge, "Outside the window a group of curious girls stood, pointing out the house" ("The Real Mary MacLane," *New York World*, August 17, 1902, 1–2).

81. Fanny Butcher, "Mary MacLane Pops up Again, Ego Oozing Out," *Chicago Sunday Tribune*, May 6, 1917.

82. "Eloise Larsen of Chicago, Victim of MacLaneism—Head of Local Mary MacLane Society Arrested for Stealing a Horse," *Butte Intermountain*, December 4, 1902, 10.

83. "The Harvest Begun," *Butte Tribune-Review*, May 17, 1902. Another suicide attempt, of a Denver girl, was reported (*Butte Intermountain*, May 24, 1902).

84. Woodward, "Dear Diary," 155.

85. *Chicagoan*, August 31, 1929.

86. Carolyn G. Heilbrun, "Non-Autobiographies of 'Privileged' Women: England and America" in *Life/Lines: Theorizing Women's Autobiography*, ed. Bella Brodzki and Celeste Schenck (Ithaca: Cornell University Press, 1988), 65.

87. Heilbrun, *Writing a Woman's Life* (New York: Norton, 1988), 37.

88. Nancy K. Miller, *The Heroine's Text; Readings in the French and English Novel, 1722–1782* (New York: Columbia University Press, 1980), ix–x, cited by Ann Romines, *The Home Plot: Women, Writing, and Domestic Ritual* (Amherst: University of Massachusetts Press, 1992), 7.

89. "'Our Mary' Talkative," *Butte Intermountain*, May 24, 1902, 5.

90. Ibid.

91. Dorst, *Looking West,* 28.

92. Robert Murray Davis, *Playing Cowboy: Low Culture and High Art in the Western* (Norman: University of Oklahoma Press, 1992), xix.

93. "Mary Elizabeth MacLane," *Great Falls Tribune,* May 4, 1902, 10.

94. "Mary MacLane, Former Fergus Falls Writer, Dies," *Fergus Falls (Minnesota) Daily Journal,* August 7, 1929, 1.

95. Carolyn J. Mattern, "Mary MacLane: A Feminist Opinion," *Montana: The Magazine of Western History* (Autumn 1977): 58. Mattern refers to a letter she received from Jane Joyce, MacLane's niece.

96. MacLane additionally seeks to shock in stating, "I have brothers and a sister and a mother in the same house with me — and I find myself somewhat alone. . . . Would it affect me in the least — do you suppose — if they should all die tomorrow?" (*The Story of Mary MacLane,* 25)

97. This invocation of Scottish Highlands may also be a marker of MacLane's little noted Canadianness; see Katie Trumpener, *Bardic Nationalism: The Romantic Novel and the British* (Princeton: Princeton University Press, 1997). Except for the occasional Canadian or Minnesotan journalist, few emphasize that MacLane was born in Canada and grew up in Minnesota, although MacLane herself did. (*The Story of Mary MacLane,* 14, 35–36) Montana trumps Manitoba and Minnesota.

98. Julia Watson, "Engendering Montana Lives: Women's Autobiographical Writing," in *Writing Montana: Literature under the Big Sky,* ed. Rick Newby and Suzanne Hunger (Helena: Montana Center for the Book, 1996), 140.

99. My reading here has been influenced by Sidonie Smith's discussion of Annie Dillard's *American Childhood.* Dillard uses the trope of skin, Smith points out, in describing her childhood roamings in Pittsburgh, a city that, like MacLane's Butte, is blue-collar and industrial but nevertheless offers its narrator a primarily suburban, white-washed experience: "This narrative skin, identified with the position of universal subject, reveals its normative whiteness and thus its neutralizing identity practices. . . . What permeates Dillard's metaphor of skin is the comfort of the white skin if not the female skin, the natural and expected fit between skin and neighborhood" (*Subjectivity, Identity, and the Body,* 138).

100. MacLane to Stone, January 19, 1909, University of Chicago.

101. Written in January 1909 for the *New York Evening Journal,* unpublished, Newberry.

102. Earl Pomeroy summarizes the reactions of late-nineteenth-century travelers: "'What a tremendous old stoneyard'. . . . 'repulsive to the eye'. . . . 'If her wealth consisted in the beauty of her external appearances, then she truly would be one of the poorest countries on the face of nature'" (*In Search of the Golden West,* 62).

103. Including John Charles Van Dyke's *The Desert* (1901); Austin's

Land of Little Rain (1903); Arthur J. Burdick's *The Mystic Mid-Region;* George Wharton James's *The Wonders of the Colorado Desert* (1906), Frank Norris' *The Octopus* (1901). Kevin Starr, *America and the California Dream: 1850–1915* (New York: Oxford University Press, 1973), 385.

104. "Mary by 'Devil' Meant Ideal," *New York World,* July 22, 1902, 8.

105. The pairing of Fanny and the devil recalls MacLane's claim that two pictures of Bashkirtseff and seventeen of Napoleon adorn her bedroom wall. Of the Napoleon pictures, she writes. "In one he is ugly and unattractive—and strong. I fall in love with him. In another he is cruel and heartless and utterly selfish—and strong. I fall in love with him. In a third he has a fat, pudgy look, and is quite insignificant—and strong. I fall in love with him" *(The Story of Mary MacLane,* 253). "Judging from biographies in popular magazines of the 1890s," Peter Gabriel Filene remarks, "A cult of Napoleon had seized the middle-class imagination. . . . as a model of individualistic success" (*Him/Her/Self: Sex Roles in Modern America* [New York: Harcourt Brace Jovanovich, 1974], 80). Napoleon appears to have especially intrigued young women for whom their gender blocked such pursuit; both Bashkirtseff and MacLane invoke him, as does Cather's Thea Kronborg.

106. Dorst, *Looking West,* 16.

107. Jonathan Goldberg, "Photographic Relations: Laura Gilpin, Willa Cather," *American Literature* 70.1 (March 1998): 69–70.

2. After *The Story of Mary MacLane*

1. Georgi-Findlay, *Frontiers of Women's Writing,* 288.

2. Cited by Graulich, "'O Beautiful,'" 192.

3. Kolodny, *The Lay of the Land: Metaphor as Experience and History in American Life and Letters* (Chapel Hill: University of North Carolina Press, 1975).

4. Austin, for example, asserts, "If the desert were a woman, I know well what like she would be: deep-breasted, broad in the hips, tawny, with tawny hair, great masses of it lying smooth along her perfect curves, full lipped like a sphinx" (*Stories from the Country of Lost Borders,* ed. Marjorie Pryse [New Brunswick: Rutgers University Press, 1987], 160). Pryse points out that the language Austin uses to describe the desert resembles the language she uses to describe her own self.

5. Comer, "Revising Critical Paradigms," *Updating the Literary West,* 31.

6. Mitchell, *Westerns,* 133.

7. Consider, for example, Zane Grey's *Riders of the Purple Sage* (New York: Grosset & Dunlap, 1912), in which Bern Venters metamorphoses from a shrinking outcast into a bloodthirsty he-man; or *The Rainbow Trail:* "The desert had transformed Shefford. The elements had entered

into his muscle and bone, into the very fiber of his heart. Sun, wind, sand, cold, storm, space, stone . . . these were as if they had been melted and merged together and now made a dark and passionate stream that was his throbbing blood" (*The Rainbow Trail: A Romance* [New York: Grosset and Dunlap, 1920]).

8. Similarly, in Stafford's *The Mountain Lion* (New York: Harcourt, Brace and Company, 1947), Molly blends in with her environment while her brother, her near twin, hunts for blood. Gripped by mining fever, the white men in Austin's desert sketches deteriorate into monomaniacs, whereas the desert enables the essential selves of her white women characters to emerge. Likewise, Cather's male characters do not mature gradually (as Thea does), but instead violently pass from one life stage to another (Rosowski, "Writing against Silences," 62).

9. Such an aesthetic is well encapsulated in the title of Ella Rhoads Higginson's 1897 story, "A Passion-Flower of the West," with its Indian maiden connotations. Its heroine rejects marriage in order to "stay out till midnight to hear the wind in the trees or the tide comin' up the beach" (*A Forest Orchid And Other Stories* [New York: MacMillan, 1897], cited by Susan Goodman, "Legacy Profile: Ella Rhoads Higginson, c. 1862–1940," *Legacy* 6.1 [1989]: 61).

10. Terry Tempest Williams, "In Cahoots with Coyote," in *From the Faraway Nearby: Georgia O'Keeffe as Icon*, ed. Christopher Merril and Ellen Bradbury (Albuquerque: University of New Mexico Press, 1998), 181.

11. Ibid., 184.

12. We might reflect here on another kind of rewriting, in considering Comer's suggestion that the work of Chicana and Native American writers is a source of the current boom in white female western writers. "Revising Critical Paradigms," *Updating the Literary West*, 19.

13. Martha Sandweiss, *Laura Gilpin: An Enduring Grace* (Fort Worth: A. Carter Museum), 62. Gilpin herself saw affinities between her work and Cather's, and had hoped to collaborate with Cather on an illustrated edition of *The Professor's House* (66).

14. For example, in *Stories from the Country of Lost Borders* Austin portrays both her narrator and the white Walking Woman as able to safely enter even the roughest of camps, in implicit contrast to the Indian girls she refers to, who kill themselves after being raped in the desert by white settlers (256).

Like MacLane, white western women sometimes represented ravaged landscapes as reflecting their own sufferings. Yet such a claim of victimhood suggests an evasion of responsibility: genocide and environmental destruction is perpetrated by others, not by them. Kolodny argues that nineteenth-century western women "avoided male anguish at lost Edens and male guilt in the face of the raping of the continent by confining themselves, instead, to the innocent . . . amusement of a garden's narrow space" (*The Land before Her*, 7). Likewise, some of their heirs "confined" their interest not to the garden but to the self. The land is central to their identity but secondary in their concerns.

15. I have borrowed these phrases from Francis Edward Abernethy, ed., *Legendary Ladies of Texas* (Dallas: E-Heart Press, 1981) and Patricia Maida, "Wild Woman of the West: A Study of the Female Image in Selected Novels," *CEA Magazine* 7.1 (Fall 1994): 21–30.

16. See, for example, Earl S. Pomeroy, "Toward a Reorientation of Western History: Continuity and Environment," *Mississippi Valley Historical Review* 41 (1955): 579–600.

17. Gertrude Atherton, *Perch of the Devil* (New York: Frederick A. Stokes, 1914). See also Mary Murphy, *Mining Cultures: Men, Women, and Leisure in Butte, 1914–41* (Urbana: University of Illinois Press, 1997), 76.

18. Romines, *Constructing the Little House*, 55.

19. Ibid., 147.

20. Austin, *Earth Horizon*, 16.

21. Murphy, *Mining Cultures*, 20–21.

22. *Butte Miner*, June 3, 1899, cited by Mattern, "Mary MacLane," 57.

23. Miller, "'Hot as Live Embers,'" 51.

24. Paul, "A Young Messalina Out of the West?" 314.

25. Garland, *Companions on the Trail*, 147.

26. Henry Tyrrel, *Christian Science Monitor*, 1917, cited by Barbara Buhler Lynes, *O'Keeffe, Stieglitz and the Critics, 1916–29* (Ann Arbor: University of Michigan Research Press, 1989), 167–68.

27. Lynes, *O'Keeffe, Stieglitz and the Critics*, 78, 170, 105.

28. *Canadian Press*, cited in "Mary MacLane, Found Dead," *New York Times*, August 8, 1929, 25.

29. "Odd Book by a Girl,"*Chicago Record-Herald*, April 26, 1902, 11.

30. "Prof. Triggs Enthuses over Mary MacLane: He Declares a Book such as the One Written by Her Could Never Have Been Written by an Eastern Woman, and He Is Right," *New York World*, June 28, 1902, 7. Concurring with Triggs, a reader stated "Those that say aught against [MacLane] do not understand the child of nature. What of the free native influence brought to bear on this child? . . . She is slightly poetic; she is thoroughly saturated with the air and aroma of Butte-Montana, and must feel like a captured bird in New York. . . . Mary MacLane has a little shocking way of expressing herself that sounds like the wild and woolly West, but she is perfectly harmless" (Fannie Lloyd, "What They Think about Mary MacLane," *New York World*, Sunday magazine, September 21, 1902, 10).

31. Mencken, "The Butte Bashkirtseff," 124.

32. Waino Nyland, *A Famous Mining Camp in Literature*, c. 1926, unpublished manuscript in Butte–Silver Bow Public Archives, 5. Similarly naming Butte a "camp," a 1929 *Overland Monthly* retrospective described the city as "peopled with an *olla podrida* — an outré mixture of dull midwestern morals and lawless paganism" (Ada Page, "Mary Goes Back to Sand and Barrenness," *Overland Monthly* 87 [November 1929]: 345).

33. "Prof. Triggs," *New York World*, June 28 1902, 7.

34. Wheeler, "Montana's Shocking 'Lit'ry Lady,'" 25.

35. Taking an offensive defense, the Butte newspaper went on to suggest that "the insane craving for sensationalism manifested by some of the eastern press in the case of this unfortunate Butte girl" revealed the East's own failings. *Butte Miner*, May 1 1902, cited by Wheeler, "Montana's Shocking 'Lit'ry Lady,'" 25.

36. *Montana Standard*, "Butte Authoress Dies in Chicago after Operation," August 7, 1929, 1. Other west-east regional digs include "It will be safe to bet that Mary MacLane will not be in Boston three weeks before she will change its spelling to Mae LacLayne" (*Denver Post*); "Mary MacLane says her language is 'just as pure as possible.' It may have been up to public expectation in Butte, but she should pack it in moth balls for a few weeks before introducing it into Boston" (*Denver Post*); "'Mary MacLane Busts Home Ties' is a headline in the New York World. Is it a typographical error or is the World trying to adopt for the moment the language of Butte as a delicate compliment to the literary phenomenon who has made that camp famous?" (*Minneapolis Tribune*). All cited in "'Our Mary' Abroad," newspaper clipping, n.d., Butte–Silver Bow Public Archives.

37. "Tell Ned that I think well of the plan to send Mary McLane to Europe. . . . [S. S. McClure] thought well of it and said he would syndicate her if desired" (Melville E. Stone Senior to "Mattie," memorandum, n.d., Newberry).

38. "Illness Ends Life of Mary MacLane: Author of Cheap Diaries Dies, Alone, in Cheap Hotel in Chicago: Once Toast of Nations," *Washington Post*, August 8, 1929, 4.

39. "Mary MacLane Busts Home Ties" *New York World*, July 8, 1902, 3.

40. "Look Out! Here comes the 'Anemone Lady,'—Also Mary MacLane," *New York World*, July 13, 1902, Sunday magazine, 7.

41. Harriet Monroe recalled, "The firm brought Mary from Butte to Chicago, and my sister and I invited her to stay awhile with us, without realizing what a real publicity siege would mean" (memorandum, n.d., University of Chicago).

42. "The temperature of literary Chicago was at 103 all the afternoon and this evening it was steadily rising. . . . 'Mary MacLane is coming!

Mary MacLane is coming!' go up the glad cries of the populace, for here in the literary centre of the Middle West Mary is appreciated to the full" ("Mary MacLane Busts Home Ties," 3). The *World* noted the following week, "Mary MacLane has scrubbed a Chicago kitchen. Another literary step forward for the Athens of the West" (Editorial comment, *New York World*, July 15, 1902, 6).

43. "Mary Will Skip New York," *New York World*, July 15, 1902, 1. The *World* continues, "Miss MacLane cannot secure any idea of the high order of civilization and culture of the East without visiting New York City."

44. MacLane, "Mary MacLane at Newport," *New York World*, August 24 1902, Sunday magazine, 1.

45. MacLane explained "'My English and my style are perfect. Hamlin Garland says I write perfect English. So why need I a course in literature? I will study chemistry'" ("Look Out!" *New York World*, July 13, 1902).

46. MacLane to Stone, July 1902, Newberry. She wrote to Stone that "Radcliffe is not superlatively anxious to receive Mary MacLane. . . . If you have some influence to use for me, it had better be used immediately." Of her rejection, the *Missoula Fruit-Grower* staunchly declared "[it] was no insult to Miss MacLane [but] rather an admission of the excessive stupidity which educated asses display upon the slightest provocation. . . . Miss MacLane needs no more education except that which can be secured by travel and observation" (July 25, 1902, 4).

47. "Mary by 'Devil' Meant 'Ideal,'" *New York World*, July 22 1902, 2.

48. "Mary MacLane to Go to Radcliffe College — Before Starting to School She will Visit New York with the 'Anemone Lady,'" *New York World*, July 1, 1902, 2.

49. Atherton, *Adventures of a Novelist*, 491.

50. Garland, *Companions on the Trail*, 5–6. In 1900 Garland himself had written "The Hustler," a story that gives a western miner's perspective of London. Garland remarked that the conceit quickly became hackneyed (13–14).

51. MacLane, "Mary MacLane at Newport," 1.

52. Gale, "The Real Mary MacLane," *New York World*. Even in her earliest high school editorial, MacLane had declared "I set down only the outside layer, because the inside is too good for you. Anyway, I want to keep it for myself" ("Look Out!"). In *I, Mary MacLane*, she lays out an elaborate theory of the relationship between lying and art, concluding of her book that "It is as if I have made a portrait not of Me, but of a Room I have just quitted" (317).

53. MacLane, *My Friend Annabel Lee* (Chicago: Herbert S. Stone & Co., 1903).

54. Shortly after *My Friend Annabel Lee* appeared, MacLane began a correspondence with the Japanese poet Yone Noguchi [Miss Morning Glory], author of *The American Diary of a Japanese Girl*. Her six letters to him are housed in the Keio University Mita Bungaku Library and are reproduced in Yone Noguchi, *Collected English Letters*, ed. Ikuko Atsumi (Tokyo: Yone Noguchi Society, 1975).

55. Wheeler, "Montana's Shocking 'Lit'ry Lady,'" 28.

56. MacLane to Stone, Autumn 1902, Newberry.

57. MacLane to Stone, Autumn 1902.

58. For example, Paul remarked "'My Friend, Annabel Lee' is . . . far less objectionable than the former Mary MacLane book, so unobjectionable, indeed, that it is scarcely likely to make a 'sensation'" ("Mary MacLane Again," *New York Times*, September 5, 1903).

59. MacLane to Stone, August 1902, Newberry. Mattern states that MacLane was fired from the *World* for not being as sensational as hoped ("Mary MacLane," 60). However, both a letter of MacLane's that predates her employment there and an article in the *Great Falls Tribune* show that MacLane and the *World* had agreed that she would write for the paper for one month only.

60. MacLane to Stone, January 12, 1909, Newberry.

61. A. Brisbane (*New York Journal*) to Stone, January 14, 1909. MacLane also had a six-week assignment with the *Denver Post*

62. "Chicago Is a Bore to Mary MacLane," *New York World*, July 9, 1902, 12.

63. "Mary MacLane Shows Better Frame of Mind in 'My Friend Annabel Lee,'" *Chicago Record-Herald*, August 29, 1903, 8.

64. For years, MacLane's family relied on Stone and Monroe for information about MacLane's whereabouts, as in an October 28, 1903, telegram from MacLane's mother to Stone that queried "Please tell me is my daughter Mary MacLane in Chicago" (Newberry).

65. MacLane to Stone, June 14, 1909, Newberry.

66. MacLane to Stone, September 26, 1906, Newberry.

67. Respectively, MacLane to Stone, September 14, 1906; March 22, 1907; October 30, 1908; all in Newberry.

68. H. G. Klenze to Monroe, May 12, 1918, University of Chicago.

69. See Shirley Neuman, "Autobiography, Bodies, Manhood" in *Women, Autobiography, Theory*, 416.

70. Smith, *Subjectivity, Identity, and the Body*, 83.

71. "The feeling of never having quite enough to eat, and being owed a thousand dollars, is not pleasant. Neither is the feeling of having to go into 14th street, with the nightly brigade of other half-hungry women, to drag my living from it" (MacLane to Stone, March 4, 1909, Newberry).

72. MacLane to Stone, June 23, 1909, Newberry.

73. Terris implies that MacLane's wish to keep her affairs with women covert led her to cover her tracks in her travels, making later research difficult. Miller, "'Hot as Live Embers,'" 50.

74. MacLane, "The Borrower of Two-Dollar Bills—and Other Women," *Butte Evening News,* May 15, 1910, 9.

75. Ann Massa, "Form Follows Function: The Construction of Harriet Monroe and *Poetry, A Magazine of Verse*" in *A Living of Words: American Women in Print Culture,* ed. Susan Albertine (Knoxville: University of Tennessee Press, 1995), 121.

76. In 1902, sexologists had only just started wielding the term "lesbian" and depicting same-sex love as pathological. Even the breathless *New York World* found little remarkable in MacLane's devotion. Despite noting that MacLane wrote of Corbin "with an intensity that would melt the crucibles at Vassar or Radcliffe" ("Look Out!"), the newspaper respectfully depicted Corbin and MacLane's relationship as that between a young girl in need of guidance and her older mentor ("Mary MacLane to Go to Radcliffe College"). Lillian Faderman uses MacLane's changing depictions of same-sex love to buttress her "morbidification of love" theory (*Surpassing the Love of Men: Romantic Friendship and Love between Women from the Renaissance to the Present* [New York: William Morrow, 1981], 299–300).

77. MacLane to Monroe, September 10, 1909, University of Chicago.

78. "Mary MacLane Meets the Vampire on the Isle of Treacherous Delights," *Butte Evening News,* March 27, 1910, 9.

79. MacLane to Monroe, May 24, 1909, University of Chicago.

80. MacLane to Monroe, March 5, 1911, University of Chicago.

81. MacLane to Stone, October 10, 1910, Newberry.

82. MacLane, "The Second *Story of Mary MacLane,*" *Butte Evening News,* April 3, 1910, 9–10. Indeed, this change in attitude had begun soon after she left Butte in 1902: on first visiting Cambridge, she declared "Many of the people I have met in Cambridge thus far . . . don't interest me in the least. . . . You would understand what I mean . . . if you had lived in Butte, where the people are so much more virile and full of life and where the large horizon broadens the imagination. You have to live in such a place to understand it" ("Folk Out in Butte Are Best After All," *New York World,* July 23, 1902, 4).

83. Stokes wrote to Monroe, "Your fine letter of April 29th is especially welcome, coming as it does after we have heard so many unfavorable comments on the book. Your feeling about it coincides almost exactly with my own and with the feeling of our editorial assistants Mrs. Atherton and Mrs. Willsie. On the other side we find Miss Amy Lowell, who asks that we do not tell the author of her dislike for the book, Henry Blackman Sell of the Chicago Daily News, whose opinion is that of a

sincere, confident reviewer, and several others who have power to hurt the sale in various ways. Moreover, there has been only meagre response to the rather extensive advertising we have done" (Frederick A. Stokes to Harriet Monroe, May 1, 1917, University of Chicago).

84. James McQuade, Review of "Men Who Have Made Love to Me," *Motion Picture World* (January 28, 1918): 525.

85. *Wid's Daily*, January 17, 1918, 873.

86. *Chicago Tribune*, October 21, 1917, cited by Wheeler, "Montana's Shocking 'Lit'ry Lady,'" 20.

87. "'I, Mary,' More to Be Pitied Than Censored,"*Chicago Daily Tribune*, January 25, 1918, 14.

88. She had similarly disappeared in 1908 from Boston: "that set the reporters to hunting me up—and there have been a great many half-column interviews and photographs since" (MacLane to Stone, November 21, 1908, Newberry). Shortly after the 1918 disappearance, Monroe contacted MacLane's family in Butte to inform them of her whereabouts. MacLane's stepfather responded "While Mrs. Klenze rec'd your very kind and welcome letter it has been such a shock to her that she is not able to answer it at present. . . . We did not approve of Mary leaving in the first place as she gave no definite plans as to how she was to get along and pay her way there, but she is very set in her ways and never tells the family of her affairs or weather [*sic*] she makes any money and of course spends it faster than she gets it. We are sorry to here [*sic*] that she did not get much from her book, and also that she rec'd very little from the movie people and was advanced all she is to get out of that on her contract. We are sorry to here she has gone in debt so bad. We are sorry she has been ill. We have not heard anything from her since over two months and up to this day we have heard nothing from her. I suppose she has forgotten all about her home, she certainly is a peculiar girl. Yes the papers here copied the Chicago news about her.

I am personally aware of the fact as you suggest that Mary can not manage her own affairs and should not be left alone there in Chicago or anywhere. Therefore I think the only thing we can do is to try and get her back home again. About nine years ago I brought her back home from New York after she had spent all she made from her first book. Now than [*sic*] as we do not know where she is, will you kindly help us arrange to have her come home" (H. G. Klenze to Harriet Monroe, May 12, 1918, University of Chicago).

89. "Mary MacLane Now in Court," *Fergus Falls Daily Journal*, July 28, 1919, 6.

90. *Fergus Falls Daily Journal*, August 9, 1929, 1.

91. MacLane to Monroe, May 14, 1926, University of Chicago.

92. Chapin, "The Devilish Mary MacLane," 19.

93. "Mary MacLane Is to be Buried in Fergus Falls," *Fergus Falls Daily Journal*, August 8, 1929, 1.

94. Rachel DuPlessis, *Writing Beyond the Ending: Narrative Strategies of Twentieth-Century Women Writers* (Bloomington: Indiana University Press, 1985), 85.

95. Smith states, "given the cultural alliance of woman's speech with the forces of unleashed sexuality in Western discourse . . . the woman who would write autobiography must uphold her reputation for female goodness or risk her immortal reputation" (*Poetics of Women's Autobiography*, 55–56).

96. Mencken, "The Butte Bashkirtseff," 124.

97. Georgi-Findlay, *Frontiers of Women's Writing*, 288.

98. Heilbrun reads this mode as only fully emerging in the 1970s. *Writing a Woman's Life*, 13.

99. Ibid., 24, 23. Heilbrun refers to the research of Jill Ker Conway and Spacks.

100. Bella Brodzki and Celeste Schenck, Introduction, *Life/Lines: Theorizing Women's Autobiography* (Ithaca: Cornell University Press, 1988), 1. I am aware that most theorists of women's autobiography have moved beyond the essentializing tendencies I criticize. I am, however, struck by how naturally women continue to be celebrated for collectivist tendencies.

101. Smith and Watson, "Introduction: Situating Subjectivity in Women's Autobiographical Practices" in *Women, Theory, Autobiography*, 17.

102. Ibid, 18.

103. Culley, "Introduction," *American Women's Autobiography*, 10.

104. Mary G. Mason, "The Other Voice: Autobiographies of Women Writers," *Women, Autobiography, Theory*, 321.

105. Jean-Jacques Rousseau, *The Confessions*, translated by J. M. Cohen (New York: Penguin, 1953), 17, cited by Brodzki and Schenck in "Introduction," *Life/Lines*, 3.

106. Carol Holly, "Nineteenth-Century Autobiographies of Affiliation," 226.

107. Avrom Fleishman, *Figures of Autobiography: The Language of Self-Writing in Victorian and Modern England* (Berkeley: University of California Press, 1983), 47.

108. Lawrence Buell, "Autobiography in the American Renaissance," in *American Autobiography*, 64.

109. Ibid., 47–48.

110. Ibid., 64.

111. Egan, "'Self'-Conscious History: American Autobiography after the Civil War," in *American Autobiography*, 79.

112. Nancy K. Miller, "Writing Fictions: Women's Autobiography in France," *Life/Lines*, 47.

113. Egan, "'Self'-Conscious History," 79.

3. Little Girls and Their "Explores"

1. In notes for a school composition, Whiteley wrote of her grandparents that "When they were married they came to Missouri . . . but Milton had a longing for the West and after they had been in Missouri only a short time they joined an emigration party, coming to California" (University of Oregon).

2. Pomeroy, *In Search of the Golden West*, 175–79.

3. Those qualities that initially made the text so appealing soon became the source of controversy over the text's authenticity. Most probably, the original child's text was rewritten by the adult Whiteley under Sedgwick's guidance. As not germane to the issues I explore, I only touch upon the matter of whether the text was first written by Whiteley at seven or at twenty. The debate is covered extensively elsewhere, the focus of Benjamin Hoff, Elizabeth Bradburne, and Elbert Bede's biographies, as well as the bulk of Whiteley archival materials. Bede's book is devoted to proving the text a hoax; Hoff and Bradburne argue for child authorship.

4. *The Fairyland around Us* is a mixture of journal entries and nature observation in which plants, animals, and other forms of life are characterized as fairies. When Whiteley printed the rough manuscript, filing with the Library of Congress under the name "Opal de Vere Gabrielle de Bourbon de La Tremoille Stanley Whiteley," it contained 126 pages of text and 498 illustrations and pictures, many taken from postcards, magazines, and books and pasted above hand-printed captions. The text also liberally quoted writers including Wordsworth, Tennyson, and Howells. Whiteley's printers, following an argument with Whiteley over money, produced the meager several hundred copies that they thought her payments deserved and then destroyed the type forms. (Hoff, *The Singing Creek where the Willows Grow* [New York: Penguin, 1994], 32) Whiteley sent these copies to her subscribers, receiving in response praise from such prominent figures as Queen Elizabeth of Belgium, Queen Victoria Eugenia of Spain, Mary Roberts Rhinehart, Booth Tarkington, Kate Douglas Wiggins, William Howard Taft, Cardinal Gibbons, Earl Curzon of Kedleston, David Starr Jordan, Douglas Fairbanks, Nicholas Murray Butler, and various university presidents. Theodore Roosevelt was said to have "sent his compliments" two days before he died. (Elbert Bede, *Fabulous Opal Whiteley: From Oregon Logging Camp to Princess in India* [Portland, Oregon: Binfords & Mort, 1954], 22)

5. Sedgwick, introduction to *The Story of Opal: The Journal of an Understanding Heart*, by Opal Whiteley (Boston: Atlantic Monthly Press, 1920), ix–x.

6. Especially since in the several years previous to the release of Whiteley's text, *I, Mary MacLane* (1917) and "Men Who Have Made Love to Me" (1918) had revived interest in *The Story of Mary MacLane*.

7. Sedgwick's account contradicts an early letter he had received from Whiteley, in which she refers to a childhood diary as the source for portions of *The Fairyland*: "Last winter I published my first book. . . . In it are parts of the journal of my childhood. . . . from it you may know how I write — and of the days in the lumbercamps" (September 16, 1919, MHS).

8. Ellery Sedgwick, *The Atlantic Monthly 1857–1909: Yankee Humanism at High Tide and Ebb* (Amherst: University of Massachusetts Press, 1994), 14.

9. Ibid., 313.

10. Sedgwick, *The Happy Profession* (Boston: Little, Brown, & Co., 1946), 155. Sedgwick misrepresents Scudder, who actually was "tenacious in soliciting," albeit of a narrower range of texts. (Sedgwick, *Yankee Humanism*, 207, 314)

11. Sedgwick, *The Happy Profession*, 200.

12. Ibid., 187.

13. Ibid., 197.

14. Mark Twain, "Marjorie Fleming, the Wonder Child," *Harper's Bazaar* 43 (Dec 1909): 1182–83.

15. William Kavanaugh Doty, introduction to *Blue Beads and Amber: A Child's Book of Verses*, by Mary Harriss (Baltimore: Norman, Remington Co., 1923), xvi–xvii.

16. *Bookman* 52 (1920): 383. Likewise, the *Literary Digest* remarked that readers might have "few infant-prodigy emotions left over from the 'Young Visiters' craze" (67 [1920]: 34).

17. Daisy Ashford, *The Young Visiters, or, Mr. Salteener's Plan*, preface by J. M. Barrie (London: Chatto and Windus, 1919).

18. Hilda Conkling, *Poems by a Little Girl*, preface by Amy Lowell (New York: Stokes, 1920).

19. *Bookman* 53 (1921): 285. Likewise: "Genius, apparently, is not a matter of years. Opal Whiteley began to write when she was six years old; Hilda Conkling wrote her 'Poems by a Little Girl' at the tender age of nine; Daisy Ashford was penning 'The Young Visiters' — of which fifty thousand have been sold — when she was about the same age" (*Bookman* 52 [1920]: 383).

20. R. M. Malcolmson, *Daisy Ashford: Her Life* (London: Chatto & Windus, 1984), 103.

21. See Howard P. Chudaroff, *How Old Are You? Age Consciousness in American Culture* (Princeton: Princeton University Press, 1989). Poems by children such as Mary Harriss and Helen Douglas Adam were grouped according to the ages at which they were composed.

22. James R. Kincaid, *Child-Loving: The Erotic Child and Victorian Culture* (New York: Routledge, 1992).

23. The boom in books written *by* children paralleled a boom in books written *for* children, which were becoming an increasingly distinct market category. The Atlantic Monthly Press had created a new line in children's books only a year before publishing Whiteley in 1920. In 1921 alone, issues of the *Bookman* included the article "What do American Children Read?" a series of book reviews by children; an essay contest for children about their favorite books; a discussion of children's book shops; and the introduction of a new feature, "Children's Book Corner." In the same year, Annie Carroll Moore began reviewing children's books in the *Bookman*. She reviewed books both by and for children, and speculated on how texts by children might better be packaged to appeal to child readers.

24. Carolyn Steedman, *The Tidy House: Little Girls Writing* (London: Virago, 1982), 62. My reading builds upon Steedman's discussion of the 1920s' vogue for reading books written by little girls (62–67).

25. I would qualify, though, the extent of Whiteley's influence suggested by Steedman's statement "the boom in the publication of children's writing in this country and in the USA in the 1920s and 1930s followed on the success of Opal Whiteley" (65). Whiteley participated in an already existing "boom."

26. Steedman, *The Tidy House*, 62. Steedman contends that "the cult of the child was really the cult of the little girl. It was almost without exception the writing of little girls that was published. This is by way of striking contrast with scientific child study, the subjects of which have usually been boys." A great deal of children's poetry was also published, but the majority of it appeared only in magazines.

27. Malcolmson, *Daisy Ashford*, 97.

28. Steedman, *The Tidy House*, 65.

29. *Dial* 67 (1919), 174; Rupert Hughes, "Viewing with Alarm," *Bookman* 49 (1919): 265.

30. *Littell's Living Age* 307, no. 3990 (Dec 1920): back cover; original letter in MHS.

31. Steedman, *The Tidy House*, 67.

32. Woodward, "Dear Diary," 99.

33. Malcolmson, *Daisy Ashford*, 102.

34. Contemporary accounts dramatize the editor's personal investment. Hoff recounts, "One summer morning in 1983, I was looking for a

book on a shelf of the local public library. I was about to reach for it when I noticed the one next to it, and pulled that out, instead, an old, worn volume entitled 'The Story of Opal: The Journal of an Understanding Heart.' . . . A few days later, at ten o'clock in the morning, I began to read it. At two-thirty the next morning, I finished the last page, closed the book, and looked out at the trees in the moonlight for a long time" (*The Singing Creek Where the Willows Grow,* 3). Likewise, Laurel Holliday, the editor of *Heart Songs: The Intimate Diaries of Young Girls,* explains, "Five years ago, when I was combing the stacks of a university library researching another book, *The Diary of Nelly Ptaschkina* uncannily fell off a shelf directly in front of me, and after glancing through it I couldn't resist reading Nelly cover to cover" ([Berkeley, Calif.: Bluestocking Press, 1978], 9). Barbara Timm Gates describes a similar discovery of Emily Shore's diary and writes in diary form the story of her research and publication of the text (*Journal of Emily Shore* [Charlottesville: University of Virginia Press, 1991], viii).

35. Steedman, *The Tidy House,* 67; Woodward, "Dear Diary," 155.

36. Bede, *Fabulous Opal Whiteley,* 30.

37. Sedgwick, introduction to *The Story of Opal,* x.

38. *Bookman* 52 (1920), 258.

39. Agnes Sligh Turnbull, introduction to *Mary Paxon, Her Book, 1880–1884* (Garden City, N.Y.: Doubleday, Doran & Co., 1937), 3; cited by Steedman, *The Tidy House,* 67.

40. Holliday, *Heart Songs,* 9.

41. Hoff, *The Singing Creek Where the Willows Grow,* 74.

42. Reverend John A. Hutton, foreword to *The Elfin Pedlar and Other Tales Told by Pixie Pool,* by Helen Douglas Adam (New York: D. D. Putnams, 1923), v.

43. Elizabeth Luling's book, therefore, is advertised as including "an introduction and Notes by Sylvia Thompson (Her Mother)." *Do Not Disturb: The Adventures of M'm and Teddy* (London: Oxford University Press, 1917).

44. Marguerite Wilkinson, *New York Times,* October 3, 1920, 14.

45. Doty, *Blue Beads,* vi.

46. Sedgwick, *Atlantic Monthly* 125 (March 1920): 289.

47. Hoff, *The Singing Creek Where the Willows Grow,* 3.

48. Barrie, introduction to *The Young Visiters,* vii.

49. Wilkinson, *New York Times,* October 3, 1920, 14; Wilkinson, "The Poems of the Month," *Bookman* 53 (1921): 246.

50. Amy Lowell, preface to *Poems by a Little Girl,* xi, xix.

51. Ibid., xviii.

52. As reviewers remarked of Ashford's text, "Its humor is certainly the humor of childhood, because it is absolutely unconscious" (*New York*

Times, August 3, 1919, 392); "The unconscious humor of the book might be the genuine product of a girl of nine; it is the seemingly conscious humor that is suspicious" (*Springfield Republican*, August 3, 1919, 17); "The fun is in the unconscious naiveté of a child, not the conscious cleverness of the assured humorist" (*Outlook* 123 [1919]: 191).

53. Lowell, preface to *Poems by a Little Girl*, xii.

54. *The Times* (London) Literary Supplement, July 1, 1920, 42.

55. *Springfield Republican*, May 27, 1920, 8.

56. Hutton, *The Elfin Pedlar*, vi.

57. As in the title of Hoff's introduction, "Magical Opal Whiteley."

58. Lowell, preface to *Poems by a Little Girl*, xii.

59. A letter to Sedgwick from Alfred R. McIntyre of Little, Brown & Co. refers to the text's original working title in stating "In glancing over the announcement of the ATLANTIC MONTHLY plans for 1920, we are much interested in The Diary of a Child, which you are going to print" (November 18, 1919, MHS).

60. Callil, introduction to *My Brilliant Career*.

61. Author's telephone conversation with Michael Brown, publisher of *Tender Darkness*, 1998.

62. Ian Taylor met with Whiteley in preparing a documentary on her. He recounts, "She said she was forced to work, even when she was ill, and the wages were being kept to help the IRA. She also said that there were UFO's landing in the area and they were tied in with the IRA. She said she didn't mind working but this was not her kind of work. Her work was that of writing" (Stewart, "Story of Opal Whiteley," University of Oregon).

63. Bede, *Fabulous Opal Whiteley*, 75.

64. *Bookman* 53 (1921): 140.

65. Banks, *New York Times Book Review*, May 22, 1994.

66. "A reductio ad absurdum of . . . the American sentimental novel" (*Athenaeum* [September 17, 1920]: 372); "The book is so incessantly sentimental as to be very tiresome reading to most English people — Americans seem to have stronger stomachs" (*Spectator* 125 [October 16, 1920]).

67. Although these displays of grief may have had little effect at the time, with the publication of *The Story* Whiteley made her childhood emotions known to an international audience. Her text recently has been repackaged along eco-feminist lines, presented by Hoff as a plea against "earth-pillaging" (*The Singing Creek Where the Willows Grow*, 359) and anthologized in *Sisters of the Earth: Women's Prose and Poetry about Nature*, ed. Lorraine Anderson (New York: Random House, 1991).

68. Steedman, *The Tidy House*, 67.

69. Lowell, preface to *Poems by a Little Girl*, viii.

70. Whiteley to Sedgwick, March 30, 1920, MHS.

71. Whiteley's mother herself appears to have had difficulty contending with life in Oregon logging camps. Reports of her vary widely. Hoff writes that she exhibited signs of mental illness akin to her daughter's, hiding in the trees when strangers visited and claiming that she was really an East Indian Princess, proof of which resided in her locked trunk (*The Singing Creek Where the Willows Grow*, 19). Bede claims that she "was spoken of by all who knew her as a woman of education and refinement" (*Fabulous Opal Whiteley*, 144) and that she encouraged Whiteley's literary and naturalist pursuits. In his correspondence, Bede also dwelled on the fact that she was said to have acted "like an Indian," in this case presumably North American.

72. Hoff, *The Singing Creek Where the Willows Grow*, 41. After leaving Eugene, Whiteley never saw any of her family again. Shortly before the publication of *The Story of Opal*, though, family members received several dozen anonymous letters that were traced to her. These letters ask that they "Tell [Opal] that she should appreciate the kindness of your mother to her when she was not her own child. Tell her its hard for most people to be kind to a child that isn't their own. . . . Tell her that you and the family feel that before she lets any of this diary be published she ought to let you all read it." The letters are primarily concerned with promising the family gifts as compensation to "the mamma," now deceased, for caring for "Françoise." All symbols of upper middle-class affluence, the gifts—which arrived as promised—are intriguing in relation to Whiteley's class drama of the orphaned princess raised by rough woodland folk, and suggest that her mother may have held class aspirations much like her own: "To-day we send you some of the silverware which [your mother] wanted bought for your hopechest. We are sending you . . . the following all engraved with your initials. A gold plated silver berry spoon a silver cream ladle a pickle fork and a butter knife. In another week we will send you some of the knives and forks and teaspoons and tablespoons and soup spoons and other pieces of silverware which your mother wanted to have in a hopechest for you. Keep things carefully that we send you for we are buying the best for you."

"Soon the jewel boxes and glove and handkerchief boxes will be sent to the girls as their mother wanted them to be sent. Also each of the two older girls a gold plated pen knife with their initials on as she wished and Cloe's bracelet. Also there will be sent some centerpieces next week which she wanted them to embroider for their hope chests. And soon will be sent to Fay music which she wanted her to have. And also we will send soon each the silk scarf she wanted them to have and more of the mechanical toys for the little boy Elwin. . . . At a later time . . . I will send to you $50.00 to help in buying a tombstone for your wife Lizzie's grave as she so faithfully took care of this child that was put in her care to bring up as her own child which she did as she agreed to" (transcripts of letters in MHS).

73. Whiteley to Sedgwick, February 20, 1920, MHS.

74. In an interview, Whiteley's grandmother stated, "I never did understand her, and switching didn't seem to make her any different. She would climb up in a big evergreen over the pigpen, and get to studying about something, and drop out of the tree into the mud. Lizzie would spank her or switch her, or if Lizzie wasn't feeling up to it, I would. I would talk to her, and she would look right at me, as solemn as an owl; and then, when I was all through, I would say, 'Will you remember what I have said?' She would say, 'I was thinking of something else. What did you say?' And I would have to spank her all over again. She certainly was a trial" (Fred Lockley, "Who Is Opal Whiteley?" *Bookman* 53 [1921]: 140).

75. In her adult life, Whiteley strove for this outside/inside integration on a more daily basis. The last chapter of the diary attests to the beginnings of the massive collection of nature specimens (eventually comprising 16,000 rocks, plants, insects, and shells) she kept within her early homes. Later in life, Whiteley replaced this nature collection with a similarly formidable collection of books. During World War II she often was seen scavenging bombed buildings for books, and in 1948 was estimated to possess 10–15,000 of them (Hoff, *The Singing Creek Where the Willows Grow*, 65, 66). Her room in London "was stacked from floor to ceiling with books and magazines, one moved up and down the lanes between books" (Elizabeth Bradburne, *Opal Whiteley: The Unsolved Mystery* [London: Putnam & Co., 1962], 22–23).

76. MacLane, *The Story of Mary MacLane*, 56.

77. Fathers, in contrast, exist in the background of these texts, more significant as absences than as presences. In the diary Whiteley rarely mentions Mr. Whiteley. She explained to Sedgwick, "about it being strange that I didn't know the papa very well—when I was little he was away at other camps much. When we were at the same camp I was keeping house and he didn't talk much to me" (Whiteley to Sedgwick, February 20 1920, MHS).

78. Allmendinger, "Anastasia of Oregon," *Arizona Quarterly* 51.1 (Spring 1995): 120. The article is reprinted in his *Ten Most Wanted: The Literature of the New West* (New York: Routledge, 1998).

79. Allmendinger, "Anastasia of Oregon," 121, 129.

80. Ibid., 121.

81. Kolodny, *The Land before Her*, 62. Allmendinger himself alludes to Kolodny's garden argument in order to refute it: "[Whiteley's] forest is more than just a garden. It is a Garden of Eden in which Opal functions like the new American Adam" (121).

82. Kathleen A. Boardman, personal correspondence with the author, March 2002.

4. The Disappearing Region

1. Bede, "Little Princess of India Story a Fiction," Cottage Grove *Sentinel*, October 24 1935; clipping in MHS.
2. Hoff, *The Singing Creek Where the Willows Grow*, 7, 10, 11.
3. Ibid., 20.
4. Jean Morris Ellis to Sedgwick, May 28, 1920, MHS.
5. Hoff, *The Singing Creek Where the Willows Grow*, 21.
6. According to *Christian Endeavor Bulletin*, April 15, 1917, cited by Inez Fortt, "The Education of an Understanding Heart," *The Call Number* (18.1): 2, University of Oregon.
7. The account continues, "'This experience happens to a university but once in a generation,' declared Warren D. Smith, head of the university geological department. 'She knows more about geology than do many students that have graduated from my department. She may become one of the greatest minds Oregon ever has produced. She will be an investment for the university'" (*Eugene Daily Guard*, 1915; cited by Hoff, *The Singing Creek Where the Willows Grow*, 21–22).
8. *Oregonian*, June 12, 1921, University of Oregon.
9. Bede, *Fabulous Opal Whiteley*, 12.
10. Hoff, *The Singing Creek Where the Willows Grow*, 23–24.
11. Stewart, "Story of Opal Whiteley," University of Oregon.
12. Fortt, " The Education of an Understanding Heart."
13. Whiteley, "Recollections of My Childhood," published by Bede in *Cottage Grove Sentinel*, 1915, University of Oregon.
14. Fortt, " The Education of an Understanding Heart."
15. Ibid.
16. Ibid.
17. This book had a deep psychic impact on Whiteley: it names its author as "Angel Mother," who later was to appear, along with "Angel Father," in Whiteley's fantasies of noble birth.
18. Whiteley to Verena [Black?], July 7, 1914, University of Oregon.
19. Fortt, "The Education of an Understanding Heart."
20. As Elizabeth Segel argues, "the interest derives from the tension between the heroine's drive to activity and autonomy, and the pressure exerted by society to thwart these drives and clip her wings. . . . The approved girls' book depicted a curbing of autonomy in adolescence; while in form purporting to be a Bildungsroman" ("As the Twig Is Bent" in *Gender and Reading: Essays on Readers, Texts, and Contexts*, ed. Elizabeth A. Plynn and Patrocinio P. Schweickart [Baltimore: John Hopkins University Press, 1986], 174).
21. Madonne M. Miner, quoting Nina Baym in "Guaranteed to Please: Twentieth-Century American Women's Bestsellers" in *Gender and Reading*, 190.

22. Barbara Sicherman, "Sense and Sensibility: A Case Study of Women's Reading in Late Victorian America" in *Gendered Domains: Rethinking Public and Private in Women's History,* ed. Dorothy O. Helly and Susan M. Reverby (Ithaca: Cornell University Press, 1992), 87.

23. "'Girl Assailed as Fakir': Book by American Mystery Child Hoax, Says Critic," newspaper clipping, n.t., n.d., University of Oregon.

24. Gene Stratton-Porter, *A Girl of the Limberlost* (Garden City, N.Y.: Doubleday & Co., 1909), 49.

25. Hoff, *The Singing Creek Where the Willows Grow,* 27.

26. Katherine Beck, personal correspondence with the author, June 1, 2001.

27. Bede, notes, University of Oregon.

28. Cited by Stephen Schwartz, *From West to East: California and the Making of the American Mind* (New York: Free Press, 1998), 178.

29. Conklin to Bede, April 23, 1920, University of Oregon.

30. Sedgwick wrote to F. L. Hoppin, "The Story of Opal is going like mad out West, but we are withholding our powder from the East lest we interfere with the sale of the book. The orders from the news company at Portland, Oregon, have jumped from 475 to 2000 copies a month, and The Oregonian is running a daily two-column story on the subject. We are a little careful not to spread the melodramatic features among Eastern papers for the present, but there is a good deal of appreciation for the literary quality of the story" (April 3, 1920, MHS).

31. Sedgwick, *The Happy Profession,* 261. One reader, for example, wrote to Sedgwick, "I want to get the whole thing and be able to lend it to my friends—I have already passed my magazines around until the covers are about off—I don't usually enthuse over such things but this is so delightful, such poetical prose, that I am waiting on the doorstep each month" (June 29, 1920, MHS).

32. *Atlantic Monthly* 126 (July 1920): 144.

33. W. F. Goodwin Thacher, foreword to Bede's *Fabulous Opal Whiteley,* n.p.

34. Bede, *Fabulous Opal Whiteley,* 85.

35. In England, Whiteley's text was published under the title "The Diary of Opal" (London: Putnam and Company, 1920). Putnam's chairman Constant Huntington wrote the *Atlantic,* "Your record of sales is very like ours, as our first edition of 5,000 was exhausted in the first week, and we are now well into the second" (October 11, 1920, MHS).

36. Bede, *Fabulous Opal Whiteley,* 3.

37. M. Simmons to Sedgwick, MHS.

38. Bede, *Fabulous Opal Whiteley,* 39. Likewise, of *The Story of Mary MacLane,* Jeannette Howard asserts that "like the comparable 'Story of Opal,' printed as authentic by the *Atlantic Monthly* in 1920, but partially

debunked by discerning critics, it was probably laced with more than a dash of fiction" (*Sex Variant Women in Literature* [New York: Vantage, 1956], 244–45).

39. Hoff, *The Singing Creek Where the Willows Grow*, 41.

40. Ibid., 72.

41. Josef Berger and Dorothy Berger, *Small Voices* (New York: Paul S. Eriksson, 1966), 32.

42. Hoff, *The Singing Creek Where the Willows Grow*, 55.

43. Sedgwick, introduction to *The Story of Opal*, xv. In full, this passage reads, "Our theme should not be Opal, but Opal's book. She is the child of curious and interesting circumstance, but of circumstance her journal is altogether independent. The authorship does not matter, nor the life from which it came. There the book is. Nothing else is like it, nor apt to be. If there is alchemy in Nature, it is in children's hearts the unspoiled treasure lies, and for that room of the treasure house, the Story of Opal offers a tiny golden key."

44. The year following, Sedgwick wrote to Bede, "After the magazine articles drew to a close, I was a good deal troubled by the increasing amount of French that showed itself in the diary. It became so great that I felt, whatever the truth of her story, certainly the appearance of so much that was strange would lead most people to disbelieve in her work. I therefore prevailed upon her to omit a great many passages from the book, hoping that if her origin and whole story were discovered, it might be possible to publish a second book, in which all this extra material could appear, buttressed by proofs from outside. These extra pages of the diary contained a very great number of cross-references to the Bourbon family and to Opal's supposed parentage" (June 7, 1921, MHS).

45. Sedgwick to Alfred R. McIntyre, November 19, 1919, MHS.

46. "Mystery Child of Lumber-Camps. Diary Written at Six on Scrap-Paper. Torn into Fragments,"*Daily Chronicle*, September 4, 1920; clipping in MHS.

47. Brodhead, *Cultures of Letters*, 120.

48. Whiteley wrote to Sedgwick, "You had spoken of wanting to get to-gether all of the material — or as much as possible — of the seven year old period. So to-day I began concentrating on that" (November 12, 1919, MHS).

49. According to a December 9, 1919 list of "Illustrations for Opal's Book," MHS.

50. Whiteley to Sedgwick, October 30, 1919, MHS.

51. Read Bain to Sedgwick, March 20 1920, MHS; [Mr.] Woodward to Sedgwick, February 13, 1920, MHS.

52. Bede recalled, "Teachers of vocal and instrumental music and of elocution gave the settlement [of Cottage Grove] a cultural atmosphere.

Business depended to a large extent upon the twice-a-month payrolls of the mills and logging camps. There were the usual mercantile establishments on Main street, the usual number of struggling churches, good grade and high schools, a newspaper, lodges of the Masons, Odd Fellows, and Knights of Pythias, and a commercial club" (*Fabulous Opal Whiteley*, 7).

53. April 5, 1920, MHS.

54. Thus, in *The Song of the Lark* Cather describes the Colorado desert as "childlike" and the Arizona canyons as home to the childhood of the human race. Austin claims in *Earth Horizon* that in the Southwest she experienced anew the mystical certainties of her childhood. In contemporary literature, Watson notes the preponderance of recent Montana writers focusing on Montana childhoods rather than adult experience ("Engendering Montana Lives"). Michael Powell similarly remarks that western sites (referring here to Oregon) "[seem] to have blossomed in literature as a very private landscape, often revealing . . . the 'nectar' of a severely tested childhood" ("Oregon," *Updating the Literary West*, 240).

55. "Anytime the Ground is Uneven: The Outlook for Regional Studies and What to Look Out For," *Geography and Literature: A Meeting of the Disciplines*, ed. William E. Mallory and Paul Simpson-Housley (Syracuse: Syracuse University Press, 1987), 2–3.

56. Doreen Massey, *Space, Place, and Gender* (Minneapolis: University of Minnesota Press, 1994), 180.

57. Stewart Holbrook, *Far Corner, a Personal View of the Pacific Northwest* (New York: Macmillan, 1952), 209.

58. Bede, *Fabulous Opal Whiteley*, 33. Parts of the Northwest are still marked by an absence of narratives and associations. Of southeastern Oregon and northern Nevada, William Kittredge remarks, "this huge drift of country is pretty much nonexistent in the American imagination" (*Hole in the Sky: A Memoir* [New York: Alfred A. Knopf, 1992], 19).

59. Max Westbrook, preface, *A Literary History of the American West* (1987), cited by Powell, "Oregon," 240.

60. Susan Goodman, "Legacy Profile: Ella Rhoads Higginson c. 1862–1940," *Legacy* 6.1 (1989): 59.

61. Romines, *Constructing the Little House*, 130–31.

62. *Portland Oregonian*, April 9, 1920; clipping in MHS. Martin was not alone in seeing *The Story of Opal* as a "reproduction" of Hawthorne's novel. The *Cottage Grove Sentinel* printed a poem that declared "A certain knight-errant 'came out of the West,'/And so did our own Opal Whiteley. . . . And still it remained for an Oregon Maid/To capture the staid old Atlantic. . . . The Story of Opal is awkward enough/Ye Editors might have known better/The Magazine Man who would fall for such stuff/Should borrow Hawthorne's 'Scarlet Letter'" ("That Opal Story

Way Back East," *Cottage Grove Sentinel,* April 30, 1920; clipping in MHS). Echoing the poem's suggestion that it was Whiteley's western origins that "captured" the magazine, another reader wrote "so winsomely she told her tale — tingeing it with the pungent odor of the staid big firs, and garbing it in the glamour of the wildness of an Oregon lumber camp — that, — well, — truth to tell, — ye Best of Editors fell. . . . So the Sacred Box was telegraphed out of its western lair, and it came, like some literary young Lochinvar" (Read Bain to Sedgwick, February 28, 1920, MHS).

63. Respectively, D. T. Awbrey to Sedgwick, February 16, 1920, MHS; Hoff, *The Singing Creek Where the Willows Grow,* 10; Edith M. Patch, "Contributors' Column," *Atlantic Monthly* 126 (July 1920): 142. The blandness of Hoff's title for Whiteley's text, *The Singing Creek Where the Willows Grow,* also strikes me as significant in this regard.

64. *Life* (1920): 702; clipping in MHS.

65. E. Bolenius to Sedgwick, MHS. Such ardent response characterizes recent Whiteley portrayals, too. The "Opal Whiteley Web Page" (http://www.efn.org/~opal) declares, "A Child Literary Genius & a Victim of Childhood Abuse, a Brilliant Nature Scientist & Religious Teacher, She has been Compared to The Indian Princess Pocahontas and St. Francis. *Was She a Mystic? a Princess? a Madwoman?*"

66. *Evening Standard,* September 2, 1920; clipping in MHS.

67. Bradburne, *Opal Whiteley,* 27.

68. J. M. Armo Sheldon to Sedgwick, October 1920, MHS.

69. Toronto reader to Sedgwick, May 6, 1920, MHS.

70. Reader to Sedgwick, May 28, 1920, MHS.

71. Steedman, *The Tidy House,* 65.

72. Bede, *Fabulous Opal Whiteley,* 45.

73. Brodhead, *Cultures of Letters,* 120.

74. Bede, *Cottage Grove Sentinel,* May 5, 1915, MHS.

75. Hoff, *The Singing Creek Where the Willows Grow,* 17.

76. MHS.

77. Whiteley to Elbert and Mrs. Bede, April 2, 1920, MHS.

78. Bradburne, *Opal Whiteley,* 48.

79. Whiteley suffered increasing paranoia and threatened to sue the *Atlantic.* Sedgwick wrote, "[She] has now assumed an attitude of hostility for which I am absolutely powerless to account. At first, I was inclined to think that her mind might be affected" (September 31 [*sic*], 1920, MHS).

80. Sedgwick, *The Happy Profession,* 264.

81. Bradburne, *Opal Whiteley,* 29, 32.

82. "A Bourbon-Orléans Princess in London," *Evening News,* March 16, 1931; cited by Bradburne, *Opal Whiteley,* 30.

83. In an interview in which she discussed her decision to become

an English citizen, Whiteley stated "My father, Prince Henri of Bourbon Orléans, died when I was very young . . . and I was 'given' to England in 1903. It was decided that I should pass my life here. Although I have not always lived here since then, I feel very English and I love England, very, very much" ("Niece of the Pretender to French Throne Applies for British Naturalisation," *Evening Standard,* May 9, 1936; cited by Bradburne, *Opal Whiteley,* 31).

    84. Hoff, *The Singing Creek Where the Willows Grow,* 15.

    85. Whiteley wrote some articles for the English magazine, *The Queen,* including one about Catherine the Great entitled, "The Greatest Hoax in History." In answer to later inquiries magazine staff members said they "'had thought her to be Russian or something'" (Bradburne, *Opal Whiteley,* 24). In 1929 *The Queen* also serialized portions of Whiteley's manuscript "The Story of Unknown India" (Hoff, *The Singing Creek Where the Willows Grow,* 64).

    86. Bradburne, *Opal Whiteley,* 60.

    87. Hoff, *The Singing Creek Where the Willows Grow,* 63. Whiteley's Indian adventures were made public in a 1932 radio show and subsequent article by Edwin C. Hill, "The Human Side of the News: Romantic and Mysterious History of Opal Whiteley — Strange Meeting in India." Hill described Whiteley as "a child who sprang from a royal house of France and a royal house of India; who came somehow to America as an orphan and was brought up in a middle class family, and who made her way back by some sort of instinct to the land and level of her origins." Unaccountably, in 1938 in another "Human Side of the News" feature, Hill reported that MacLane, too, sojourned in India at the home of a maharaja: "Her second book, 'Men Who Have Made Love to Me,' was the loudest shilling shocker of its day. One of the great maharajahs of India staked her to a de luxe trip to his palace, to read the book to him, with an interpreter translating as she read. The reading was a great success, not only with the maharaja, but with his harem. Mary returned to her gilded New York hotel suite with a casual aside to the reporters, that she had missed only her Martinis — that she needed at least fifty a day to sustain her" ("The Human Side of the News," 1938, King Features Syndicate).

    88. Hoff, *The Singing Creek Where the Willows Grow,* 62. After the trip, Whiteley sent her travel journal to Sedgwick, entitled "The Sun King and His Kingdom of Mystery in Unknown India," along with pictures of herself seated on an elephant at the onset of a tiger hunt. Sedgwick recalled, "Since Opal's narrative identified two of the greatest Maharajahs who had been her hosts, I wrote to both their courts. In due time two letters returned, emblazoned with regal crests, each informing me the writer's royal master bade the secretary reply that it had been his high

privilege to entertain H. R. H. Mlle. Françoise de Bourbon, and that a series of fêtes had been given to do her honor." Sedgwick did not publish Whiteley's journal ("The dew of the morning had vanished" [*The Happy Profession*, 265]). In the years following Whiteley continued working on the book about India, as well as her memoirs and several books with religious themes (Hoff, *The Singing Creek Where the Willows Grow*, 65). After over a decade as a ward of the city of London, in 1948 she was institutionalized in Napsbury Hospital in Hampstead, where she remained until her death in 1992.

89. Bede, *Fabulous Opal Whiteley*, 128.

90. *Evening Oregonian*, clipping in MHS.

5. "Betwixt and Between"

1. One exception is *Sister of the Road: Autobiography of Box-Car Bertha*, itself posited as the invention of its male amanuensis.

2. James Clifford remarks that servants are often used to represent the "people" of a nation as well as cultural order and continuity. *The Predicament of Culture* (Cambridge: Harvard University Press, 1988), 4.

3. Harry A. Franck, *A Vagabond Journey Around the World: A Narrative of Personal Experience* (Garden City, N.Y. Century Co., 1910), xv.

4. Nellie Y. McKay, "The Narrative Self: Race, Politics, and Culture in Black American Women's Autobiography" in *Women, Autobiography, Theory*, 101. Harrison's text also can be read productively as biracial literature, as set forth by Werner Sollors in *Neither Black Nor White Yet Both* (New York: Oxford University Press, 1997).

5. Henry Louis Gates Jr., Introduction to *"Race," Writing, and Difference*, ed. Gates (Chicago: University of Chicago Press, 1986), 5.

6. Ibid., 6.

7. James A. Snead, "Spectatorship and Capture in *King Kong:* The Guilty Look" in *Representing Blackness: Issues in Film and Video*, ed. Valerie Smith (New Brunswick: Rutgers University Press, 1997), 26.

8. Due to incorrect information in the text's preface, discussions of Harrison have inaccurately represented her as having been born in 1891, left Mississippi at sixteen, and begun her international travels at thirty-six. Passport records reveal, however, that she was born in Columbus on December 26, 1887, and lived there until 1917; she traveled around the world between the ages of forty and forty-eight, not thirty-six and forty-four. We cannot know if it was Harrison who led others to believe that she began her travels at the more romantic younger ages, or if her editors chose to represent her so. Harrison does suggest that she regularly claimed to be younger than she was: "the calender say I am another year

old but 1925 find me the same age I was 15 years ago and I expect to be that same age at least 10 years more anyway" (18). She died in Honolulu in 1967 at the age of eighty.

9. Smith, *Subjectivity, Identity, and the Body,* 62.

10. See Stephen Fender, *Plotting the Golden West: American Literature and the Rhetoric of the California Trail* (Cambridge: Cambridge University Press, 1981).

11. Gates states that eighteenth-century black literary tradition depended upon the belief that "the recording of an authentic black voice — a voice of deliverance from the deafening discursive silence which an enlightened Europe cited to prove the absence of the African's humanity — was the millennial instrument of transformation though which the African would become the European, the slave become the ex-slave, brute animal become the human being" (*"Race," Writing, and Difference,* 11–12).

12. According to Morris, as a child Harrison "lived with a bright vision of templed cities in foreign lands which she had seen pictured in the stray pages of a magazine" (ix).

13. *Publisher's Weekly* (April 25, 1936): 1670.

14. Adele Logan Alexander, introduction to *My Great, Wide, Beautiful World* (New York: G. K. Hall and Co., 1996). Alexander glosses the text's central themes before going on to compare Harrison's journeys with those of Eslanda Goode Robeson and Odysseus. Outside of my own work, Alexander's brief and occasionally inaccurate introduction stands as the only published Harrison scholarship.

15. "Juanita, Unique Authoress, Meets 'Unseen Sweetheart,'" *Honolulu Star-Bulletin,* March 25, 1936, 4.

16. Sedgwick, *The Happy Profession,* 215.

17. Stepto, *From Behind the Veil,* 45, cited by Claudine Raynaud, "'Rubbing a Paragraph with a Soft Cloth'? Muted Voices and Editorial Constraints in *Dust Tracks on a Road*" in *De/colonizing the Subject: The Politics of Gender in Women's Autobiography,* ed. Sidonie Smith and Julia Watson (Minneapolis: University of Minnesota Press, 1992), 56.

18. Culley, *American Women's Autobiography,* 7–8.

19. Thomas Cripps, "'Race Movies' as Voices of the Black Bourgeoisie: *The Scar of Shame*" in *Representing Blackness,* 55.

20. According to David Van Leer, minority autobiographers do not write the "narrative of individual triumph" of traditional autobiography and do not serve as "models or exemplars, but only counter-examples" ("Visible Silence: Spectatorship in Black Gay and Lesbian Film" in *Representing Blackness,* 166).

21. Darlene Clark Hine, "Black Migration to the Urban Midwest: The Gender Dimension, 1915–1945," in *The Great Migration in Historical Per-*

spective, ed. Joe William Trotter Jr. (Bloomington: Indiana University Press, 1991), 139.

22. Shirlee Taylor Haizlip, *The Sweeter the Juice: A Family Memoir in Black and White* (New York: Simon & Schuster, 1994), 15.

23. Smith, *Subjectivity, Identity, and the Body*, 105, 125.

24. Raynaud, "'Rubbing a Paragraph with a Soft Cloth'" and "*Dust Tracks on a Road*: Autobiography as a 'Lying' Session" in *Studies in Black American Literature*, vol. 3, ed. Joe Weixlman and Houston A. Baker Jr. (Greenwood, Fl.: Penkevill, 1988), 111–38.

25. Smith, *Subjectivity, Identity, and the Body*, 124, 105.

26. The parallels between Harrison's title and closing words and those of Hurston's *Dust Tracks on a Road*, published only five years later, are striking. Avowing that she has "touched the four corners of the horizon," Hurston concludes, "I do not wish to . . . [live] in a space whose boundaries are race and nation. Lord, give my poor stammering tongue at least one taste of the whole round world"([Urbana: University of Illinois Press, 1984], ed. Robert E. Hemenway, 330–31). These two African American writers of rural southern roots chose to chronicle their lives through literal and metaphorical travel, despite occupying such different authorial positions—Hurston as a highly educated professional writer and scholar, Harrison as a working domestic and traveler. With her resistance to racial essentialism, the more prolific, public, and widely studied Hurston illuminates Harrison. At the same time, Harrison provides an essential context for Hurston, herself often read as anomalous.

27. Harrison both dedicated her book to Myra Dickinson and listed George Dickinson, rather than a family member, as her emergency contact on her 1950 passport application.

28. David Fine, "Beginning in the Thirties: The Los Angeles Fiction of James M. Cain and Horace McCoy" in *Los Angeles in Fiction: A Collection of Original Essays*, ed. Fine (Albuquerque: University of New Mexico Press, 1984), 44.

29. Michael Rogin, *Blackface, White Noise: Jewish Immigrants in the Hollywood Melting Pot* (Berkeley: University of California Press, 1996), 14.

30. Gates, *"Race," Writing, and Difference*, 6.

31. A similar sense of difference can be detected in Harrison's reference to the "55 colored nice fat Mamas" (253) visiting their sons' graves in France.

32. Harrison was similarly struck in a ball room in Nice by "Dark colord girls in their evening cloths dancing in the Arms of Hansom White Frenchmen" (22).

33. Patricia Yaeger, *Dirt and Desire: Reconstructing Southern Women's Writing, 1930–1990* (Chicago: University of Chicago Press, 2000), 58–60.

Yaeger reads Harrison's account of a train wreck in Eastern Europe and the childhood wreck it reminds her of as offering valuable insight into Harrison's sense of racial and regional identity. While I argue that it is rewarding to read Harrison as a western writer, Yaeger argues that we should "widen the network of texts we read as 'southern'" to include that of writers like Harrison, who never refers directly to the South but whose life is deeply affected by her southern past. (297n. 1)

34. Certainly, Sedgwick's portrait of Harrison in *The Happy Profession* suggests that at least in hindsight he perceived Harrison with this kind of racist condescension. Nevertheless, his actual publication of her text probably reflects less a desire to cater to racist stereotypes than his longstanding penchant for publishing the first-person accounts of odd women.

35. Respectively, "'Gelouries!'" *Time* (May 18, 1936): 83–85; Donald Gordon, "Current Books," *American Magazine* (July 1936): 78; Sedgwick, *The Happy Profession*, 211. The first opens, "'Gelouries!' Juanita Harrison is a 45-year-old Negro lady's-maid who never stays long in one place. She invariably resigns her domestic job before she is fired."

36. Martha Gruening, in *New Republic*, June 3, 1936; Virginia Kirkus, quoted in advertisement, *Publishers Weekly* (April 25, 1936): 1670.

37. Another states, "There is nothing on our shelves, certainly, that is quite like this spontaneous, shrewd, and unselfconscious story of the Odyssey of an American negress. . . . Juanita is an absolutely natural human being" (Katherine Woods, "Traveling for Adventure," *Saturday Review* [June 20, 1936]: 10).

38. Cited by Cheryl A. Wall, *Women of the Harlem Renaissance* (Bloomington: Indiana University Press, 1995), 4.

39. Cited by Clifford, *The Predicament of Culture*, 1, from "To Elsie" (1923): "The pure products of America go crazy—/mountain folk from Kentucky/or the ribbed north end of/Jersey."

40. Cited by Marilyn Wesley, *Secret Journeys: The Trope of Women's Travel in American Literature* (Albany: State University of New York Press, 1999), 39.

41. Clifford, *The Predicament of Culture*, 14.

42. In the case of the popular culture figure of the hobo, for example, Wesley notes that "the vaunted wanderlust and celebrated freedom of the vagrant lifestyle is countered by actual domestic investment [and] sentimental attachment. . . . One of the likely sources for the derivation of the term *hobo* is 'home-bound'" (*Secret Journeys*, 80, 82).

43. See Wall, *Women of the Harlem Renaissance*, 18, for a discussion of the differences between these traditions.

44. The exception, her childhood train wreck.

45. Thanks to David Ginsburg for enabling this study by his assiduous investigation of Harrison's life.

46. Amy Kaplan, "Manifest Domesticity," *American Literature* 70.3 (September 1998): 581–606.

47. Romines, *Home Plot,* 17–18.

48. See Janis Stout, *Through the Window, Out the Door* (Tuscaloosa: University of Alabama Press, 1998), 12.

Conclusions

1. Fetterley, "Politics of Recovery," 605.

2. Caren Kaplan, "Resisting Autobiography: Genres and Transnational Female Subjects" in *De/colonizing the Subject,* ed. Smith and Watson, 115.

3. Fleishmann, *Figures of Autobiography,* 36.

4. Smith, *Poetics of Women's Autobiography,* 8.

5. Buss, *Mapping Our Selves,* 18.

6. Joanna Russ, *How to Suppress Women's Writing* (Austin: University of Texas Press, 1983), 80.

7. Ibid., 86.

8. Lejeune, "'Journal de Jeune Fille,'" 118, 119.

9. Esther F. Lanigan, *Mary Austin: Song of a Maverick* (Tucson: University of Arizona Press, 1997); Joanne M. Braxton, *Black Women Writing Autobiography* (Philadelphia: Temple University Press, 1989), 146.

10. As in the following review of *Around the World in Eleven Years:* "[C]hildren have something to teach their parents. 'Europe Simplified for Adults' this might have been called. Which brings me back to Miss Harrison, who is quite illiterate and has no pretensions to grammar or spelling, but more than makes up for this by her superabundant sense of life, by her capacity for the mere 'joy of living.' The rhythm of her race is in her blood, and she dances her way across continents" (John Cournos, "Exploring We Go," *Yale Review* (1936): 840).

Works Cited

Books and Articles

Abbe, Patricia, Richard Abbe, and Johnny Abbe. *Around the World in Eleven Years*. New York: Frederick A. Stokes, 1936.
———. *Of All Places!* New York: Frederick A. Stokes, 1937.
Abbott, Porter. *Diary Fiction: Writing as Action*. Ithaca: Cornell University Press, 1984.
Abernethy, Francis Edward, ed. *Legendary Ladies of Texas*. Dallas: E-Heart Press, 1981.
Adam, Helen Douglas. *The Elfin Pedlar and Other Tales Told by Pixie Pool*. Introduction by Rev. John A. Hutton. New York: Putnam's, 1923.
Alexander, Adele Logan. Introduction to *My Great, Wide, Beautiful World*, by Juanita Harrison. New York: G. K. Hall and Co., 1996.
Allmendinger, Blake. "Anastasia of Oregon." *Arizona Quarterly* 51.1 (Spring 1995): 111–32.
———. *Ten Most Wanted: The Literature of the New West*. New York: Routledge, 1998.
Amiel, Henri-Frédéric. *Fragments d'un Journal Intime*. 4th ed. Geneva: Charles Schuchardt, 1885.
Ammons, Elizabeth. *Conflicting Stories: American Women Writers at the Turn into the Twentieth Century*. New York: Oxford University Press, 1991.
Anderson, Lorraine, ed. *Sisters of the Earth: Women's Prose and Poetry about Nature*. New York: Random House, 1991.
Ardis, Ann L. "Mary Cholmondeley's Red Pottage." In *Writing the Woman Artist: Essays on Poetics, Politics, and Portraiture*, edited by Suzanne W. Jones, 333–50. Philadelphia: University of Pennsylvania Press, 1991.
Ashford, Daisy. *The Young Visiters, or, Mr. Salteener's Plan*. Preface by J. M. Barrie. London: Chatto and Windus, 1919.
Atherton, Gertrude. *Adventures of a Novelist*. New York: Liveright, 1932.

———. *Perch of the Devil.* New York: Frederick A. Stokes, 1914.

Austin, Mary. *Earth Horizon: Autobiography.* Boston: Houghton Mifflin, 1932. Reprint, with an afterword by Melody Graulich. Albuquerque: University of New Mexico Press, 1991.

———. *The Land of Little Rain.* Boston: Houghton Mifflin and Co., 1903.

———. *Lost Borders.* New York: Harper and Brothers, 1909.

———. *A Woman of Genius.* New York: Doubleday, Page and Co., 1912. Reprint, with an afterword by Nancy Porter. Old Westbury, New York: Feminist Press, 1985.

Banks, Ann. Review of *Only Opal,* by Jane Boulton. *New York Times Book Review,* May 22, 1994.

Banta, Martha. *Imagining American Women: Ideas and Ideals in Cultural History.* New York: Columbia University Press, 1987.

Bashkirtseff, Marie. *Journal de Marie Bashkirtseff.* Cassell and Company, 1890. Reprint, with an introduction by Rozsika Parker and Griselda Pollock. Translated by Mathilde Blind. London: Virago, 1985.

Bede, Elbert. *Fabulous Opal Whiteley: From Oregon Logging Camp to Princess in India.* Portland, Oregon: Binfords & Mort, 1954, 1978.

Bederman, Gail. *Manliness and Civilization: A Cultural History of Gender and Race in the United States, 1890–1917.* Chicago: University of Chicago Press, 1995.

Berger, Josef, and Dorothy Berger. *Small Voices.* New York: Paul S. Eriksson, 1966.

Boardman, Kathleen A. "Western American Literature and the Canon." In *Updating the Literary West,* 44–70. Fort Worth: Texas Christian University Press, 1997.

Boulton, Jane, ed. *Opal: The Journal of an Understanding Heart.* New York: Macmillan, 1976; New York: Tioga Publishing Co., 1984.

———. *Only Opal: The Diary of a Young Girl.* Illustrated by Barbara Cooney. New York: Philomel Books, 1994.

Boynton, H. W. "Cleverness." *Atlantic Monthly* (December 1902): 852–56.

Bradburne, Elizabeth. *Opal Whiteley: The Unsolved Mystery.* London: Putnam and Co., 1962.

Braxton, Joanne M. *Black Women Writing Autobiography: A Tradition within a Tradition.* Philadelphia: Temple University Press, 1989.

Brodhead, Richard. *Cultures of Letters: Scenes of Reading and Writing in Nineteenth-Century America.* Chicago: University of Chicago Press, 1993.

Brodzki, Bella, and Celeste Schenck. Introduction. *Life/Lines: Theorizing Women's Autobiography,* edited by Bella Brodzki and Celeste Schenck, 1–15. Ithaca: Cornell University Press, 1988.

Bruns, Rose A. *The Damndest Radical: The Life and World of Ben Reitman,*

Chicago's Celebrated Social Reformer, Hobo King, and Whorehouse Physician. Chicago: University of Illinois Press, 2001.

Buell, Lawrence. "Autobiography in the American Renaissance." In *American Autobiography: Retrospect and Prospect*, edited by Paul John Eakin, 47–69. Madison: University of Wisconsin Press, 1991.

Bunkers, Suzanne L., and Cynthia A. Huff. "Issues in Studying Women's Diaries: A Theoretical and Critical Introduction." In *Inscribing the Daily: Critical Essays on Women's Diaries*, edited by Suzanne L. Bunkers and Cynthia A. Huff, 1–20. Amherst: University of Massachusetts Press, 1996.

Buss, Helen M. *Mapping Our Selves: Canadian Women's Autobiography in English*. Montreal: McGill-Queen's University Press, 1993.

Canfield, Mary Cass. "I, Mary MacLane." *Grotesques and other Reflections on Art and the Theatre*, 48–60. New York: Harper and Brothers, 1927. (First published as "Mary MacLane and the Apparent Agonies of Introspective Pathology" in *Vanity Fair* [June 1917], under the byline "Peter Savage.")

Cather, Willa. *The Song of the Lark*. Boston: Houghton Mifflin Co., 1915.

Chave, Anna C., "O'Keeffe and the Masculine Gaze." In *From the Faraway Nearby: Georgia O'Keeffe as Icon*, edited by Christopher Merril and Ellen Bradbury, 29–31. Albuquerque: University of New Mexico Press, 1998.

Chudaroff, Howard P. *How Old Are You? Age Consciousness in American Culture*. Princeton: Princeton University Press, 1989.

Clifford, James. *The Predicament of Culture*. Cambridge: Harvard University Press, 1988.

"Come Buy! Come Buy! The Modern Publisher's Frantic Effort to Dispose of His Goods." *Munsey's Magazine* 27 (1902): 467.

Comer, Krista. "Feminism, Women Writers, and the New Western Regionalism: Revising Critical Paradigms." In *Updating the Literary West*, 17–34. Fort Worth: Texas Christian University Press, 1997.

———. *Landscapes of the New West: Gender and Geography in Contemporary Women's Writing*. Chapel Hill: University of North Carolina Press, 1999.

Conkling, Hilda. *Poems by a Little Girl*. Preface by Amy Lowell. New York: Frederick A. Stokes, 1920.

Cournos, John. "Exploring We Go." [Review of *Around the World in Eleven Years*.] *Yale Review* (1936): 839–42.

Creston, Dormer. *The Life of Marie Bashkirtseff*. London: Eyre & Spottiswoode, 1943.

Cripps, Thomas. "'Race Movies' as Voices of the Black Bourgeoisie: *The Scar of Shame*." In *Representing Blackness: Issues in Film and Video*, edited by Valerie Smith. New Brunswick: Rutgers University Press, 1997.

Cronon, William. *Nature's Metropolis: Chicago and the Great West.* New York: Norton, 1992.

Culley, Margo, ed. *A Day at a Time: The Diary Literature of American Women from 1764 to the Present.* New York: Feminist Press, 1985.

———. Introduction. *American Women's Autobiography: Fea(s)ts of Memory,* edited by Culley. Madison: University of Wisconsin Press, 1992.

Davis, Robert Murray. *Playing Cowboy: Low Culture and High Art in the Western.* Norman, Oklahoma: University of Oklahoma Press, 1992.

Derleth, August. *Still Small Voice: The Biography of Zona Gale.* New York: D. Appleton-Century Company, 1940.

Doran, George H. *Chronicles of Barabbas: 1884–1934.* New York: Harcourt, Brace and Co., 1935.

Dorst, John D. *Looking West.* Philadelphia: University of Pennsylvania Press, 1999.

DuPlessis, Rachel. *Writing beyond the Ending: Narrative Strategies of Twentieth-Century Women Writers.* Bloomington: Indiana University Press, 1985.

Duvert, Elizabeth. "With Stone, Star, and Earth: The Presence of the Archaic in the Landscape Visions of Georgia O'Keeffe, Nancy Holt, and Michelle Stuart." In *The Desert Is No Lady: Southwestern Landscapes in Women's Writing and Art,* edited by Janice Monk and Vera Norwood. New Haven: Yale University Press, 1987.

Egan, Susanna. "'Self'-Conscious History: American Autobiography after the Civil War." In *American Autobiography: Retrospect and Prospect,* edited by Paul John Eakin, 70–94. Madison: University of Wisconsin Press, 1991.

Egerton, George. *Keynotes & Discords.* London: Elkin Mathews and John Lane, 1893 and 1894. Reprint, with an introduction by Martha Vicinus. London: Virago, 1983.

Faderman, Lillian. *Odd Girls and Twilight Lovers: A History of Lesbian Life in Twentieth-Century America.* New York: Columbia University Press, 1991.

———. *Surpassing the Love of Men: Romantic Friendship and Love between Women from the Renaissance to the Present.* New York: William Morrow, 1981.

Faragher, John Mack. *Women and Men on the Overland Trail.* New Haven: Yale University Press, 1979.

Fender, Stephen. *Plotting the Golden West: American Literature and the Rhetoric of the California Trail.* Cambridge: Cambridge University Press, 1981.

Fetterley, Judith. "Commentary: Nineteenth-Century American Women

Writers and the Politics of Recovery." *American Literary History* 69.3 (1994): 600–611.

Filene, Peter Gabriel. *Him/Her/Self: Sex Roles in Modern America.* New York: Harcourt Brace Jovanovich, 1974.

Fine, David. "Beginning in the Thirties: The Los Angeles Fiction of James M. Cain and Horace McCoy." In *Los Angeles in Fiction: A Collection of Original Essays,* edited by Fine. Albuquerque: University of New Mexico Press, 1984.

Fleishmann, Avrom. *Figures of Autobiography: The Language of Self-Writing in Victorian and Modern England.* Berkeley: University of California Press, 1983.

Foote, Mary Hallock. *A Victorian Gentlewoman in the Far West; the Reminiscences of Mary Hallock Foote.* San Marino, Calif.: Huntington Library, 1972.

Forrt, Irene. "The Education of an Understanding Heart." *Call Number* 18.1: 2. [University of Oregon newsletter]

Foster, Jeannette Howard. *Sex Variant Women in Literature.* New York: Vantage, 1956.

Franck, Harry A. *A Vagabond Journey around the World: A Narrative of Personal Experience.* Garden City, N.Y.: Century, 1910.

Franklin, Miles. *My Brilliant Career.* Reprint, with an introduction by Carmen Callil. London: Virago, 1981.

Friedman, Susan Stanford. "Women's Autobiographical Selves: Theory and Practice." In *Women, Autobiography, Theory,* edited by Sidonie Smith and Julia Watson, 72–82. Madison: University of Wisconsin Press, 1998.

Fuller, Henry B. "Unquenchable Fires." [Review of *I, Mary MacLane.*] *Dial* (May 2, 1917): 400–401.

Gale, Zona. "The Real Mary MacLane." *New York World,* Sunday magazine, August 17, 1902, 1–2.

Gannett, Cinthia. *Gender and the Journal: Diaries and Academic Discourse.* Albany: State University of New York Press, 1992.

Garland, Hamlin. *Companions on the Trail: A Literary Chronicle (1900–1914).* New York: Macmillan, 1931.

———. *Crumbling Idols: Twelve Essays on Art and Literature.* Chicago: Stone and Kimball, 1894.

Gates, Henry Louis, Jr. Introduction. *"Race," Writing, and Difference.* Chicago: University of Chicago Press, 1986.

Georgi-Findlay, Brigitte. *The Frontiers of Women's Writing: Women's Narratives and the Rhetoric of Westward Expansion.* Tucson: University of Arizona Press, 1996.

Gladstone, William. "Journal de Marie Bashkirtseff." *Nineteenth Century* 26 (1889): 606.

Goethe, Johann Wolfgang. *The Sorrows of Young Werther.* Translated by William Rose. London: Scholartis Press, 1929.

Goldberg, Jonathan. "Photographic Relations: Laura Gilpin, Willa Cather." *American Literature* 70.1 (March 1998): 63–95.

Goldman, Anne. *Take My Word: Autobiographical Innovations of Ethnic American Working Women.* Berkeley: University of California Press, 1996.

Goodman, Susan. "Legacy Profile: Ella Rhoads Higginson c. 1862–1940." *Legacy* 6.1 (1989): 59–63.

Gordon, Donald. "Current Books." [Review of *My Great, Wide, Beautiful World.*] *American Magazine,* July 1936, 78.

Graulich, Melody. "'O Beautiful for Spacious Guys': An Essay on the 'Legitimate Inclinations of the Sexes.'" In *The Frontier Experience and the American Dream: Essays on American Literature,* edited by David Mogen, Mark Busby, and Paul Bryant, 186–201. College Station: Texas A & M University Press, 1989.

Grey, Zane. *The Rainbow Trail; A Romance.* New York: Grosset and Dunlap, 1920.

———. *Riders of the Purple Sage.* New York: Grosset & Dunlap, 1912.

Gruening, Martha. Review of *My Great, Wide, Beautiful World. New Republic,* June 3, 1936.

Haizlip, Shirlee Taylor. *The Sweeter the Juice: A Family Memoir in Black and White.* New York: Simon & Schuster, 1994.

Halverson, Cathryn. "Redefining the Frontier: Mourning Dove's *Cogewea, The Half-Blood.*" *American Indian Culture and Research Journal* 21.4 (1997): 105–24.

Harrison, Juanita. *My Great, Wide, Beautiful World.* New York: Macmillan, 1936. Reprint, with an introduction by Adele Logan Alexander. New York: G. K. Hall and Co., 1996.

Harriss, Mary Virginia. *Blue Beads and Amber: A Child's Book of Verses.* Introduction by William Kavanaugh Doty. Baltimore: Norman Remington Co., 1923.

Heilbrun, Carolyn G. *Writing a Woman's Life.* New York: Norton, 1988.

———. "Non-Autobiographies of 'Privileged' Women: England and America." In *Life/Lines: Theorizing Women's Autobiography,* edited by Bella Brodzki and Celeste Schenck. Ithaca: Cornell University Press, 1988.

Higginson, Ella Rhoads. *A Forest Orchid and Other Stories.* New York: Macmillan, 1897.

Hine, Darlene Clark. "Black Migration to the Urban Midwest: The Gender Dimension, 1915–1945." In *The Great Migration in Historical Perspective,* edited by Joe William Trotter Jr., 127–46. Bloomington: Indiana University Press, 1991.

Hoff, Benjamin. Introduction and afterword to *The Singing Creek Where the Willows Grow: The Rediscovered Diary of Opal Whiteley.* New York: Ticknor & Fields, 1986. Reprinted as *The Singing Creek Where the Willows Grow: The Mystical Nature Diary of Opal Whiteley.* New York: Penguin, 1994.

Hoffman, Katherine. *An Enduring Spirit: The Art of Georgia O'Keeffe.* Metuchen, N.J.: The Scarecrow Press, 1984.

Holbrook, Stewart. *Far Corner: A Personal View of the Pacific Northwest.* New York: Macmillan, 1952.

Holliday, Laurel, ed. *Heart Songs: The Intimate Diaries of Young Girls.* Berkeley, Calif.: Bluestocking Press, 1978.

Holly, Carol. "Nineteenth-Century Autobiographies of Affiliation: The Case of Catharine Sedgwick and Lucy Larcom." In *American Autobiography: Retrospect and Prospect,* edited by Paul John Eakin, 216–34. Madison: University of Wisconsin Press, 1991.

Hughes, Rupert. "Viewing with Alarm." *Bookman* 49 (1919): 263–67.

Hurston, Zora Neale. *Dust Tracks on a Road.* 1942. Reprint, edited by Robert E. Hemenway. Urbana: University of Illinois Press, 1984.

Johnson, Lionel. "Marie Bashkirtseff." In *Post Liminium: Essays and Critical Papers by Lionel Johnson,* edited by Thomas Whittemore. London: Ellkin Mathews, 1911.

Johnson, Susan L. "A Memory Sweet to Soldiers: The Significance of Gender in the History of the American West." *Western Historical Quarterly* 24.4 (November 1993): 495–517.

Kaplan, Amy. "Manifest Domesticity." *American Literature* 70:3 (September 1998): 581–606.

Kaplan, Caren. "Resisting Autobiography: Genre and Transitional Female Subjects." In *De/colonizing the Subject: The Politics of Gender in Women's Autobiography,* edited by Sidonie Smith and Julia Watson, 115–38. Minneapolis: University of Minnesota Press, 1992.

Kimmel, Michael. *Manhood in America: A Cultural History.* New York: Free Press, 1996.

Kincaid, James R. *Child-Loving: The Erotic Child and Victorian Culture.* New York: Routledge, 1992.

Kirkland, Caroline. *A New Home—Who'll Follow? or, Glimpses of Western Life.* 1839. Reprint, edited by Sandra A. Zagarell. New Brunswick: Rutgers University Press, 1990.

Kittredge, William. *Hole in the Sky: A Memoir.* New York: Alfred A. Knopf, 1992.

Kolodny, Annette. *The Land before Her: Fantasy and Experience of the American Frontiers, 1630–1860.* Chapel Hill: University of North Carolina Press, 1984.

———. *The Lay of the Land: Metaphor as Experience and History in American*

Life and Letters. Chapel Hill: University of North Carolina Press, 1975.

Kramer, Sidney. *A History of Stone and Kimball and Herbert S. Stone and Co.* Chicago: University of Chicago Press, 1940.

Lamar, Howard R. "The Unsettling of the West: The Mobility of Defeat." In *Crossing Frontiers: Papers on American and Canadian Western Literature*, edited by Dick Harrison, 35–54. Edmonton: University of Alberta Press, 1979.

Lee, Robert Edson. *From West to East: Studies in the Literature of the American West*. Urbana: University of Illinois Press, 1966.

Lejeune, Phillipe. "The 'Journal de Jeune Fille' in Nineteenth-Century France," translated by Martine Breillac. In *Inscribing the Daily: Critical Essays on Women's Diaries*, edited by Suzanne L. Bunkers and Cynthia A. Huff, 107–22. Amherst: University of Massachusetts Press, 1996.

Limerick, Patricia Nelson. *The Legacy of Conquest: The Unbroken Past of the American West*. New York: Norton, 1987.

"Literary Chat." [Review of *Journal de Marie Bashkirtseff*.] *Munsey's Magazine* 27 (1902): 282.

"Literature and Trash." *Munsey's Magazine* 27 (1902): 283.

Lockley, Fred. "Who Is Opal Whiteley?" *Bookman* 53 (1921): 137–40.

Luling, Elizabeth. *Do Not Disturb: The Adventures of M'm and Teddy*. Introduction by Sylvia Thompson. London: Oxford University Press, 1917.

Lynes, Barbara Buhler. *O'Keeffe, Stieglitz and the Critics, 1916–29*. Ann Arbor: University of Michigan Research Press, 1989.

MacLane, Mary. "The Autobiography of the Kid Primitive." *Butte Evening News*, April 3, 1910, 9–10.

———. "The Borrower of Two-Dollar Bills—and Other Women." *Butte Evening News*, May 15, 1910, 9.

———. ["Caruso in the Metropolitan."] Untitled and probably unpublished feature article written in January 1909 for the *New York Evening Journal*; manuscript in Newberry.

———. *I, Mary MacLane: A Diary of Human Days*. New York: Frederick A. Stokes, 1917.

———. "Mary MacLane at Coney Island." *New York World*, August 31, 1902, Sunday magazine, 1.

———. "Mary MacLane at Newport." *New York World*, August 24, 1902, Sunday magazine, 1.

———. "Mary MacLane Meets the Vampire on the Isle of Treacherous Delights." *Butte Evening News*, March 27, 1910, 9.

———. "Men Who Have Made Love to Me." *Butte Evening News*, April 24, 1910, 9–10; *Morrison's Chicago Weekly*, February 2, 1911.

———. "Men Who Have Made Love to Me." Screenplay for Essanay Studios, Chicago, 1917.

———. *My Friend Annabel Lee.* 1903. Reprint, New York: Duffield & Co., 1908.

———. "The Second Story of Mary MacLane." *Butte Evening News,* January 23, 1910, 9.

———. *The Story of Mary MacLane.* Chicago: Herbert S. Stone & Co., 1902.

———. *The Story of Mary MacLane — By Herself — New Edition With a Chapter on the Present.* New York: Duffield & Co., 1912.

Maida, Patricia. "Wild Woman of the West: A Study of the Female Image in Selected Novels." *CEA Magazine* 7.1 (Fall 1994): 21–30.

Malcolmson, R. M. *Daisy Ashford: Her Life.* London: Chatto and Windus, 1984.

Marx, Edward. "The 'Miss Morning Glory' Novels of Yone Noguchi at One Hundred." MLA conference presentation, December 2001.

Mason, Mary G. "The Other Voice: Autobiographies of Women Writers." In *Women, Autobiography, Theory,* edited by Sidonie Smith and Julia Watson, 321–24. Madison: University of Wisconsin Press, 1998.

Massa, Ann. "Form Follows Function: The Construction of Harriet Monroe and *Poetry, A Magazine of Verse.*" In *A Living of Words: American Women in Print Culture,* edited by Susan Albertine, 115–32. Knoxville: University of Tennessee Press, 1995.

Massey, Doreen. *Space, Place, and Gender.* Minneapolis: University of Minnesota Press: 1994.

Mattern, Carolyn J. "Mary MacLane: A Feminist Opinion." *Montana: The Magazine of Western History* (Autumn 1977): 54–63.

McKay, Nellie Y. "The Narrative Self: Race, Politics, and Culture in Black American Women's Autobiography." In *Women, Autobiography, Theory,* edited by Sidonie Smith and Julia Watson, 96–107. Madison: University of Wisconsin Press, 1998.

McKown, [Mrs.] T. D. *The Devil's Letters to Mary MacLane.* Chicago: Interstate Book Co., 1903.

McQuade, James. Review of "Men Who Have Made Love to Me." *Motion Picture World,* January 28, 1918, 525.

Mencken, H. L. "The Butte Bashkirtseff." In *Prejudices: First Series,* 123–28. New York: Alfred A. Knopf, 1919.

———. "The Cult of Dunsany." *Smart Set* (July 1917): 138.

Merton, Madge [pseud.]. *Confessions of a Chorus Girl.* New York: Grafton Press [c. 1903].

Miller, Barbara. "'Hot as Live Embers — Cold as Hail': The Restless Soul of Butte's Mary MacLane." *Montana Magazine* (April–October 1982): 50–53.

Miller, Jim Wayne. "Anytime the Ground Is Uneven: The Outlook for Regional Studies and What to Look Out For." In *Geography and Literature: A Meeting of the Disciplines,* edited by William E. Mallory and Paul Simpson-Housley, 1–20. Syracuse, New York: Syracuse University Press, 1987.

Miller, Nancy K. *The Heroine's Text; Readings in the French and English Novel, 1722–1782.* New York: Columbia University Press, 1980.

———. "Writing Fictions: Women's Autobiography in France." In *Life/Lines: Theorizing Women's Autobiography,* edited by Bella Brodzki and Celeste Schenck. Ithaca: Cornell University Press, 1988.

Miner, Madonne M. "Guaranteed to Please: Twentieth-Century American Women's Bestsellers." In *Gender and Reading: Essays on Readers, Texts, and Contexts,* edited by Elizabeth A. Flynn and Patrocinio P. Schweickart, 187–211. Baltimore: Johns Hopkins University Press, 1986.

Mitchell, Lee Clark. *Westerns: Making the Man in Fiction and Film.* Chicago: University of Chicago Press, 1996.

Monk, Janice, and Vera Norwood, eds. *The Desert Is No Lady: Southwestern Landscapes in Women's Writing and Art.* New Haven: Yale University Press, 1987.

Monroe, Harriet. "Fire of Youth." [Review of *I, Mary MacLane.*] *Poetry: A Magazine of Verse* (June 1917): 154.

Moore, Annie Carroll. Review of *Poems by a Little Girl. Bookman* 51 (1920): 314.

———. Review of *The Story of Opal. Bookman* 52 (1920): 258–59.

Morris, Mildred. Preface to *My Great, Wide, Beautiful World,* by Juanita Harrison. New York: Macmillan, 1936.

Mott, Frank Luther. *Golden Multitudes: The Story of Best-Sellers in the United States.* New York: Macmillan, 1947.

Mourning Dove. *Cogewea: The Half-Blood: A Depiction of the Great Montana Cattle Range.* Boston: Four Seas Co., 1927. Reprint, with an introduction by Dexter Fisher. Lincoln: University of Nebraska Press, 1981.

Murphy, Mary. *Mining Cultures: Men, Women, and Leisure in Butte, 1914–41.* Urbana: University of Illinois Press, 1997.

Neuman, Shirley. "Autobiography, Bodies, Manhood." In *Women, Autobiography, Theory,* edited by Sidonie Smith and Julia Watson, 415–24. Madison: University of Wisconsin Press, 1998.

Noguchi, Yone [pseud. "Miss Morning Glory"]. *The American Diary of a Japanese Girl.* New York: Frederick A. Stokes, 1902. Excerpted as "The American Diary of a Japanese Girl." *Frank Leslie's Popular Monthly* 53 (November 1901–April 1902): 69–82, 192–201.

———. *Collected English Letters.* Edited by Ikuko Atsumi. Tokyo: Yone Noguchi Society, 1975.

Nyland, Waino. A Famous Mining Camp in Literature. Unpublished manuscript c. 1926, Butte–Silver Bow Public Archives.

Page, Ada. "Mary Goes Back to Sand and Barrenness." *Overland Monthly* 87 (November 1929): 345.

Pain, Barry. *Another Englishwoman's Love-Letters*. G. P. Putnam's Sons, 1901.

Parker, Rozsika and Griselda Pollock. Introduction. *The Journal of Marie Bashkirtseff*, by Marie Bashkirtseff. Translated by Mathilde Blind. London: Virago, 1985.

Pascoe, Peggy. *Relations of Rescue: The Search for Female Moral Authority in the American West, 1874–1939*. New York: Oxford University Press, 1990.

Paxon, Mary. *Mary Paxon, Her Book, 1880–1884*. Introduction by Agnes Sligh Turnbull. Garden City, N.Y.: Doubleday, Doran and Co., 1937.

Pearce, T. M., ed. *Literary America, 1903–1934: The Mary Hunter Austin Letters*. Westport, Conn.: Greenwood, 1979.

Phelps, Elizabeth Stuart [pseud. Mary Adams]. "Confessions of a Wife." *Century* 41–43 (April–November 1902).

Pomeroy, Earl S. *In Search of the Golden West: The Tourist in Western America*. New York: Alfred A. Knopf, 1957.

———. "Toward a Reorientation of Western History: Continuity and Environment." *Mississippi Valley Historical Review* 41 (1955): 579–600.

Powell, Michael. "Oregon." In *Updating the Literary West*. Fort Worth: Texas Christian University Press, 1997.

Pritchard, Melissa. "A Graven Space: O'Keeffe and the Masculine Gaze." In *From the Faraway Nearby: Georgia O'Keeffe as Icon*, edited by Christopher Merril and Ellen Bradbury, 137–39. Albuquerque: University of New Mexico Press, 1998.

Pruitt, Elisabeth, ed. *Tender Darkness: A Mary MacLane Anthology*. Belmont, Calif.: Abernathy & Brown, 1993.

Pryse, Marjorie. Introduction to *Stories From the Country of Lost Borders*, by Mary Austin. New Brunswick: Rutgers University Press, 1987.

Raynaud, Claudine. "*Dust Tracks on a Road*: Autobiography as a 'Lying' Session." In *Studies in Black American Literature*, vol. 3, edited by Joe Weixlman and Houston A. Baker Jr., 111–38. Greenwood, Fl.: Penkevill, 1988.

———. "'Rubbing a Paragraph with a Soft Cloth'? Muted Voices and Editorial Constraints in *Dust Tracks on a Road*." In *De/colonizing the Subject: The Politics of Gender in Women's Autobiography*, edited by Sidonie Smith and Julia Watson. Minneapolis: University of Minnesota Press, 1992.

Risley, R. V. "The Story of Mary MacLane." *The Reader: An Illustrated Monthly Magazine of Literature* 1 (November 1902): 97.

Rogin, Michael. *Blackface, White Noise: Jewish Immigrants in the Hollywood Melting Pot.* Berkeley: University of California Press, 1996.

Romines, Ann. *Constructing the Little House: Gender, Culture, and Laura Ingalls Wilder.* Amherst: University of Massachusetts Press, 1997.

———. *The Home Plot: Women, Writing, and Domestic Ritual.* Amherst: University of Massachusetts Press, 1992.

Rosemont, Penelope. "Marvelous Mary MacLane." In *Free Spirits: Annals of the Insurgent Imagination,* edited by Paul Buhle et al., 31–33. San Francisco: City Lights Books, 1982.

Rosowski, Susan J. *Birthing a Nation: Gender, Creativity, and the West in American Literature.* Lincoln: University of Nebraska Press, 1999.

———. "Writing against Silences: Female Adolescent Development in the Novels of Willa Cather." *Studies in the Novel* 21.1 (Spring 1989): 60–77.

Rousseau, Jean-Jacques. *The Confessions,* translated by J. M. Cohen. New York: Penguin, 1953.

Russ, Joanna. *How to Suppress Women's Writing.* Austin: University of Texas Press, 1983.

Sandweiss, Martha A. *Laura Gilpin: An Enduring Grace.* Fort Worth: A. Carter Museum, 1986.

Schlereth, Wendy Clauson. *The Chap-Book: A Journal of American Intellectual Life in the 1890s.* Ann Arbor: University of Michigan Research Press, 1982.

Schwartz, Stephen. *From West to East: California and the Making of the American Mind.* New York: Free Press, 1998.

Sedgwick, Ellery. *The Happy Profession.* Boston: Little, Brown, & Co., 1946.

Sedgwick, Ellery I. *The Atlantic Monthly 1857–1909: Yankee Humanism at High Tide and Ebb.* Amherst: University of Massachusetts Press, 1994.

Segel, Elizabeth. "As the Twig Is Bent." In *Gender and Reading: Essays on Readers, Texts, and Contexts,* edited by Elizabeth A. Flynn and Patrocinio P. Schweickart, 165–86. Baltimore: John Hopkins University Press, 1986.

Shaw, Bernard. "The Womanly Woman." In *The Quintessence of Ibsenism,* 33–49. New York: Brentano's, 1922.

Shore, Margaret Emily. *Journal of Emily Shore.* London: Kegan, Paul, Trench, Trubner, and Co., 1891. Reprint, edited by Barbara Timm Gates. Charlottesville: University of Virginia Press, 1991.

Shores, Robert T. *The Story of Willie Complain.* Butte, Mont.: Intermountain Publishing Co., 1902.

Showalter, Elaine. *Sister's Choice: Tradition and Change in American Women's Writing.* Oxford: Clarendon Press, 1991.

Sicherman, Barbara. "Sense and Sensibility: A Case Study of Women's Reading in Late Victorian America." In *Gendered Domains: Rethinking Public and Private in Women's History*, edited by Dorothy O. Helly and Susan M. Reverby, 71–89. Ithaca: Cornell University Press, 1992.

Sidgwick, Frank, ed. *The Complete Marjory Fleming*. New York: Oxford University Press, 1935.

Slotkin, Richard. *Gunfighter Nation: The Myth of the Frontier in Twentieth-Century America*. New York: Atheneum, 1992.

Smith, Patsy. Review of "Men Who Have Made Love to Me." "Among the Women." *Variety* (February 8, 1918).

Smith, Sidonie. *A Poetics of Women's Autobiography: Marginality and the Fictions of Self-Representation*. Bloomington: Indiana University Press, 1987.

———. *Subjectivity, Identity, and the Body: Women's Autobiographical Practices in the Twentieth Century*. Bloomington: Indiana University Press, 1993.

Smith, Sidonie and Julia Watson. "Introduction: Situating Subjectivity in Women's Autobiographical Practices." In *Women, Autobiography, Theory*, edited by Sidonie Smith and Julia Watson, 3–52. Madison: University of Wisconsin Press, 1998.

Snead, James A. "Spectatorship and Capture in *King Kong:* The Guilty Look." In *Representing Blackness: Issues in Film and Video*, edited by Valerie Smith. New Brunswick: Rutgers University Press, 1997.

Sollors, Werner. *Neither Black Nor White Yet Both*. New York: Oxford University Press, 1997.

Spacks, Patricia Meyers. *The Female Imagination*. New York: Alfred A. Knopf, 1975.

Stafford, Jean. *The Collected Stories of Jean Stafford*. New York: Farrar, Straus and Giroux, 1969.

———. *The Mountain Lion*. New York: Harcourt, Brace and Company, 1947.

Stanton, Donna C. "Autogynography: Is the Subject Different?" In *Women, Autobiography, Theory*, edited by Sidonie Smith and Julia Watson, 131–44. Madison: University of Wisconsin Press, 1998.

Starr, Kevin. *America and the California Dream: 1850–1915*. New York: Oxford University Press, 1973.

Steedman, Carolyn. *The Tidy House: Little Girls Writing*. London: Virago, 1982.

Stout, Janis. *Through the Window, Out the Door*. Tuscaloosa: University of Alabama Press, 1998.

Stratton-Porter, Gene. *A Girl of the Limberlost*. Garden City, N.Y.: Doubleday, Page, and Co., 1909.

Thompson, Bertha [pseud. Box-Car Bertha]. *Sister of the Road: The Auto-biography of Box-Car Bertha. As Told to Dr. Ben L. Reitman.* New York: Macaulay Company, 1937.

Toth, Emily. *Unveiling Kate Chopin.* Jackson: University of Mississippi Press, 1999.

Trumpener, Katie. *Bardic Nationalism: The Romantic Novel and the British.* Princeton: Princeton University Press, 1997.

Turner, Frederick Jackson. *The Significance of the Frontier in American History.* 1893. Reprint, edited by Harold P. Simonson. New York: Ungar, 1963.

Twain, Mark [Samuel Clemens]. *Eve's Diary, translated from the original MS.* New York: Harper and Brothers, 1906.

——. "Marjorie Fleming, the Wonder Child." *Harper's Bazaar* 43 (December 1909): 1182–83.

Untermeyer, Louis. Review of *Poems by a Little Girl* by Hilda Conkling. Dial 69 (August 1920): 186.

Van Doren, Carl. *Contemporary American Novelists 1900–1920.* New York: Macmillan, 1922.

Van Leer, David. "Visible Silence: Spectatorship in Black Gay and Lesbian Film." In *Representing Blackness: Issues in Film and Video,* edited by Valerie Smith. New Brunswick: Rutgers University Press, 1997.

Wall, Cheryl A. *Women of the Harlem Renaissance.* Bloomington: Indiana University Press, 1995.

Watson, Julia. "Engendering Montana Lives: Women's Autobiographical Writing." In *Writing Montana: Literature under the Big Sky,* edited by Rick Newby and Suzanne Hunger, 121–62. Helena: Montana Center for the Book, 1996.

Weber, Ronald. *The Midwestern Ascendancy in American Writing.* Bloomington: Indiana University Press, 1992.

Wesley, Marilyn. *Secret Journeys: The Trope of Women's Travel in American Literature.* Albany: State University of New York Press.

Wheeler, Leslie A. "Montana's Shocking 'Lit'ry Lady.'" *Montana Magazine* (Summer 1977): 20–33.

Whiteley, Opal. *The Story of Opal: The Journal of an Understanding Heart.* Boston: Atlantic Monthly Press, 1920. First serialized in *Atlantic Monthly* 125–26 (March–August 1920).

——. *The Diary of Opal Whiteley.* London: Putnam's, 1920.

——. *The Flower of Stars.* Washington, D.C., 1923.

Wilkinson, Marguerite. "The Poems of the Month." *Bookman* 53 (1921): 246.

Williams, Terry Tempest. "In Cahoots with Coyote." In *From the Faraway Nearby: Georgia O'Keeffe as Icon,* edited by Christopher Merril and Ellen Bradbury. Albuquerque: University of New Mexico Press, 1998.

Winslow, Anna Green. *Diary of Anna Green Winslow: A Boston School Girl of 1771*, edited by Alice Morese Earle. Boston: Houghton, Mifflin and Co., 1894.

Wister, Owen. *The Virginian: Horseman of the Plains.* New York: Macmillan, 1902.

Woods, Katherine. "Traveling for Adventure." [Review of *My Great, Wide, Beautiful World.*] *Saturday Review* (June 20, 1936): 10–11.

Woodward, Helen Beal. "Dear Diary—Will Secret Scribblings Bring Fame to a New Marie Bashkirtseff or Mary MacLane?" *Mademoiselle* (April 1943).

Writer's Program of the W. P. A. in the State of Montana. *Copper Camp: Stories of the World's Greatest Mining Town—Butte, Montana.* New York: Hastings House, 1943.

Yaeger, Patricia. *Dirt and Desire: Reconstructing Southern Women's Writing, 1930–1990.* Chicago: University of Chicago Press, 2000.

Ziff, Larzer. *The American 1890s: Life and Times of a Lost Generation.* New York: Viking, 1966.

Unsigned Magazine Reviews and Articles, Harrison

Review of *My Great, Wide, Beautiful World. Publishers Weekly* (April 25, 1936): 1670.

"'Gelouries!'" [Review of *My Great, Wide, Beautiful World.*] *Time* (May 18, 1936): 83–85.

Unsigned Magazine Reviews and Articles, MacLane

"Chronicle and Comment." [Review of *The Story of Mary MacLane.*] *Bookman* (April 1902): 115.

"A Montana Marie Bashkirtseff." *Literary Digest* 25.4 (1902): 99.

Review of "Men Who Have Made Love to Me." *Wid's Daily* (January 17, 1918): 873.

Review of *The Story of Mary MacLane. Critic* 51 (1902): 7.

Review of *The Story of Mary MacLane. Publishers Weekly* 61 (January–June 1902): 1349.

"The Story of Mary MacLane." *Literary World* 33 (1902): 102.

Unsigned Magazine Reviews and Articles, Whiteley

Story of Opal advertisement. Bookman Advertiser 52 (1921).

Story of Opal advertisement. *Littell's Living Age* 307. no 3990 (December 1920): back cover.

Review of *The Diary of Opal Whiteley*. *Athenaeum* (September 17, 1920): 372.
Review of *The Diary of Opal Whiteley*. *Spectator* 125 (October 16, 1920).
Review of *The Story of Opal*. *Literary Digest* 67 (October 30, 1920): 34.
Review of *The Story of Opal*. *Outlook* 126 (1920): 201.

Unsigned Reviews and Articles on Other Child Writers

Booklist 17 (October 30, 1920). [Ashford]
Bookman 50 (1919): 30. [children's books]
Bookman 50 (1919): 395. [Edward Grey]
Bookman 52 (1920): 383. [child writers]
Bookman 53 (1921): 285. [child writers]
Dial 67 (August 1919): 174. [Ashford]
Dial 69 (August 1920): 186. [Conkling]
Outlook 123 (1919): 191. [Ashford]
Outlook 125 (1920): 615. [Ashford]

Newspapers

Anaconda Standard
Butte Intermountain
Butte Miner
Butte Tribune-Review
Chicago Daily News
Chicago Daily Tribune
Chicago Record-Herald
Chicagoan
Detroit Free Press
Evening Post
Fergus Falls (Minnesota) Daily Journal
Great Falls (Montana) Tribune
Honolulu Star-Bulletin
Minneapolis Tribune
Missoula Fruit-Grower
Montana Standard
New York Herald
New York Times
New York World
Springfield Republican
The Times [London]
The Times [London] Literary Supplement
Washington Post

Archival Collections

Butte–Silver Bow Public Archives.

Records of *Poetry: A Magazine of Verse*, University of Chicago Library, Special Collections Research Center.

Stone & Kimball Publishing Co. archives, The Newberry Library.

Opal Whiteley Papers, Division of Special Collections and Archives of the University of Oregon Libraries.

Opal Whiteley, special subject file of the Ellery Sedgwick Papers, Massachusetts Historical Society.

Index

WISCONSIN STUDIES IN AUTOBIOGRAPHY

American Women's Autobiography: Fea(s)ts of Memory
Edited, with an introduction, by Margo Culley

FRANK MARSHALL DAVIS
Livin' the Blues: Memoirs of a Black Journalist and Poet
Edited, with an introduction, by John Edgar Tidwell

JOANNE JACOBSON
Authority and Alliance in the Letters of Henry Adams

CORNELIA PEAKE MCDONALD
A Woman's Civil War: A Diary with Reminiscences of the War, from March 1862
Edited, with an introduction, by Minrose C. Gwin

KAMAU BRATHWAITE
The Zea Mexican Diary: 7 Sept. 1926–7 Sept. 1986
Foreword by Sandra Pouchet Paquet

GENARO M. PADILLA
My History, Not Yours: The Formation of Mexican American Autobiography

FRANCES SMITH FOSTER
Witnessing Slavery: The Development of Ante-bellum Slave Narratives

Native American Autobiography: An Anthology
Edited, with an introduction, by Arnold Krupat

American Lives: An Anthology of Autobiographical Writing
Edited, with an introduction, by Robert F. Sayre

CAROL HOLLY
Intensely Family: The Inheritance of Family Shame and the Autobiographies of Henry James

People of the Book: Thirty Scholars Reflect on Their Jewish Identity
Edited by Jeffrey Rubin-Dorsky and Shelley Fisher Fishkin

G. THOMAS COUSER
Recovering Bodies: Illness, Disability, and Life Writing

JOSÉ ANGEL GUTIÉRREZ
The Making of a Chicano Militant: Lessons from Cristal

JOHN DOWNTON HAZLETT
My Generation: Collective Autobiography and Identity Politics

WILLIAM HERRICK
Jumping the Line: The Adventures and Misadventures of an American Radical

Women, Autobiography, Theory: A Reader
Edited by Sidonie Smith and Julia Watson

CARSON MCCULLERS
Illumination and Night Glare: The Unfinished Autobiography of Carson McCullers
Edited by Carlos L. Dews

MARIE HALL ETS
Rosa: The Life of an Italian Immigrant

YI-FU TUAN
Who Am I?: An Autobiography of Emotion, Mind, and Spirit

HENRY BIBB
The Life and Adventures of Henry Bibb: An American Slave
With a new introduction by Charles J. Heglar

SUZANNE L. BUNKERS
Diaries of Girls and Women: A Midwestern American Sampler

JIM LANE
The Autobiographical Documentary in America

SANDRA POUCHET PAQUET
Caribbean Autobiography: Cultural Identity and Self-Representation

CATHRYN HALVERSON
Maverick Autobiographies: Women Writers and the American West, 1900–1936